AF513353

Shantanu Datta is a journalist, writing on politics, films, books and music since 1987. He started off as a trainee in *The Telegraph* in Calcutta and went on to head editions of *The New Indian Express* and *The Indian Express* in Bangalore, Pune and Mumbai, after a stint in *IE*, Delhi. He is now with *The Telegraph Online*, back in the city where it all began. This is his first book.

Calling Elvis

Conversations With Some of Music's Greatest: A Personal History

SHANTANU DATTA

SPEAKING TIGER

SPEAKING TIGER BOOKS LLP
4381/4, Ansari Road, Daryaganj
New Delhi 110002

First published by Speaking Tiger Books in paperback 2020

Every effort has been made to trace individual copyright holders and obtain permission. Any omissions brought to our attention will be remedied in future editions.

ISBN: 978-81-944468-9-7
eISBN: 978-81-944729-2-6

10 9 8 7 6 5 4 3

All rights reserved.

Typeset in Adobe Devanagari by Jojy Philip
Printed at EIH Limited, Manesar

No part of this publication may be reproduced, transmitted, or stored in a retrieval system, in any form or by any means, electronic, mechanical, photocopying, recording or otherwise, without the prior permission of the publisher.

This book is sold subject to the condition that it shall not, by way of trade or otherwise, be lent, resold, hired out, or otherwise circulated, without the publisher's prior consent, in any form of binding or cover other than that in which it is published.

In loving memory of my parents
Shila & Sudhir Datta

For Shreya and her mother

‘Someday everything is gonna be smooth like a rhapsody
When I paint my masterpiece’

—Bob Dylan

Contents

Prologue

The door would be kept open slightly through which a sliver of light would pass through reassuringly so that he wouldn't be in the dark. A four-year-old boy would be in his cot, trying to sleep to the comforting strains of his favourite song, *Ogo nodi apon begey pagol para*, coming from the record player in the other room where his parents were.

The ballad of the river would play on.

Next morning, the boy would be standing on a Vespa scooter, within the safe arcs of his father's arms, riding down College Tilla to a pick-up point where the school bus to Shishu Bihar would be waiting.

The familiar chatter of fifty-odd kids greeted the boy on board. Soon, the bus was off. *Japaan*, love in Tokyo, the children screamed.

He joined in with gusto.

Le gayi dill, gudiya Japaan ki, le gayi dill… paagal mujhe kar diya!

Introduction

Sun, Sun, Sun Here It Comes

I met him for thirty-three and one-third seconds. It was a Sunday evening in January 1983. Seated two rows in front of us at Netaji Indoor Stadium, he was there to witness the coming together of Pandit Ravi Shankar and Ustad Ali Akbar Khan, who would be playing together in Calcutta after twelve years, a historic concert in the annals of Indian classical music and an occurrence so momentous in stature that my mother allowed me to attend even though it was barely a month from my class XII boards.

After Raga Imon, alaap, jor, followed by gat and jhala, the musicians took an unscheduled break. Shankar had descended from the stage erected at the centre of the stadium, and we noticed George Harrison leave his seat in the gallery. My influential friend, who had snagged two VIP passes for the marquee event, joined me as I followed the Beatle down the ramp to the cafeteria. There he was with a cup, of tea I presume, while two men of distinctly large proportions stood guard. By then, around twenty of us had gathered there. We milled around him in the hope of exchanging pleasantries.

I think I'll start charging ten rupees for every autograph, he said, smiling as he went about signing on whatever we held out for him.

We'll give you twenty, I remember muttering.

True to form, I think I said the stupidest thing ever told to a Beatle. Who talks money when you are meeting George Harrison, the quiet one, for the first, and probably, the only time?

By then word had spread and more people began trooping in. It was my turn. I held out a piece of paper and Harrison started to sign. My heart was beating fast. There was a bit of jostling. Suddenly, Harrison let his cup drop. It broke, spilling tea all over the floor, almost naturally clearing the way for him. He went up to his seat, leaving that piece of paper with me. I looked at it; my hands were trembling.

That evening Ravi Shankar and Ali Akbar Khan were accompanied by Ustad Allahrakha and his son Zakir Hussain on tablas. They played for over five hours. It was a unique jugalbandhi, wrote Sankarlal Bhattacharya in the *Anandabazar Patrika* the next day, commending organisers Jalsaghar for the near-perfect arrangements: great sound that ensured every nuance of the sitar and sarod was experienced by the over 13,000 disciplined listeners, about 200 of whom were seated right in front of the platform for musicians to bridge the divide between Performer and Listener. It was 10.30 p.m. and many had got up to leave. Last bus worries notwithstanding, they stood near the exits, but could not leave. The music held them back. I recall vividly how at one of the many climactic moments of the concert, when the father-son duo had wrapped up a thundering sawal-jawab routine to a rapturous ovation from the gathering, Zakir walked up to Allahrakha and touched his feet. A gentle tap on his head and the hint of a smile from the old man that followed said it all. From the dark reaches of my seat in the stadium, George Harrison in silhouette, music and its all-encompassing ambitions of tradition and modernity unveiled itself to me at that moment.

Living on a college campus for around three years when I was around six-seven in the early '70s, I remember loving the *Bratacharir Gaan* that students would conduct a drill to every morning. Kaji Nazrul Islam's freedom cry of *Kara Louhokopat*, which they would often sing, was awe-inspiring and took on a new dimension, for me during the Bangladesh war. When we moved to our own home, Puja functions at the para would showcase some of the most important Baul and folk singers of the time, in addition to renowned exponents of Rabindrasangeet like Subinoy Roy. Prahlad Brahmachari and Purna Das Baul would sing late into the night as would Nirmalendu Choudhury, and later on his son. Their repertoire would inevitably include *Gole male, gole male pirit koro naa*, a naughty take on the eccentricities of love, and *Amar jemon beni temni robey chul bhijabona* on the dilemmas of getting your feet wet. In between, there was *Mone pore Ruby Rai,* The Ventures and *Dhire se jana bagiayan mein* on 45s & 78s.

If these diverse experiences formed the chorus of my early life, La Martiniere filled in the verses with hymns at morning assembly, the songs we got to learn as members of the school choir under Tony Menezes, and the 'education' I received from some very generous friends who loaned me albums to devour.

The Beatles' *Hard Day's Night*, which I hung on to for months from a friend who used to live on Keyatola Road, started it all. The sheer joy of discovering music, whatever the genre, was what got to me. Johnny Wakelin's *Black Superman*, Jose Feliciano's *California Dreamin'* and Musical Bandbox every Sunday on radio; Hindi film songs that would be aired every afternoon on Vividh Bharati;

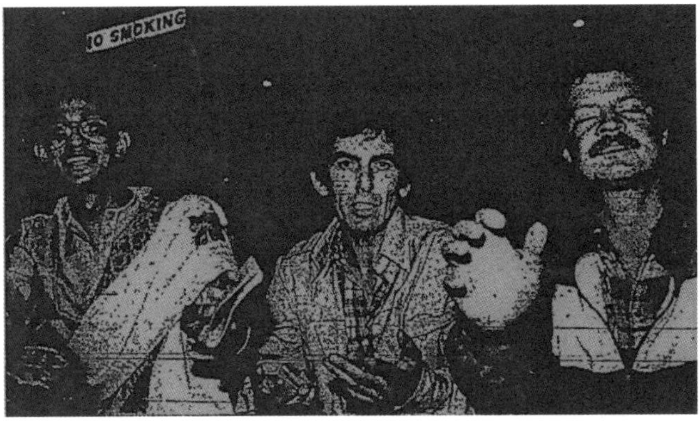

MY SWEET LORD: GEORGE HARRISON (centre), minus his long hair, *The Telegraph* noted on the front page of Monday, January 17, 1983, enjoys the Ravi Shankar-Ali Akbar Khan concert at Netaji Indoor Stadium in Calcutta. (Aloke Mitra, courtesy *The Telegraph*)

and musicals like *Goopi Gayen Bagha Bayen*, *The Sound of Music*, *The Man from Lamancha* and later, songs from *Bobby* and *Hare Krishna Hare Rama* that would be played, as if on loop, on all five days of the Pujas.

Then Presidency College provided the intro, and outro, to this vast never-to-be bookended collection of art forms. Books, paintings, theatre, more music, and film. The innocence of Jamini Roy's 'Mother and Child', the intellectual ambivalence about revolution in Guenter Grass's *The Plebeians Rehearse The Uprising*, the chiselled perfection of Satyajit Ray's *Charulata*, the humanism of Vittorio DeSica's *Bicycle Thief*, the madness of Warner Herzog's *Aguirre, the Wrath of God*, the stark symbolism of Bergman's *Seventh Seal* and the final freeze-frame in *Butch Cassidy and the Sundance Kid*.

'The next time I say, "Let's go someplace like Bolivia, let's GO someplace like Bolivia!"'

That's the point. I did not have to go to Bolivia. I stayed put in Calcutta, moving, if only for about a decade or so, to Delhi, Bangalore, Pune and Mumbai. Wherever we were, the music played. Eric Clapton, J.J. Cale, CSNY, ELP and Floyd tracks swapped play time with the likes of Kishore Kumar and R.D. Burman. The trumpet interlude in Kishore's—our Elvis—*Ek Ladki Bheegi Bhaagi Si* invokes jazz, right? And what is it that makes R.D.'s perhaps not-so-well known train song, *Dhanno ki aakhon mein,* an intoxicating rock ballad?

In the late '90s, during the early part of my stint at *The Indian Express* in Delhi, I used to write a fortnightly column, 'Calling Elvis', the title of the Dire Straits song that celebrates all that is great about music. Mark Knopfler's tribute is about Elvis's songs, his daring, his audacity, his free spirit, and above all, his path-breaking forays into the soundscape of American, and subsequently, world music that would forever change the way performers benchmarked their ideals—and perhaps, their sideburns too. Who else but Elvis could inspire a musician in faraway Calcutta, someone whose tutelage in a family of classical giants did not deter him to play *Teddy Bear* on the sitar? Ananda Shankar's subsequent renditions of the Rolling Stones *Jumpin' Jack Flash* became the signature tune to one of our favourite western music programmes on All India Radio.

'Calling Elvis' chronicled all that by collating factoids and anecdotes about classic rock acts that refused to fade away, a la Jethro Tull, Kiss and Peter Frampton. It was about the discovery of the French Algerian pop-rockstar Khaled, Bob Dylan playing *Times They Are a Changin'* at a corporate do for a hefty fee, Bruce Springsteen's ode to Steinbeck's *Grapes of Wrath* by turning musical minimalist with *The Ghost of Tom Joad* and a lot more.

Decades later, *Calling Elvis* has morphed into a collection of interviews and musical experiences, a kind of 'Best of...' if you please, to take stock of a continuing journey, an amalgamation of all that I was privileged to have been exposed to. They came to India and, somehow, I was there; their names leaping out of vinyl centre-circles that go round and round on the turntable, becoming real people. John McLaughlin, Wayne Shorter, Herbie Hancock, Carlos Santana, Mark Knopfler, Sting... Am I showing off? Ten years ago maybe I would be. Now, I am just grateful.

Being face-to-face with Ian Anderson and Martin Barre in Bombay, discussing the importance of decency in protest music with Arlo Guthrie at the US ambassador's residence in New Delhi, meeting Roger Waters in London, talking to Keith Richards days before Rolling Stones performed in Bangalore and getting introduced to Jean-Luc Ponty, courtesy Dr L. Subramaniam, are serendipitous happenings in a music lover's life; especially when their eminences are still playing and touring. Just as their performances in India serve as cultural touchstones, they also offer a glimpse into our understanding of diverse musical genres, in the process reinforcing the essentially secular nature of our receptacles and certain key tenets of our tradition such as openness, inclusivity and coexistence, a default setting attuned to collaborations.

Calling Elvis is, therefore, a humble tribute to all performers who keep reinventing themselves. Dilip Balakrishnan did it in the '60s through the '80s of Calcutta as did Mohiner Ghoraguli. Not to forget Osibisa, a UK rock band of African immigrants, who sang *Ram Dhun* at ITF Pavilion around Diwali in 1981 to be followed, decades later, by Pete Seeger singing '*Raghupati raghava raja ram...*' Today, Srikanta Acharya is adding contemporary sophistication to

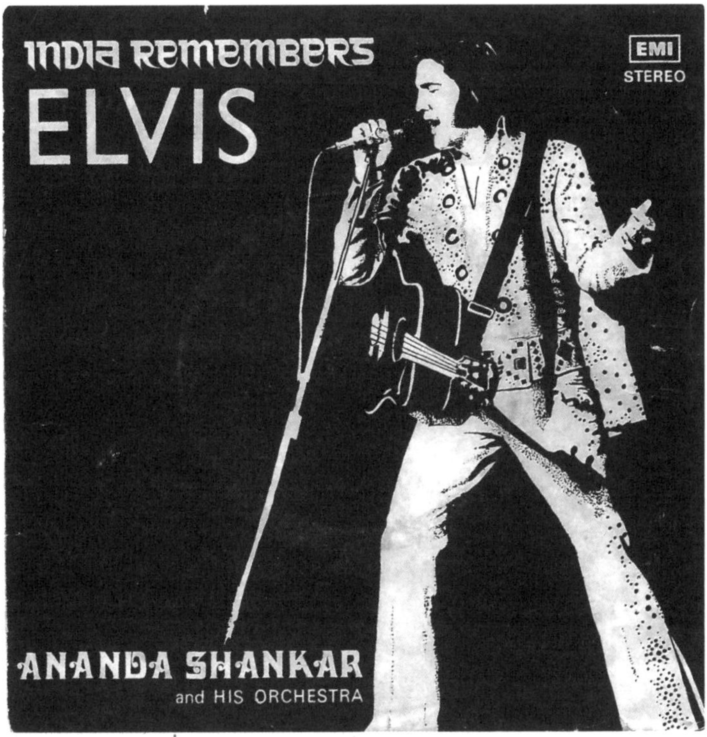

Rabindrasangeet as he rediscovers Tagore while Amyt Datta is conjuring images of the Mediterranean on his guitar. They keep coming.

As tributes go, this one by one who grew up in Calcutta, and drew on experiences our magnanimous country throws up every day, may seem woefully inadequate, given my own shortcomings and the varied nature of the conversations. But it is a tribute nevertheless. If you have read this far, thank you. Now, do turn the pages. Tune in. If for nothing else, then for the singers of the world, their tunes and symphonies yet to come.

1

A Day in the Life

The first indications that musical mountains had begun to shake rattle and roll came sometime in the cusp of 2016-17. At a desert in California in October 2016, over 70,000 people gathered over two successive weekends to hear Paul McCartney and Neil Young play the Beatles' *A Day in the Life* which segued into John Lennon's *Give Peace a Chance.* Bob Dylan asked *Why Change Me Now?* The Who harped on *My Generation,* and Roger Waters sang *Pigs*. Those lucky to be there felt like one happy family, emotional and hopeful, something otherwise difficult to be, months before the US was to elect its 45th president.

The Rolling Stones played too and did a bluesy cover of *Come Together*, a song Mick Jagger nonchalantly described as being penned by an 'unknown beat group.' Watching the video of the performance accompanying a report in *Rolling Stone* magazine, I was reminded of what Keith Richards had told me during a telephone conversation before their first-ever gig on Indian soil, in Bangalore, sixteen years ago. 'John was a very dear friend of mine. I miss him dearly,' he said over the telephone from Singapore when I asked him about John (Lennon) and George (Harrison) who were particularly fond of the Stones. 'I think the Beatles learnt and took quite a lot from us just as we did from them. Often, we used to say we should have all been in the same band. Now, John and George are not with us—nothing in the world is perfect. You know that, don't you?'

That's the amazing thing about music. It signposts our lives in myriad ways. Sometimes, it headlines an experience. At other times, it merely captions, or footnotes even, an event or a feeling, making them more memorable than they would have ever been without.

By early 2019, a lot had changed in the world. Donald Trump was in the White House, facing an enquiry over Russia's ties to his election campaign even as he presided over a thirty-five-day shutdown of the US government, the longest ever, over funding plans for a wall across the Mexican border to thwart illegal immigration. By the end of the year he was facing impeachment. Britain was in crisis over its exit from the European Union. Israel-Palestine relations were at rock bottom, the war in Syria was raging while China was flexing its muscles across the border. Closer home, amid the backdrop of the futility of demonetisation of high-value currency notes, the nation braced for a bitterly fought general election. The BJP-led government announced a bouquet of poll sops in its last Union Budget and the motley and shaky 'gathbandhan' of Opposition parties hoped to turn the tide but in vain. The politics of religious intolerance was gaining in strength as were efforts to undermine democratic institutions. In Calcutta, Mrinal Sen, the last of the triumvirate of the city's cinema greats, passed away. His favourite hero Anjan Dutt, who had managed to redefine himself as a performer, singing life-affirming songs about urban concerns in the '80s and '90s, was among the few still drawing big crowds at college dos.

Elsewhere in the world, the big daddies were rocking. The California Desert Trip, featuring rock stalwarts such as the Stones, Waters and Dylan, seemed to kickstart the old engines. Don Henley of the Eagles, the Doobie Brothers, Steely Dan and Deep Purple hit the road. Even Dead & Company, a throwback band comprising the original members of Grateful Dead, Bob Weir, Mickey Hart and Bill Kreutzmann, were joined by the amazing John Mayer to play live concerts. There was a renewed sense of purpose in the resurgence of the electric guitar, its pick-up turned to 'high' to pierce the halo provided by the bass and drums, the lyrics shouting out warnings of a future that looked more uncertain with each passing day.

The McCartney-Young rendition of *A Day in the Life* at the desert in faraway US took me back to the Beatles Blue Album. A couple of spins of the song that begins with its protagonist reading the news got me thinking. When was it that I decided to stop playing on stage? Was it the time I braved it to go solo with the song, playing guitar and even attempting the orchestral crescendo of the original on my Hobner (a faux Hofner) acoustic with a pick-up and then having to face a hostile audience at the Calcutta National Medical College fest even though I felt I wasn't all that bad? Or was it the sheer frustration of having to hail cabs, only to be repeatedly refused, to lug my drum kit back home to Salt Lake after a performance during Freshers' Welcome at Presidency College? Or was it that our bass amp would give way after almost every show and I had had enough of being saddled with inferior quality equipment, the only kind available in Calcutta then? Was it a decision at all? Or was it fait accompli that I ended up writing on musicians instead of being one?

Whatever happened did so quite like that unexpected nano-second of silence when the overture in *A Day in the Life* snaps out and the bridge sets in: I wake up, get out of bed, comb my hair, go down and drink a cup, of tea I am sure, then, realising I am late, I rush to catch the bus. I do. Then I go upstairs but don't have a smoke—because I don't smoke—and somebody speaks, and I go into a dream… I am with a group of music buffs, standing in front of George Harrison who happens to be in Calcutta! But is it a dream?

That audacious experiment with *A Day in the Life* at CNMC was inspired by Dilip Balakrishnan, the life and soul of High, one of India's foremost rock bands to successfully attempt original compositions that, thanks to HMV, today share space with the Beatles, Jethro Tull, Pink Floyd, Rolling Stones and Bob Dylan CDs in our music cabinets at home. Dilip was playing with bassist Lew Hilt at Kalamandir basement sometime in the early '80s. The do was titled Axis, as 'Hiltu da' would remind me decades later, and in all likelihood, announced via a five-line mention in the personal column of *The Statesman*. They had analogue recordings as back-up as they played a few covers, including *A Day in the Life*, and their own compositions like *Politician, Shambhu, Monkey Song,* all High standards. The second half of the concert was titled Tolkien Suite. Dilip, as sophisticated as he was eccentric, had put J.R.R's verses to music. It was a rock symphony of unlimited possibilities.

Freedom needs no introduction
Got to keep moving same direction
Freedom needs no by-election
Got to keep moving same direction

Who is Dilip?

If I said he was a versatile musician who could sing with a Mick Jagger-like swagger and play guitar, keys, synthesizer and harmonica; was developing a musical canon that had shades of Robbie Robertson and The Band with a dash of Steve Winwood, Jerry Garcia and the Fab Four; had set J.R.R. Tolkien's *Lord of the Rings* to music; and that he was a Calcutta boy, it would seem make-believe.[1]

It's not.

The '60s saw the enchanted beginnings of rock n' roll in India. And in the beginning, there was Dilip Balakrishnan, a thin guy with specs who used to bob around weirdly and sing his own songs. Singer, songwriter, composer and rhythm n' blues man, Dilip formed and led Great Bear and High, two of Calcutta's most loved bands ever. 'Dilip's music belonged to a highly pedigreed lineage,' wrote friend and longtime bandmate Nondon Bagchi in *The Telegraph*. 'The influences could be felt—Grateful Dead, Stones, Beatles and Pink Floyd

THE GREAT BEAR: DILIP BALAKRISHNAN (concert flier, courtesy Lew Hilt)

to name a few—but melodies, always his trump card, were totally original. No question of imitation or derivation. You could simply sense the lineage, and his individual stamp was clearly etched. Add to this his feel for the perfect moment at which to infuse a little Indian classical flavour into the melodic and rhythmic improvisations and there you have it.'

It was as if rock had found a nurturing parent in India. And naturally, the following was select. If Great Bear was Calcutta's first truly progressive rock band, then High was its logical progression. And though they did decent covers of the Beatles, Stones, Jimi Hendrix, Jethro Tull and Led Zeppelin, Great Bear was the first band to play Dilip's hour-long original suite of songs inspired by Lewis Carrol. '*White Knight's Tale* is my favourite,' Dilip told *Junior Statesman* in 1972. 'People who are a bit nonsensical really get me. I can identify with their eccentricity. Sometimes, it's sad, sometimes funny. I had a melody and I had no words until suddenly I was reading Lewis Carroll… The eccentric lyrics fitted to the graveyard, sombre atmosphere of the melody.'

Flowers swaying to the wind
Singing softly—spinning dreams

I heard whispers from the leaves
Living on trees and living their dreams
Little boats come floating down the streams
Listening to the happy songs of flower spinning dreams

White Knight's Tale established Dilip as one of the earliest creative forces of rock music in India. By the time he formed High with buddies Nondon (drums), Lew Hilt (bass, guitar, vocals) and Subir Chatterjee (guitar), Dilip was writing and composing prolifically, building a collection of over 150 songs and soundtracks for two documentaries shown on Doordarshan, *Dharamtala ka Mela* and *The Future of Our Cities*, the former, wrote Professor Ananda Lal in *The Statesman* in 1990, earning him appreciation from Satyajit Ray no less.

At the core of Dilip's musical ideas was the Beatles, considered by Nondon as the most significant discovery of his life. 'It was a very strong chemical reaction indeed, far deeper and more personal than for most of us; perhaps because it really reached the latent song-writer's flair deep within him, or perhaps because for him it happened in a more personal way. Dilip was never really a Park Street regular and this whole Beatles thing happened more in his own private world, and it really got a hold on him. It was not enough to listen. He had to participate.'[2]

We get a glimpse of that in Dilip's interview to *Junior Statesman* in which he talks of a family of chickens that used to live behind his home. 'Whenever the cock used to yell I used to yell back which used to make it come looking for the sound. I was just playing a game but then I began to feel what it was feeling. I could, again, identify the eccentric. And there's this picture of John Lennon opposite my bed and I used to stare at it and it stared back. All of this gave rise to *Me and Him*. Me is me and him is me trying to be the chicken or John Lennon. It's a song about my reflections in and about other beings.'

According to friends, Dilip had five boxes to check: make the charts, go on stage someday with son Tejan, solve the power crisis, be in the south of the equator in year 2000 and act as Gollum, Tolkien's ambivalent creature who once possessed the Ring. He couldn't. For Dilip passed away on June 19, 1990 in Chicago battling cancer.

High stopped playing.

It was easy—when we were both young
Life wasn't so complicated
It wasn't hard for us to dream
But now it seems so hard
To make the dreams so real

Nondon, Lew, Subir did get together a year later (April 4 & 5, 1991) at Vidya Mandir in Calcutta to celebrate Dilip's music. That concert would be one of my earliest assignments for *The Telegraph*. Help poured in from all quarters, Abeer Chakraborty of Response had told me then. Navin 'Seagull' Kishore did the lights and brochure while P.C. 'Shiva' Mukherjee, one-time bandmate of Dilip, provided the sound—all for free. Nondon recalled how the new line-up came into being after working together in Jamshedpur to help a school put up a rock opera. 'We gelled so well that on our way back on the train we decided on the concert,' he said.

The concerts were fabulous. The band was tight and emotionally charged. Three pieces from *A White Knight's Tale* were played along with most High favourites. 'The moment I finish my solo, I find myself waiting for Dilip to come in on vocals, only to be instantly stung back to reality. This happened at least thrice on stage. God, it gave me goosebumps,' recalled Subir.

Many musician friends joined in too, among them Shillong's long-haired rockstar Lou Majou, conguero and percussionist Monojit 'Kochu' Datta, and his guitarist brother Amit, also with long hair then. Amit would later become Amyt. His guitar would go places. We would be hearing him, and his music, a lot more in the years to come.

HIGH ON FRIENDSHIP

Lew is playing *Autumn Leaves* on his Ibanez fretless bass. There is a sweetness to the notes being plucked out of the red guitar that is not hooked up to an amp, a kind of Bossa Nova vibe to his playing. We are about halfway through what will be a memorable evening at the Gurgaon home of a musician friend, an accomplished harmonica player with an encyclopedic knowledge of maestros and their craft.

'Dilip Balakrishnan changed my life completely,' says Lew with an air of certainty that seems to have been reinforced over the years. It strikes me immediately that we are talking about a '70s musician of Calcutta, twenty-seven years after a concert was held in celebration of the original music he and his friends created and thirty-six years after Axis, that Kalamandir basement gig. Lew is taken aback when I mention *A Day in the Life*, one of several John Lennon songs Dilip and he played that evening on December 23, 1982 as a tribute to one half of the Lennon-McCartney duo who was shot dead in New York on December 8, 1980. 'Unfortunately, there weren't many who were thinking about music the way we were. So Dilip said we would do the show by ourselves,' he explains. It is not lost to us how incredibly courageous that effort was in the Calcutta of

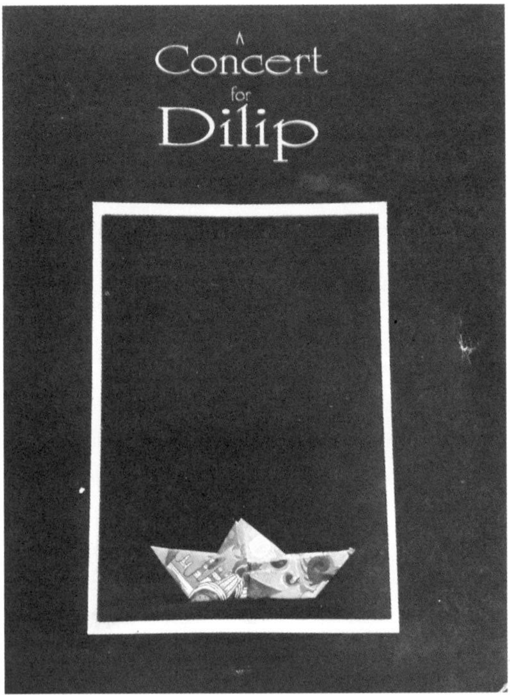

KEEPSAKES: Brochures for the memorial concert and Axis (courtesy Lew Hilt)

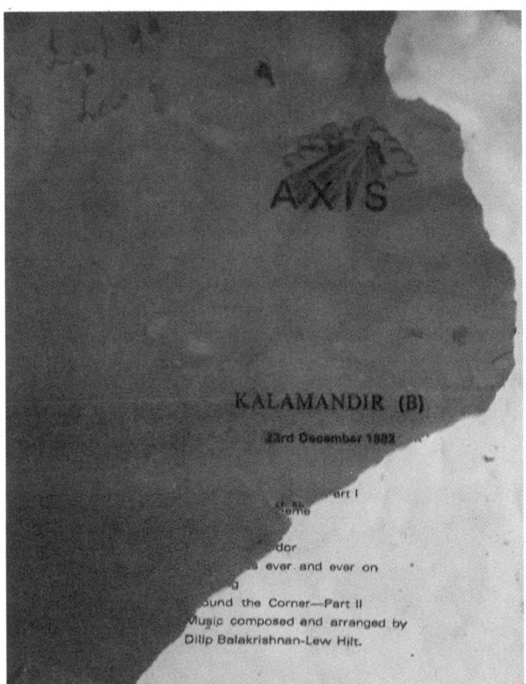

the early '80s where decent professional equipment was rare. Recording and re-recording tracks on a four-track tape recorder was painstaking, no doubt, but it was just the kind of thing Dilip and Lew would gladly do. 'We shared life. Both of us had one aim and that was the music,' he notes, pointing to a souvenir, tired and tattered over time, that was brought out for the Axis concert:

> 'A Mixed Bag: Music composed and arranged by Lew Hilt-Dilip Balakrishnan. Songs: *It's Going to Get You, A Time to Get High, Airline, A Song for Carl, Is it Love, Little Boy.*[3]
>
> 'The Tolkien Suite: Lyrics by Tolkien from *The Hobbit* and *The Lord of the Rings*. Introduction, *Around the Corner—Part I, The Hobbit Theme, Gollum's Song, Land of Mordor, Road Goes Ever and Ever on, Entsong, Around the Corner—Part II*; Music composed and arranged by Dilip Balakrishnan-Lew Hilt.
>
> 'A Tribute to John Lennon: A selection of songs by Lennon presented by Dilip and Lew in memory of one of modern music's greatest composers.'

It is fitting that Lew cites famous musical duos to describe his collaborative ties with Dilip. But he is promptly dismissive of any one-to-one comparisons. 'To try and explain to you about the person Dilip was, I refer to John Lennon & Paul McCartney, Mick Jagger & Keith Richards. I am not saying we were equal to them. No, no never. The thing is that there was always two. If one got stuck, the other pitched in.'

Of all the memories, Lew is most nonchalant about the particularly affectionate, but unprintable, name Dilip had for him. '"Hey bas****, are you only going to play that f***ing A-chord or play some other notes?", he would often say when he wanted stuff out of me.'

Lew was warming up. The fish fry from Bijoli Grill was hot. Our spirits were high. The conversation meandered to Salvador Dali, Kurosawa, Lady Luck and, happy smokes. Of course.

> **How did you hook up with Dilip?**
>
> It all started in 1966-67 when I was playing with this very established band, The Cavaliers, with Neil Sen and Robin Sen. Neil was the guitar player and singer. We were playing at St Xavier's auditorium one morning. Satanic Reflections, the band that preceded us, were playing some weird stuff. And there was this guitar player and singer, who I remember being quite impressed with. That was Dilip Balakrishnan.

So, I spoke to Neil and said, 'Why don't we get this guy to sing for us. That way you will be a bit more at ease'—being the lead singer as well as the lead guitar player was taking a toll on him. He agreed and asked me to speak to him. I still remember Dilip was playing a Bangalore-made guitar that day. Anyway, when they took a break I went up to him and asked him to play with us. Dilip agreed, his surprise quite natural as we were The Cavaliers, an established band with a fan club of sorts. I told him we were to be playing the next set.

Dilip rattled off a few songs, asking us whether we did them or not. Lo and behold, we were doing all of them. So, Dilip joined Cavaliers and went on to change the repertoire of our band. Basically, we were a pop band. But now that Dilip was the singer, he could choose and veer towards songs like *Pictures of Matchstick Men* (Status Quo). These were all heavy-duty bands. Not many had heard them those days.

SHAMBHU: LEW HILT plays Autumn Leaves on his Ibanez fretless bass (author's personal collection)

Then came Great Bear?

Yes, a year and a half later, being the creative musician he was, Dilip formed Great Bear with Nondon Bagchi, John Brinnand, Devdan Sen and P.C.

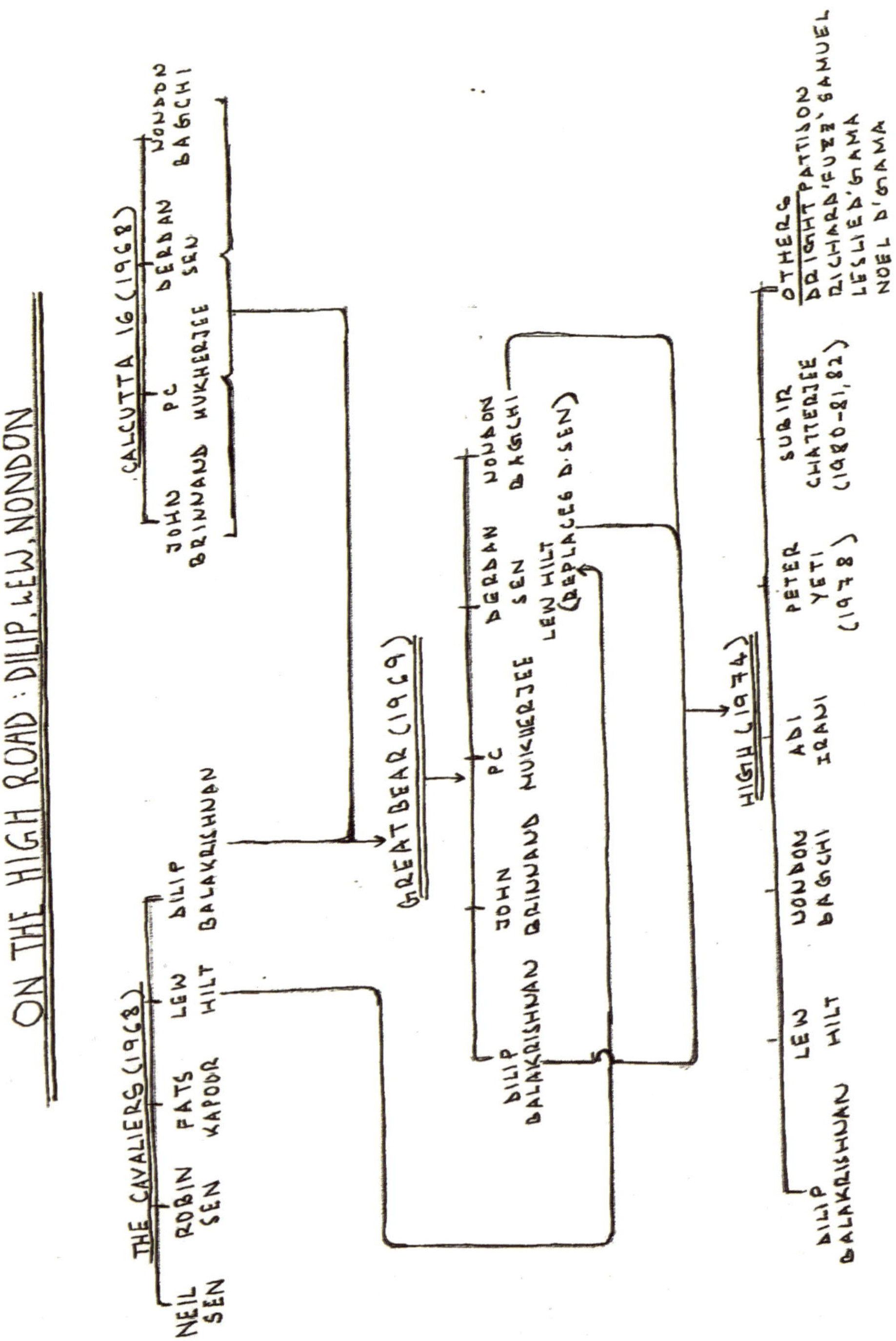
ON THE HIGH ROAD : DILIP, LEW, NONDON
THE CAVALIERS (1968)
NEIL SEN
ROBIN SEN
FATS KAPOOR
LEW HILT
DILIP BALAKRISHNAN
CALCUTTA 16 (1968)
JOHN BRINNAND
PC MUKHERJEE
DEBDAN SEN
NONDON BAGCHI
GREAT BEAR (1969)
DILIP BALAKRISHNAN
JOHN BRINNAND
PC MUKHERJEE
DEBDAN SEN
LEW HILT (REPLACES D. SEN)
NONDON BAGCHI
HIGH (1974)
DILIP BALAKRISHNAN
LEW HILT
NONDON BAGCHI
ADI IRANI
PETER YETI (1978)
SUBIR CHATTERJEE (1980–81, 82)
OTHERS
DWIGHT PATTISON
RICHARD 'FUZZ' SAMUEL
LESLIE D'GAMA
NOEL D'GAMA

Mukherjee. They had broken away from the normal trend of music. They were listening to a lot of Jethro Tull, Led Zeppelin, Cream and Blind Faith and doing covers of some of the more complex songs, say, *Whole Lotta Love*, *Lemon Song* (Zeppelin), *Sunshine of Your Love*, *White Room*, *Those Were the Days* (Cream) and the twenty-five-minute long blues-jazzy *Do What You Like* (Blind Faith). But they weren't getting too many gigs. Devdan left the band and Dilip pulled me in. That changed my way of thinking about the bass. It was no more the usual dung-dung-dung-dungdung-dung-dung-dung (hums the rock n'roll riff). It had to be dhik-dhikchakdhi-chak-chak (breaks into a slap, pinch, funk bass routine). Wow, he opened up a new way of bass playing for me.

But Great Bear broke up?

Dilip was dabbling in songwriting very briefly and we tried a lot to compose music of our own. After all, how long can you go on copying someone… so, where are you as a musician? Soon, John went away. Nondon got a job in *The Statesman*, and I went away to Jamshedpur to do god knows what… and the band broke up circa 1973.

You all got back together around 1974.

Yes, Dilip, Nondon, Adi Irani, a brilliant guitarist of the time, and myself got together to form High, a name that we would remember for life and a band that would go on to have a deep influence on rock music in India.

What were the songs you would play?

We were doing covers, but not run of the mill covers. If everyone was doing Hendrix's *Hey Joe*, we would do *Up from the Skies*, *If 6 Was 9*, *Belly Button Window*; and songs of Colosseum, Mountain, Frank Zappa, Allman Brothers, Grateful Dead and Traffic. All these were very intricate songs with different time signatures, different tempos. It took a lot of work. Nobody had heard of a local band doing such songs. And within this line-up of songs, we would slip in one of our own, most of which were written by Dilip and myself. All Dilip's ideas with a little help from his friend—because I was the core guy as I had studied music. So, I could help with the chord work. He had the lyrics, he had the melody, but sometimes you need somebody to come up with, say, a bass line. You know, like Roy Orbison (singing the *Pretty Woman* bass line). And finally, we realised that while performing covers, we could start slipping in more of our own songs in a concert. And people did not mind. Because it was something new. And it was original.

Tell me about your Narendrapur sojourns.

Dilip and I used to go to our friend Dr Anjan Roy's baganbari (bungalow). We would go there usually on a Friday with canned food (baked beans), coffee and happy smokes. Dilip had acquired a four-track tape recorder by that time. We also took a small amplifier, two small speakers, a lot of speaker wire and two acoustic guitars, but no bass guitar. We would play all day and record. Basically, playing off each other with lead riffs and chord changes and see where this would lead to.

Come sunset, we would put the speakers out, far away in the lawn—hence the long speaker wires. Light up some happy smokes, pour a happy drink and listen to all we had played. We would make a note of all that sounded good, and over a period of time we actually got the music right. These visits were among the most beautiful experiences of my life.

One of Dilip's most beautiful songs, *A Place in the Sun*, was written at Narendrapur. It talks of a campfire and dogs on the run, a reference to the fires we would often light up and the pack of strays that would come for the bones we would throw them.

High was getting there, and in no time started to fill up auditoriums such as Rabindra Sadan with 'High-heads'—much like Deadheads—coming to hear them play original music. Neither could they afford, nor did they have access to professional hi-fi equipment. Yet High's music was able to surmount those challenges. Lew remembers a gig in 1976 where a foreigner, who had been dancing to the tunes all through, came up to the band after the end of the show and was startled to find Ahuja amplifiers on stage. It tripped him off, recalled Lew, that the band had played a collection of songs of Frank Zappa, Rolling Stones, Mountain, Grateful Dead and the Beatles, all rock acts big enough to use only customized equipment, on that desi contraption.

Around a year later High disbanded for some time. Dilip, who was then working for Metalbox, got transferred to Kerala, while Lew went somewhere else and then returned for what would be another life-changing experience with Louiz Banks. Lew would be with him for around four years, even accompanying him to Bombay where they would play stuff like Weather Report and Chick Corea. But when Banks got into Hindi music, Lew decided to move on. There were residencies in Goa and Madras, but these were short-lived and Lew found himself back in Calcutta around 1984, playing with the likes of Pam Crain, Don Saigal and Carlton Kitto. He then joined P.C. Mukherjee's Shiva and stayed on with the band for seventeen long years.

While he was with Banks, Lew graduated from being a 'rocker' with no idea of music theory to a more complete musician. 'The offer to play with Banks was a very big stepping stone in my musical career,' admits Lew, and names a number of stellar musicians who had contributed to his flowering as a bass player. 'I must also thank Braz Gonsalves (sax), Carlton Kitto (guitar), Benny Rosario and Steve Sequeira (piano/keyboards) for helping me broaden my musical horizon,' he admits, and I instantly recall how Banks had also mentioned most of these names during my conversations with him. 'These are the fabulous musicians who opened it out for me; told me, for instance, where to find a sharp fifth or a sharp ninth on my guitar,' he recalls, admitting that a basic knowledge of Indian classical, ie, *sa re ga ma paa dhaa ni sa*, acquired from a certain Mrs Shanti Gurtu while at St Xavier's School Patna, helped.

Before joining Shiva, Dilip and Lew got back together once again. Only, this time Lew was equipped with 'this little knowledge' of a sharp fifth and a sharp ninth. It was around this time that Axis happened at Kalamandir basement.

These days, Lew lives in Gurgaon, having moved there with his family around the turn of the millennium. He comes to Calcutta often, sometimes for the odd gig with friends, but primarily to fulfil acting commitments for friendly film directors—and musicians—like Anjan Dutt (*Ranjana Ami Ar Ashbona*).

Lew is convinced Dilip changed his life with friendship, music and a lot more.

'Occasionally, he'd come by with tickets to a British Council film screening of, say, a *Kagemusha* (Akira Kurosawa) or a book on the famed Spanish surrealist, Salvador Dali. That blew my mind… I had no idea one could paint like that. It changed my way of painting too.'

At times, they would walk across from his home near Ballygunge Stores to Birla Mandir, that was being built then. They would smoke cigarettes and sit amid the construction workers hammering away and listen to the sounds of spades to ground, mallets to bricks. At some point the clip, clap and bang would all come together. Every sound would be in sync, as if part of some strange symphony. 'It was weird. We would love it,' says Lew. Moments later though, that symphony would turn into cacophony, break up into incomprehensible disarray, only to come back in sync all over again. 'We would just sit there and listen. Sometimes, for hours. Not a word was spoken.'

Like many of his musician peers, Lew believes Dilip was one of the greatest and most innovative musicians the country has seen. 'He was always ahead, charting new territory, trying out new sounds—he loved recording the chirping of the birds. He had a natural sense of melody. And his writing compares with the best. Just think of what he could have done if he were here today.'

Lew remembers the day Dilip left for Chicago to be treated for cancer. He helped him get dressed. 'That was the last time I saw him. When I received news of his dying, a big part of me died. Ever since, every time I try to create something musically, the first face I see is that of Dilip's… Here's to you, my friend, Dilip Balakrishnan forever.'

OUTRO

Among my collection of music memorabilia is the souvenir published for the 1991 memorial concert at Vidya Mandir. It has a charcoal black cover with a photograph of a paper boat made out of a painting. I now know that it was Lew's painting. Wow.

In 2009, Saregama did bring out High Again, a CD of their songs, remastered from original recordings on cassette tapes. Lew signed my copy. I had got Nondon Bagchi to sign it at Dalhousie Institute earlier, when he had come there to perform with his band, Hip Pocket.

We play the CD fairly regularly at home. Of late, I am hooked to *M for Gerry.* Lew described it as a 'solid' jazz piece, dedicated to Gerry Mulligan, the American cool jazz saxophone player and arranger. I am struck by its sheer complexity, convinced that *M for Gerry* works as a six-minute-long allegro in a jazz-rock symphony which, if a flute solo was to be added, may have found place in a Jethro Tull album of the '60s like *Stand Up*.

But it would be twenty-seven years after that momentous memorial concert that I would get to hear a Dilip Balakrishnan song played on stage again. Easy Riders, a group of talented youngsters led by the affable Sumit Bhattacharya, that started off in the '90s, was making a 'slight return' after twenty years at Phoenix on Shakespeare Road. None of the band members had ever heard Dilip live. All they had were some bootleg tapes. That night they sang *Politician, Monkey Song* and *It's Been a Long Time*. My partner and I exchanged glances. She had been there at Vidya Mandir too. A Good Song is always a Good Song, we agreed.

> *I am standing at the crossroads*
> *And I don't know which way to turn*

I've been on this road a long time, a long way to run
Though I know I'll never make it to California
I know I'm gonna find me a place in the sun.

IN CHARGE: The High CD brought out years after the memorial concert (author's personal collection)

2

Stormwatch at Keyatola

A fairly regular after-school ritual at a friend's house on Keyatola Road near Gol Park, Calcutta, would be to listen to *Stormwatch*, Jethro Tull's 1979 album with songs that were, as Ian Anderson would write in the sleeve notes of its re-mastered release in 2003, 'a mixture of moody and dark pieces reflecting the troubled state of the economy... oil price escalation, energy crisis and other depressing world events...'

It was the early '80s and we were old enough to get a whiff of that for sure: *Dark ages shaking the dead, closed pages, better not read.* But what blew our minds was Barriemore Barlow's drumming, his ability to mesh speed and power with intricacies and subtleties I would discover in jazz later. It was the first Tull album I listened to in its entirety, subsequently leading me to *Bursting Out, Heavy Horses, Thick as a Brick, Benefit, This Was* and, well, pretty much their entire catalogue.

Jethro Tull was a musical revelation. And it occurred at a time when music at home was in the form of All India Radio and its daily fix. *Vande Mataram* at dawn, followed by Debdulal Bandhopadhya's news headlines to keep you abreast of the unfolding realities of the day, 'Man Chahey Geet' and 'Aap Ki Pharmaiesh' of Hindi songs in the afternoon, and on Sundays, 'Musical Bandbox' with Jija Bhattacharya. 'Now the song you have all been waiting for, *Una Paloma Blanca* by George Baker, for the listening pleasure of Errol and Dorothy, wishing them on their 50th wedding anniversary are son John and daughter-in-law Joyce... for Sumit and Bhola and their cousin from Delhi Aparishim... And finally, for Montu, Rontu, Biltu and Poltu, not to forget little Jhontu!'

Rabindrasangeet and Atulprasad, S.D. Burman and Timir Baran played on our Garrard changer often, as did *Come September* and *Tiger Rag*; in those days the signature tune played before the start of every movie at Lighthouse at Esplanade. The playlist of our growing up years was complemented at La Martiniere for Boys. Singing *Mor Bina Othe Kon Shure Baajey* for Bengali cultural evening,

Immortal Invisible God Only Wise at morning assembly and *California Dreamin'* in the evening, courtesy a leisure room set up for us boarders back in 1976. It was a carpeted enclosure beside the school dining hall with a few cane sofas and a large gramophone. The collection of records, 45s, 78s and 33&1/3rds, included ones by Mamas and Papas, Simon & Garfunkel, Doobies and Bread.

All the leaves are brown and the sky is grey,
I've been for a walk on a winter's day,
I'd be safe and warm if I was in LA;
California dreamin' on such a winter's day

Jethro Tull jolted us out of our comfort zone. So, decades later in 1994, when we heard Tull would be playing in Bombay, it was a very big deal.

What? No.

You joking, right?

No.

Yes, 'Pied Piper' Ian Anderson and his merry men would be in India. *Bursting Out* started to play in the mind all over again, that timeless collection, a double album of the band's marquee numbers recorded live from a series of performances across Europe featuring Tull's classic '70s line-up of Ian Anderson, Martin Barre, John Evans, Barry Barlow, David Palmer and John Glascock. Night after night we would play the record at that generous friend's Keyatola home. The songs had got into our veins. Curious co-passengers on the crowded S-14 back home to Salt Lake would wonder what it was this lanky boy was humming.

Ian's wordplay before each song would remain with us forever. As would Montreux Jazz Fest founder and promoter Claude Nobs's incredulous multilingual introduction, reflective of the shock and awe of someone announcing a near-impossible event that was somehow about to unfold.

... *Benvenuto Italia* (welcome to Italy)... *Bonsoir* (good evening). *Ce soir...*

Good evening, sit back, relax and make yourselves coms-fortable to enjoy an evening with Jethrohtaahl!

'David's gone for a piss,' we hear Ian tell the audience well into the record. A song later, as the keys wizard from the Royal College of Music returns on stage, he is greeted thus: 'Ah David's back. David, did you give it a good shake?'

And Barriemore Barlow—HOW DOES HE PLAY LIKE THAT?

Barrie wasn't part of Jethro Tull's 25th anniversary band that toured the world, including Bombay, Madras and Bangalore, in 1994. He left the band soon after *Stormwatch*. But their longest serving bandmate, Martin 'Lancelot'

Barre, was there. And so, I made sure we were at Bombay's Rang Bhavan in the February of that year, we including my Significant Other, also a devoted Tull fan.

We were way down the pecking order at *The Telegraph* then to be sent out on assignment. But our then-editor, Shekhar Bhatia, who I later found out was a Jethro Tull faithful himself, allowed us leave. My mother loaned me money for one-way air tickets since we could not get seats on the Bombay Mail at such short notice. Finally, we did make it to the city of Taj Mahal Palace Hotel, Kala Ghoda and Rhythm House, Prithvi Theatre, double-decker buses in close kinship with Calcutta, and pav bhaji—and got to meet Ian the night before the first show at what was a press conference on the poolside of the Oberoi. A day later, before their second outing, we met Martin.

Ian was both witty and serious. He ribbed Michael Jackson for getting all the play on MTV, but spoke with intent on their musical roots, his reasons for taking up the flute, and the one time he shared writing credits with a woman, his first wife, on a song. *Aqualung* went on to become one of Jethro Tull's many signature tunes, in the process saving Ian a lot in alimony.

Martin spoke to us for over an hour. He told us about how the band was blown away by the Bombay crowd's familiarity with all the old songs as opposed to the US where only Tull's newer, post-'70s hits seemed to resonate, and how once Dire Straits frontman Mark Knopfler called him up to discuss nuances about his guitar sound.

MINSTRELS IN THE GALLERY

Why did you choose India?[1]

Ian Anderson: I have had three very brief visits to India before. Travelling as we have done thirty to forty times in the US, coast to coast, the same number of times in Europe, that's where we make our living, make money as concert performers. But we try every year to visit new places which could be Eastern Europe, South America, India. And these are places where we are not necessarily worried about making money.

Martin Barre: We're just happy to play here. For reasons of economics we couldn't bring our own equipment. We had our backline, but couldn't have the PA, and all the lights because we would then lose all the money we've made in twenty-five years. And when we come here we don't make money, we don't lose money. It's very exciting to play to people who don't get lots of western music.

Twenty-five years is a long time. To what do you owe Jethro Tull's longevity?

Ian: I think like the Grateful Dead, we've been very lucky to get a very loyal audience. Jethro Tull is an acquired taste, it's not for everybody. It's not a band you see every time you switch on MTV. In fact, it's not a band you see anytime you switch on MTV (laughing)—no, that's not true, once in a while you do see us.

People who like Jethro Tull tend to be quite passionate about it and so, a very loyal, strong kind of audience always stays with us. Also, like the Dead, if you go to one of our concerts usually you'll find the audience split into two different age groups. One is the 35-45 and the other between 16 and 25, people who weren't even born when we just started making records.

And I think that's pretty true for Jethro Tull, the Grateful Dead and a few other bands. It would be true if Jimi Hendrix was alive, it would be also true if Jim Morrison was alive.

Martin: Yes, we are different. And this difference pays off because people who like us always like us. We are like left of centre. The following we have is also left of centre and not mainstream, not for people who like Phil Collins, Rod Stewart and the Top 20. We are not a fashion item like, say, a band that is very big for a year, two years then they are nothing. Out of fashion. Whereas we are never 'in fashion', therefore, we're never 'out of fashion'. That's why we have people like you, who've known us for years. And, maybe, when, and if, we come back you'll come and see us again.

You bet. How do you raise the enthusiasm to play, say, *Locomotive Breath*, for what must be the millionth time?

Martin: For me, there are two halves to the music; one is the performance, the other is the reception. And if people just sat there, then we'd never play again. But because people react so strongly to it, their energy comes back into you. You are fed by their energy. It's like playing the blues. How does BB King play those same three chords all night for the last fifty years? It's a feeling really, not so much the restrictions of music, it helps you open up. There are bits of music I play every week that I have played for years and years and I am never tired of that. And that's the music I play for pleasure.

Ian: Realistically, of the over 200 songs we have recorded, only 25 per cent are useful live performance songs. *Locomotive Breath* is okay. *Living in the Past* is one that's due for a little light retirement for a year or so. *Aquaiung* has paled, but somehow it's a song that a Jethro Tull concert would be incomplete without.

Tull songs have very complicated arrangements. How do you work them out?

Ian: In most of the music we've done, it is usually 100 per cent me, or 90 per cent me. But certainly there have been albums where many of the individual band members have been very involved in contributing bits and pieces of music. You can imagine *Eleanor Rigby* words and music Lennon-McCartney, you kind of figure that they do 50-50—we know that it isn't, they agreed to split everything 50-50 even though one hadn't done anything on one song. But, in our case if you come across Anderson-Barre the implication is, roughly speaking, we have done a 50-50 contribution.

Albums like *Thick as a Brick, Songs from the Wood, Minstrel in the Gallery* all have credits at the bottom on the valuable inputs by different band members. But, yes, it's mostly me, that's my job; if not one of my many talents, it certainly is one of my many jobs.

Martin: Sometimes Ian has a whole idea of a song, sometimes he has a few chords, when we sit down and work out everything. There's no set rule. Some things are complicated, others are very fluid. It's just the way we write. When I write music I find it very difficult to write something simplistic. I don't like things to go straight. I like things to go at a tangent and come back again. And as long as it is relevant, then I think it's okay to do it. For example, *Thick as a Brick* took us two months of rehearsal and two months to record.

During 1977-78, *Songs from the Wood, Heavy Horses* had a lot of folk elements. That was a very fertile period for Tull. What about other influences?

Martin: I don't think that any one style of music dictates what we play. Again, the way I play music, I don't think of a style and write in that style. I just play. Sometimes something might be triggered by a folk melody, an idea might be from a jazz chord and then the next one follows. It's a mood to me. If you ask me, I'd say I am a blues rock player because I don't really like folk and jazz music that much. But I like classical music, I like rock music. I like blues, but again, I don't particularly listen to it.

However, there's a lot more to it. I don't think that these days it's possible to have just one style and not encompass anything else. I think you have to have a good background of all styles of music and then all those influences come around in one direction.

Ian: We started off being a blues group, then very quickly there was a strange metamorphosis where we became eclectic and a lot of influences came from

OH, BOMBAY: IAN ANDERSON poses for the author before the media interaction at the Oberoi; with Garry Lawyer

all different places, not just for me, but to all the band members. All of them had their own specific interest in different kinds of music.

And there have been a lot of members in Jethro Tull, twenty-two in twenty-five years. It is very confusing and sometimes I am not sure what it is we are doing. There's an old term 'progressive rock'. I still don't think there's really a better term for what we do than that rather old-fashioned classification for a good old-fashioned band.

How have the changes in Tull's line-up affected the group?

Martin: Mostly positive, because it's usually an improvement. The only way it has been derogatory is that Jethro Tull doesn't have an image as a group anymore when most people don't know the names of who is in the group. But there was a time when everybody knew who were the members of the group, the personalities were all very strong. It was very much a group identity up to *Bursting Out* (1978), the time when David Palmer, John Evans, Barry Barlow, John Glascock went away. We never really got steady after that. I think that was the time when it changed a lot. And now Ian is the image of the group. I am not moaning, but it's just the way it is supposed to be because the record company finds it easy to promote Ian rather than a fast-changing group of faces.

What news of Barriemore Barlow?

Martin: Well, he doesn't play much these days. He has his studio and manages bands. I don't get to see him often.

You are the longest serving Tull member and Ian has said that if you are not there he'd have to think twice before using the name, Jethro Tull. How is it that you have stuck on?

Martin: I don't think about it. I do as well as I can. There's no reasoning behind it. It's a choice that Ian has. I think he enjoys working with other people, it is enjoyable and I have done things away from the group. And I think Ian will, too, and hopefully we will just go back on the road with Jethro Tull, and hopefully Ian will want me to do it.

But I don't hold a gun to his head. I know that ultimately Ian will do what's best for him and I want him to do that. It would be wrong to have Jethro Tull as an entity for old time's sake because we have to do a good job and it is up to every musician to understand that. If you don't do a job you're supposed to do, it's time to go, it's time to look somewhere else for a job.

What is your relationship with Ian like?

Martin: We are going really well, even though we have very separate lifestyles. We live very far from each other, coincidentally, and we are very different when we tour. I go running and don't see very much of the others and Ian does the interviews. There's no tension or bad feelings. Arguing, fighting and getting angry is okay when you are twenty, but when you are forty you have a job to do and you do it.

The Jethro Tull lead guitar is very distinct. It's heavy and penetrating. What guitar do you play?

Martin: It's a Tom Anderson made in Los Angeles. It's nothing special, only that it's made in very small quantities. And I say I like a certain type of wood in the body and certain type in the neck and they put it together.

About the sound, the way you play a guitar involves so many variables, the plectrum, the way you hit the strings, the way you finger the left hand, about a hundred thousand variables. That's why nobody can sound like Jimi Hendrix, no one can sound like Eric Clapton or BB King.

And nobody can sound like Martin Barre.

Martin: Well (laughs), nobody wants to sound quite like Martin Barre!

But I know at least one person who wants to… A man named Mark Knopfler, who apparently said so in 1987 when Tull released the *Crest of a Knave* album.

Martin: Oh yeah (feigning ignorance initially)? Yes, he did like my sound and asked guys at Tom Anderson for a similar sounding guitar. But he knows more than anybody else that you may like the sound of a guitar; you need to play it differently.

Ian, why did you choose the flute?

Ian: As I did say earlier, I am just a guy who plays the flute, I stand at the front and take most of the applause and all of the abuse. Well, not many people play it, with the exception of Moody Blues and the guy who used to be in the band called Traffic—he's dead, by the way, there's no competition. And I think there may be four people, including a Dutch guy in a band called Focus that I can think of, having a reputation of being a flute player within a rock context.

It may sound like a joke, but the flute *is* a terrible instrument to play in a rock band. In reality, I have been an acoustic musician for nearly twenty-five years, ever since I left school really. Playing acoustic music in the middle of a bunch of completely crazy, power-crazed noisy maniacs—you know the other four guys in the band—I don't hear what I play most of the nights. Some people say it is a good thing. And I find it very difficult, frustrating.

The last time you were here you were presented with a flute and a tape of Hariprasad Chaurasia. Have you managed to hear it? Has any of that influence found its way into your music?

Ian: No. But I do listen to most of the recordings of local indigenous music people very kindly give me when I am touring. And like everything else, I am sure a little bit of it comes out in the things I play. And at the moment I do have some music that I am working on which does have—I am not going to insult you by saying it has an Indian flavour—but it certainly does have more to do with this region of Planet Earth than the Tower of London.

In fact, the last thing I did before leaving my studio in London was to send four of my Arabic drums and a set of tablas to another drummer to learn and play. So you can hear these influences one way or the other, but don't look for a scholarly approach to it because that's not my style. I react to music emotionally, in my own naive way. I don't read music in the conventional sense… I don't even understand what I am doing most of the time.

You've never worked with a female singer, have you?

Ian: A good point. For years I found myself without any favourites among female singers. But recently, I have started to enjoy a few people. I had a lot of fun playing on a record for a beautiful singer called Wendy Mahai. Milla from Yugoslavia is another great singer and songwriter.

But I have to be very careful, it's very tense working with a girl face to face. I am a little old-fashioned, you know. The only time I did that was with my first wife. What happened was that she had a few lines, sort of poetry, and in an attempt to reinforce our relationship, I said 'let's make this into a song'. And I expanded on the lines she had written and gave her the lyric-writing credit for *Aqualung*. I think the royalties, accruing from the seven million sales of the record, saved me quite a lot on alimony. It was a way of saying goodbye.

What are your plans for the immediate future? Is there another Jethro Tull album coming?

Ian: As soon as I finish this next bit of touring I will be working on a classical album (really relishing the word) as a flute player, as a writer working with some other musicians. Also, Chrysalis Records wants me to do a blues-rock album and there's a bunch of things that I am working on, not really Jethro Tull material, but might be a solo project. But, yes, there will definitely be another Jethro Tull album. Probably won't be a very good one, but there will be a Jethro Tull album and you can pretend you love it.[1]

Jethro Tull released *Roots to Branches*, their 19th studio album in September 1995. It was the last to feature Dave Pegg on the bass and the last album to be brought out by Chrysalis Records, their longtime record label. Ian calls it the '90s version of *Stand Up*, Tull's 1968 album whose ascendance to the British charts was communicated to him by none other than Joe Cocker while the band was at breakfast at a hotel in Manhattan. 'Because it (*Roots to Branches*) has a lot of things that I feel represented the key elements of Jethro Tull; there's lots of riffy guitars and quite a broad palette of influences, from the blues and classical to the Eastern motifs that were apparent on *Stand Up*... the only thing about it that lets me down is that I made it sound a little too '70s. Looking back, I think it should have been a bit more varied.'[2]

The Bombay concerts were mind-blowing; we actually got to attend both evenings, thanks to the promoter who took a liking to this crazy journalist duo that had come from Calcutta. Dutifully, I filed a report for *The Telegraph* half expecting it to be spiked. But it did get published.

A NIGHT OF COBWEBBY CLASSICS

The Pied Piper from 1968 Blackpool stole the show. Playing to a packed Rang Bhavan, British rock mega star Ian Anderson and his Jethro Tull rocked Bombay for over two hours that just slipped by.[3]

The over 2,000, mostly over-30s crowd was overwhelmed. Witness to this historic first-ever event in the country, they were stunned, and would only manage wide-eyed whispers at hearing live Jethro Tull tracks they spent their lives listening to.

So, while *Thick As A Brick* did have the more younger and enthusiastic front-rowers jump and squeal, the over-35s just swayed to the beat and silently lipped those words penned by a child prodigy. Of course, it was Ian Anderson gyrating, ranting and raving all the way, fluttering and tonguing his flute in his own inimitable style.

'God, what a night,' someone burst out.

My Sunday Feeling catapulted Ian onto stage wearing black tights (a looser version of his heydays) and a sprightly green jacket that was dispensed with soon after. His flute, versatile as ever, was energetic; Martin Barre's guitar sharp, dignified; Doanne Perry's drums tight, dexterous and reminiscent of Barriemore Barlow; Dave Pegg's bass intricately bouncy and Andy Giddings's keyboards smooth and melodious.

The sparkling wit, the naughty humour came, as always, as a bonus. 'In this track you will find our drummer Mr Doanne Perry getting very excited. A pulsating, throbbing mass of erectile tissue. So much that he might soil himself and in the process, a few up front,' was the first major dig of the evening while introducing *For A Thousand Mothers*.

Bouree by JS Bach ('whoever the f... he was, he's dead anyway') had Mr Piper squatting on stage while his sweaty brow was furrowed in concentration. *So Much Trouble*, a blues from their younger days was sheer brilliance. In fact, *So Much Trouble* was no trouble at all. Ian's blues harp, Martin's acoustic guitar (no, no one remembered to check on his 'forced and unforced errors' which Ian had jokingly predicted) and Perry's cymbals had feet tapping in no time.

By then Jethro Tull was in the air. So was the grass. What was earlier an occasional whiff, became a regular, periodic wave. There was no seating, but no one was complaining. Ian was in full blast and more wisecracks followed. The customary digs at Michael J over, he settled on Doanne once again, this time asking all in the crowd not to hold his American origins against him.

An instrumental version of *Whistler* with Martin's heavy lead gave Ian his drink of water and a few minutes' of respite. And with *Sossity; You're a Woman* it was nostalgia working overtime. Even three of the current Tull members weren't with the band when this cobwebby classic was recorded for the 1960 *Benefit* album. Only Martin Barre was, since December 1968. Bassist Dave Pegg of Fairport Convention replaced John Glascock after his death in 1979, while drummer Doanne Perry from Los Angeles and keyboardist Andy joined later.

But the music was reassuringly vintage Tull. *Songs From The Wood* became an interesting medley—a few verses from *Heavy Horses* and *Too Old to Rock, Too Young To Die* hemmed in for old times' sake. Hearts were beating fast and the crowd yearned for more. It wasn't disappointed. *Aqualung, Locomotive Breath* and *A New Day Yesterday* followed in succession.

A crisp yet flashy *Cross-Eyed Mary* was the encore gift, along with two huge white Jethro Tull balloons that set sail amidst the audience. The song over, a moment's blackout and Jethro Tull was gone. The only persons happy were the staff of BPL, the primary sponsor, and Mr Vikram Singh, whose Performance Arts Trust was the promoter responsible for the history just made. The Tull show was over without a hitch.

Back on the empty stage was a diagonal clothes line and clinging onto it was an impressive array of T-shirts and lingerie along with a white-on-black hoarding that read: 'Jethro Tull Argentine girls love you.' Now, that's an understatement.

On the way out of Rang Bhavan, there was a kind of hushed silence. Each one of us—I remember talking to singer Garry Lawyer and catching a glimpse

of Arjun Rampal, Mehr Jessia, DJ Anish Trivedi—felt thankful that night. What was it that had kept us so close to Tull, we wondered as we ambled our way back, partly on foot and then in a black-and-yellow Fiat taxi, to Hotel Sea View on Marine Drive. Was it about the 'haystack madness' of *Moths*, the novelty of *Aqualung*, the head-banging of *Locomotive Breath* or the sense of foreboding in *Stormwatch*? It had to be about the *Minstrel in the Gallery*, invoking, much like the Baul, the lonesome performer seeking a connection with his audience and Keeper. It must also be for Ian's flute, poetry and the imagery of the unadulterated joys of *Living in the Past*, of *Velvet Green* and the jagged edges of Martin's guitar, alternately inspiring moments of quiet introspection and overt celebration.[3]

Agreed, Jethro Tull is an acquired taste. For me, it will always be about the cultural sophistication of Bombay via Keyatola Road. If Calcutta's Park Street was mostly about homegrown talent, Bombay's jazz scene had been honed well over four decades into the early '60s. On that visit, we would find ourselves munching on sandwiches every morning at Gaylords near Churchgate Station, little realising then that it was, at one time, among the many night clubs—like the Ambassador, Napoli, Ritz, Bistro and Volga—offering jazz every night. It is said, the sound of jazz bands was the loudest in Bombay outside of the US, prompting none other than the legendary pianist, Dave 'Take Five' Brubeck, to try and record a few numbers during one of his visits to the port city.

These days Rang Bhavan is no longer a concert venue. Rhythm House has shut shop. But hey, there's a bridge across the sea linking Bandra with Worli, and traffic, South Bombaywallahs will tell you, has eased. Another one, the Versova-Bandra Sea Link of 17.7 km, which is three times the length of the Bandra-Worli Seal Link, is being built at an estimated cost of Rs 7,000 crore. It is expected to cut down the ninety-minute commute time between Versova and Bandra to ten minutes.

But we continue to talk of rising petrol prices amid job losses, farm distress and growing economic uncertainty. *Dark Ages*, as prophesied in *Stormwatch*, are well and truly upon us.

Jagged fires mark the picket lines
The politicians weep
And mealy-mouthed
Through corridors of power on tip-toe creep.
Come and see bureaucracy

Make its final heave
And let the new disorder through
While senses take their leave.

THIS WAS: JETHRO TULL circa 1970, perhaps their best line-up with John Evan (from left), Martin Barre, David Palmer, John Glascock, Ian Anderson, and the 'sporty' Barriemore Barlow (from the 25th anniversary tour Press kit)

OUTRO

Jethro Tull, with Ian, Martin and a varying line-up of bandmates, would return to India many times. In 2005, while we were living in Pune, I went to Mumbai, to catch them. Years later, Tull came to Calcutta and played at Science City auditorium. We had tickets for the November 27, 2008 show, but did not go. It was the day after the terrorist attack on Taj Palace in Mumbai.

After quitting Tull in 1980, Barriemore Barlow moved on as record producer. He plays occasionally and appeared with Ian and the band at the Royal Festival Hall in London in 2008.

My last question to Ian—every Tull interview just must end with it—was about their song, *Too Old To Rock 'n Roll: Too Young To Die*. A prescient ode to the performer, I asked. Ian's response was meditative.

'The reality is, yes, of course, we have become too old to rock 'n roll. The only good news is that Mick Jagger and Tina Turner will be too old a couple of years before I will, because they are even older than me. And, jokes apart, like me, they are known for their physical performance. It's a tough decision when you do that sort of thing for a living. But I think we're going to carry on long before you guys are saying, "Hey, give it a rest now" because something in you can't stop. By my standards the more frustrated I become for not being able to do it, the more I am going to keep trying to do it. Anyway, cheers, the show really must go on.'

Of course. Jethro Tull embarked on a 50th Anniversary Tour in 2018. Last heard, Martin Barre wasn't in it.

3

Big Pink on Campus

The VCR wouldn't switch on. We were all waiting, music fiends and a few guests whom we had invited to Presidency College for a screening of *Woodstock*, the 1970 released Oscar-winning 185-minute documentary. Finally, we had to assemble all over again the next day. Even Amit Datta, his brother Monojit 'Kochu' Datta, already among the established crop of musicians of Calcutta, returned to the main building to see such eminences as Richie Havens, Santana, Jimi Hendrix, Joe Cocker, CSNY, Joan Baez, Arlo Guthrie and many, many more perform for three days beginning August 15, 1969 at Max Yasgur's 600-acre farm near Bethel, New York. It was an epic gathering of musicians, comparable only with the earlier Monterey Pop (1967) and the later Live Aid (1985), who performed live for a rain-soaked audience of thousands—186,000 tickets were sold initially but the surge of 'devotees' was such that the Woodstock Music and Art Fair was opened up to the public for free.

It's 2019, fifty years since Woodstock when Jimi Hendrix signed off with his distortion-riffed overhaul of *The Star-Spangled Banner*, encompassing in one rock act the overwhelming concerns of the time, the Vietnam war, economic divide and race relations. Richie Havens sang about freedom, Arlo about coming to Los Angeles, CSNY about those wooden ships, 'scared shitless' as they were; Joe Cocker went endearingly berserk telling us how to get by with a little help from friends while Country Joe McDonald immortalised the Fish Cheer (Gimme an F!...).

Michael Wadleigh, who had for his documentary got together 100 of the best known camera and sound men, including a gentleman by the name of Martin Scorsese, released a 224-minute director's cut in 1994 to add some of the performances that had been omitted, including sets by Grateful Dead, Ravi Shankar, CCR and The Band.

We watched Woodstock in 1985-86, less than two decades after the historic concert that defined counterculture and instilled in a generation a sense of focus and purpose, foregrounding ideals forever worth fighting for. Within months, we held another screening, this time of *The Last Waltz*, The Band's farewell concert of 1976. Directed by Scorsese, it featured Messrs Robbie Robertson and a stellar cast of performers like Mr Dylan (of course), Neil Young, Neil Diamond, Dr John and Ronnie Hawkins who set the stage on fire.

It was about a decade to the day of that historic gig at San Francisco's Winterland Ballroom. Yet, for some of us, that was the day we were introduced to them for the first time. Levon Helm singing about *The Night They Drove Old Dixie Down*, his head turned to his right as he worked the snare drum; Neil Diamond beseeching one and all to *Dry Your Eyes*; Dr John gushing about *Such a Night* and Ronnie posing that all-important question, *Who Do You Love?*

Eric Clapton confessed many years later how The Band's 1968 album, *Music From Big Pink*, an incomparable collection of songs about faith and hopelessness, rooted in rock but blending seamlessly with country, folk and blues, had pointed to what music should sound like. They were clearly the avant-garde, he said, at one time even contemplating going up to Catskill Mountains of West Saugerties, New York, to find out if there was a place for him in, well, The Band. Among the songs they played that night and at Woodstock was *The Weight* (1968).

I pulled into Nazareth, was feelin' about half past dead
I just need some place where I can lay my head
'Hey, mister, can you tell me where a man might find a bed?'
He just grinned and shook my hand, 'no' was all he said
Take a load off, Fanny
Take a load for free
Take a load off, Fanny
And (and) (and) you put the load right on me

Ki re, paarbi toh (You'll manage, right)? Our pianist tapped me on the shoulder from the bench behind me, sharing, in a sense, my wide-eyed wonder at Levon singing while playing the drums. Effortless. She is today a music teacher somewhere in Southeast Asia, while the other members of our college band—later christened Hipgnosis, the name shamelessly filched from a book bought from a second hand shop on College Street about the late Storm Thorgerson and Aubrey Powell, the duo responsible for most of rock music's iconic album covers (Pink Floyd, Led Zeppelin, Genesis)—have gone into management, finance and, would you believe it, journalism.

The Last Waltz embedded in us music's higher calling, the purity of performance, the singer becoming one with the song, the Baul with his ektara, the trumpet with the drums, the guitar with the violin. That muggy afternoon at Presidency College changed our lives, forcing us to embark on what would become a fresh journey of discovery. A long road, two-way of course, that, happily, never ends.

The Ventures, Palkir Gaan, SD Burman's *Khatmal*, Rabindrasangeet and Yehudi Menuhin-Ravi Shankar jugalbandhi—every house in Calcutta had the *East Meets West* album neatly displayed in the drawing room showcase—were playing at home on 45, 78 and 331/3 rpm. Beatles, Doors, Jethro Tull, Traffic, Pink Floyd and CCR were on All India Radio's musical Bandbox. Now it was time to look out, broaden horizons: The American University Centre (AUC) Jazz Club, with fortnightly listening sessions at the Lincoln Room on Chowringhee, was our window; Miles Davis, John Coltrane, Dizzy Gillespie, Herbie Hancock, Weather Report with Jaco Pastorius and Omar Hakim, Jean-Luc Ponty, ELP (Emerson, Lake & Palmer) and the rest.

Multiple doors began to open in a mindscape of song, colour and smoke. To the extent that I found myself at Woodstock too—promise!—when Richie Havens was at Gol Park's open-air theatre (OAT) in the early '80s to sing *Freedom* just as he had done at Max's farm in 1969.

Sometimes, I feel like a motherless child

The concert was delayed. Load-shedding. A power shutdown that all of us in the Calcutta of '70s and '80s had learnt to cope with. Wishbone Ash were to come on later. But we were there for Richie. It seemed a never-ending wait. We got impatient. Screams, shouts and expletives were hurled at the government of the day, the Communist Party of India (Marxist)-led Left Front.

Policemen on duty came rushing in. They weren't many, but fanned out nevertheless. They had lathis, but said nothing, hoping we would quieten down. No one did. They walked around a bit. When they ran towards the stage, someone from the back would shout out another expletive, this time with the name of the intended target. The moment the policemen reached the rear end of OAT, another group from the front shouted out more names. We got raucous—not proud of it now. But the cops let us be. They did not beat us with their lathis, did not arrest us into silence.

On hindsight that was inflection point, however slight, in the way the Left Front government would navigate cultural spaces it perceived as problematic. For Richie, unbeknownst to him, was singing in the backdrop of 'apasanskriti' or crass culture, a term used to signify a vilification campaign launched by the

FREEDOM: RICHIE HAVENS at Woodstock
(pencil sketch on textured paper by Suman Choudhury)

ruling party against anything popular, especially if it was ordained with western influences. Championed by the late RSP leader, Jatin Chakraborty, who was a minister in chief minister Jyoti Basu's cabinet, apasanskriti's prime target was Usha Uthup, a multilingual singer with fluency in English, Bangla, Hindi, Tamil, Malayalam and even Swahili.

So when Usha, a Tamilian by birth who married a man from Kerala and went on to live in Calcutta, sang *Malaika*, possibly the most recognisable Swahili love song in celebration of angelic beauty, and then mixed it up with a *Dum Maro Dum* followed by the smouldering 1956 R&B classic, *Fever*, the elders in the Party saw red. I suspect it incensed them even more to see how easily Usha was able to work up the crowds with her elegant renditions of danceable numbers in her trademark Kanjeevaram sari and bold bindi on her forehead. Why, I still remember her singing at La Martiniere during our school's annual fete sometime in 1977-78 while we were manning a skittles stall.

Usha fought tooth and nail against apasanskriti, often requesting crowds at her shows not to turn belligerent while dancing to her tunes so as not to attract undue attention of the powers that be. She even met Chakraborty who, it was made known then, ultimately asked cadres to pipe down. Truce.

At the OAT that night, the lights came on about an hour later. And Richie trooped in, hunched, hugging his guitar. We all sang about freedom.

Freedom, freedom, freedom…
Sometimes, I feel like a motherless child
A long, long, long way, way from my home

College students have a lot to say. They get belligerent and shout a lot. But, at that music concert the police in Bengal let us be. At Presidency College then, the students' union comprised a bunch of Independents, in other words, not offshoots of political parties although youth wings of the Congress, Left parties and even the BJP were present on campus trying to exert their influence with varying degrees of success. There was the odd sloganeering, but by and large, the campus was peaceful with no particularly dominant ideology holding sway. The police were never on campus. They let us be. It seems so long ago.

Richie's songs and vigorous guitar playing that night brought Woodstock home to us in Calcutta. More than a decade later, I would get to hear folk patriarch Pete Seeger in Delhi and learn how protest need not always be combative. Decency, humour and compassion count too.

'There is no such thing as a wrong note as long as you can sing it,' Pete Seeger said, his gentle tone immediately endearing him to an audience that had spilled on to the aisles of the main auditorium of Siri Fort in Delhi. It was 1996, a month before Christmas, and Pete was singing paeans to love, peace, brotherhood and nature in India thirty years after he sang *We Shall Overcome* to a crowd of over 15,000 faithful in Calcutta.

The Siri Fort concert was about the power of simplicity and its effectiveness when rooted in truth.

You've got to walk that lonesome valley
You've got to walk it by yourself
No one else can walk it for you
You've got to walk it by yourself...

Woody Guthrie's song of life was one of the many Pete performed that night. He had learnt them from him while touring with the Almanac Singers in the '40s after giving free performances at union meetings and strikers' rallies. 'A small little man who never had much money, but wrote some of the world's greatest songs ever,' Pete described the friend several years his senior.

The money question would recur several times that night. It would return years later, when Woody's son Arlo would surface magically in Delhi.

RAGHUPATI RAGHAV ON THE BANJO

They all sang along.[1]

With Pete Seeger it is difficult not to. Embellishing his selection with high-note harmonies by grandson Tao Rodriguez, Pete strummed his banjo and guitar to strike up the ever-popular *If I had a hammer* question, reminisce Jose Marti's *Guantanamera,* count *1,2,3* on the *Vietnam Song* and run through the *Midnight Special.* In between there were stories, lots of laughter, more stories and a knee-slapping, foot-stomping jingle that had the 77-year-old bringing the house down with thunderous applause.

And they all sang along.

The money tune came next. It was zesty, what with Tao's freewheeling harmonies aided by the snappy guitar rhythm: ...*Money can still be handy too (but) let's not allow 'king money' to rule.*

The audience, essentially 30-plus, was loving it.

'How does he do it?'

'What energy, it's amazing...' were all that the chattering classes could manage.

But it was truly magical. How could one man, 77 years old, and helped only by a guitar and a grandson, captivate his listeners thus? And that too when there are none of the now-generation psychedelic pyrotechnics, no multi-coloured lights and no fancy bass-boosting sound system.

The truth is Pete doesn't need all that. He never did. For having spent over five decades directing music towards social change for peace, equality and decency, his philosophy was always about heart-and-soul, and about the power of simplicity. No wonder they always sing along.

During the early '60s, after he was able to reorganise the Newport Folk Festival to use profits to help folk performers, he privately published *How to Play the Five-String Banjo* but refused to copyright the book because the 'banjo belongs to everyone'. Pete's humanity was so unusual it seemed threatening. Always a popular target of the US witch-hunt—he was sentenced to prison and blacklisted during the McCarthy era—particularly suspicious was his custom of learning songs from every country where he gave concerts.

Back at Siri Fort, Tao held on to this tradition as he rendered an Argentinian song about god, war and the future. Pete was on harmony this time as the grandson's soul-stirring high-pitched singing had the audience fall head over heels. A standing ovation was the young man's reward.

A slow and soft tune on Pete's recorder helped the ever-cooperating audience hum one note for effect, which was then followed by what the Guru had picked up from an Indian student, *Ram Dhun*. Tao dwelled on the high notes once again as Pete celebrated his comeback.

Raghupati Raghav Raja Ram/Patita Pavan Sita Ram....

And they all sang along.

Over two hours had slipped by rather quickly. By then there were more songs with tabla player Ashim Chakraborty joining the duo. But the audience was getting restless. Some of the favourites were yet to come. '*Turn, Turn*', someone screamed from the far corner of the balcony. '*Last Train to Nuremberg, Garbage*', it went on. Amidst all the shouts for encores, chief guest Ustad Amjad Ali Khan presented the customary floral tributes on behalf of hosts, Indian Council for Cultural Relations. And as Pete thanked the 'wonderful singing audience,' he obliged with The Anthem.

We shall overcome,
We shall overcome, someday
Oh deep in my heart I do believe
We shall overcome someday...

And they all sang along.

I learnt that song in Bangla in the '70s as a ten-year-old while living on a college campus on Beltola Road in Bhawanipore, hearing students sing it with zest, welcoming a group of families from Bangladesh who had fled the war of 1971 and had been sheltered there, courtesy my aunt, the principal of Beltola Basic Training College. Not sure if I grasped its true import then, but as the years passed I realised how my mother and I could well have been among them. Not fleeing war, but finding ourselves without a roof over our heads after life in Agartala took an unexpected turn.

WE SHALL OVERCOME: PETE SEEGER by E.P. Unny (author's personal collection)

That song, anthem really, would be heard on various occasions in Calcutta; at student marches protesting too few teachers in government colleges, at Left Front political rallies against the bourgeois Press or funnily enough, at residents' meetings to demand, not eight-hourly, but four-hourly, water supply from Calcutta Corporation and at a Dharamtala sit-in defence of the Bengali's inalienable right not to work and enforce a state-wide shutdown (bandh). Calcutta still loves a good protest. We had to take it in our stride. Still do.

But Delhi is way different.

As the very select swish set settled down and sipped wine on the lawns of Roosevelt House, the US ambassador's official residence at Chanakyapuri, he walked in, and some of the ladies whispered, 'Who is Arlo Guthrie?'

That evening in 1998, thirty years after he strummed his guitar to a spaced-out audience at Woodstock, Arlo and ambassador Richard Celeste were undoing the past, giving new meaning to what someone had said about 'the times' long ago. Sometime between 1983 and 1991, when Celeste was governor of Ohio, he had invited Pete Seeger and the Weavers, that included a young Arlo, to play, making up for a McCarthy-era censure of their concert circa the '50s. Now, having learnt that Arlo was travelling, he invited him to India.

The times they are a-changin'.

Son of the legendary Woody Guthrie, long-time touring partner to Pete Seeger and darling of the swinging '60s, Arlo was in 1998 as old as India. Fifty, looking a fit forty, his shoulder-length mane a startling mix of grey and blond. He was also heavier than what we remember him looking like in the Woodstock footage, the twenty-something man with guitar singing about *Coming into Los Angeles*.

Accompanied by son Abe on keys, he sang his songs. Old and new. And, of course, *Alice's Restaurant*, that eighteen-and-half-minute story-tune released in 1967, which recounts his infamous arrest for littering three years earlier.

That arrest record kept him out of the army during the Vietnam War: he wasn't moral enough to fight and kill people.

'You know, back in those days, I would bet serious money against doing this song at the US Ambassador's house,' he joked. 'And today, even more strange things are happening. Back home, they are making a stamp out of my father. Boy, if he were alive to see this!'

America's greatest and certainly most influential folk poet, Woody Guthrie wrote over a thousand songs, hundreds of poems and books during a life spent in relative poverty. 'I was only seven when he went into hospital, and twenty–twenty-one when he died,' says Arlo of his father. Having made more money with his first album than his father did in his entire life, Arlo looked at things differently. Many feared the money would 'spoil' him. It didn't. Armed with a wry sense of humour, Arlo's view of contemporary reality caught the fancy of the times. The '67 Newport Folk Festival established him and Woodstock made him. He was big.

In Delhi, when I caught up with him, it was as though he took off from where he left us—the Woodstock stage.

THE PROTEST SINGER, HIS SPORTS CAR

How did you end up playing at the US ambassador's house?[2]

Richard Celeste is an old friend from years ago. As Governor of Ohio, he invited Pete Seeger and his Weavers and myself to do a few shows to undo what had happened in the '50s, when a Weavers concert was cancelled in Ohio because of the McCarthy blacklist. So we met, stayed at his official home and rehearsed, and performed our show. He's been a friend ever since.

As for this visit, we were stopping over en-route Australia. Once in Delhi, Richard asked us whether we'd mind playing for a few friends. Sure, we said, and played.

Do you still write songs satirising the Army and the establishment?

The nice thing about *Alice's Restaurant* is that even today the biggest single source of sales of that record is the US military. I think the kind of humour that's not humiliating is the best kind—I learnt this from my father. You can't take everything so seriously that you lose yourself in it. After the crisis there still has to be you. This was the problem many Left-wing and Right-wing people had. They got lost in the ideology and then there was no them.

Where do you think folk music is headed?

I think my father, Pete and the others invented a different kind of music. Music that sounds traditional but talks contemporary. They took old songs and re-wrote them, or wrote new songs about immediate things. Guys like Bob Dylan and Bruce Springsteen are continuing that tradition, and I have great respect for them when they make records that they know are not going to be on MTV. But a huge number of people are buying them. There is a big resurgence of folk music not just in the US, but also in Europe.

How important is money to you? I am told success led you to buy a penthouse and that your mother didn't approve of such 'self-indulgence'?

I don't know that story, but I'll tell you another one. When I first made some money, I wanted to buy a sports car. Pete's son Danny had a red MGA, one of those which Elvis drove in the movies. And I wanted it. But my mother said,

WOODSTOCK'S DARLING: ARLO GUTHRIE in India, sometime in the late '90s when he appeared magically in New Delhi for a concert at the residence of then US ambassador Richard Celeste

'No. Folk singers cannot drive sports cars. You should get a sensible car.' But I said, 'Mom, I'm not a folk singer, I'm a guy. I'll drive this sports car, have girlfriends, it'll be cool.' And she said, 'No. Absolutely not.' And then I said, 'Mom, I'm buying it from Pete.'

That silenced her. If there had been anyone else in the world that I could get this car from, she would have kept going. But because I was buying it from Pete, there was nothing else she could say. So I bought the car, and had a great time for years. And she never spoke to me about it again, as if it didn't exist.

I made more money with my one record than my father had made in his entire life. And I don't think my mother understood that. I didn't. It had nothing to do with what's right or wrong. It's just the way it was. But I am sensible, too, and I bought myself a place in Massachusetts, and thirty years later, I still live there; I have been married to the same girl for thirty years.

Any plans of a real concert in India?

Yeah. Maybe as soon as January. I am also trying to get some Woodstock friends like Richie Havens, Country Joe and John Sebastian.

The last Pete Seeger and Arlo Guthrie show was in November 30, 2013 at Carnegie Hall, only a few months before Pete passed away at the age of ninety-four. I did not have the good fortune of seeing them live on stage together, but thanks to the internet, I caught them performing an Elvis Presley song sometime in 1993.[3]

Always one to spin a yarn, Arlo talks of a time when the two of them were performing in Denmark at a folk festival after the fall of the Berlin Wall. Arlo jokes about how Pete looked at him sternly and how the banjo looked quite threatening, when he chose to sing the Elvis song since 'Pete had already sung all the songs, like the *We Shall Overcome* types that used to mean a lot of things to a lot of people decades ago.' And that when Arlo started to sing, *I Can't Help Falling In Love With You*, everyone sang along. All 30,000 people, including Pete, who also 'knew' the tune. As Arlo goes on with his story, we get a glimpse of Pete, leisurely reclining on what seems to be a platform hosting the drum set, smiling away. He gets up and starts to play the Elvis tune on his banjo as Arlo sings and the audience willingly joins in.

That night, Arlo said a few things about protest, music and Elvis; and what he meant to the world.

'There they were 30,000 drinking, screaming, crying and laughing… people all singing an old Elvis tune somewhere in Europe. Boy there was something wonderful about that, you know. I suddenly realised how proud I was to come from a country where our songs are loved, known and sung all over the world by all kinds of people. Also, I learnt a little bit about what folk songs are about and even what they are not about. Sometimes it's not even about anything… Here we were singing an old Elvis tune that didn't have much to say about the state of the world or something like that, but more was being said by who was singing it and how they were feeling.'

OUTRO

We are still waiting for an Arlo Guthrie concert in India, although Arlo has been touring extensively with the family band comprising son Abe and daughters Cathy, Annie and Sarah Lee, and their children. At their annual Thanksgiving Concert in November 2017, there were thirteen family members on stage!

In 2012, he held The Family Reunion tour to honour the centennial of his father Woody Guthrie's birth. Arlo lost his wife Jackie Hyde shortly after the tour, a few days after their 43rd wedding anniversary.[4]

As for Alice's restaurant, Arlo seems to have had other plans. As the song tells us, 'Alice didn't live in a restaurant. She lived in the church nearby the restaurant…'

And so, the old Trinity Church,[3] where Alice once lived and where the saga began, is now home to The Guthrie Center and The Guthrie Foundation. The center has a not-for-profit interfaith church foundation dedicated to providing a wide range of humanitarian services locally and internationally.

Meanwhile, *Alice's Restaurant* is half a century old, to commemorate which Arlo released a two-CD-set that captured the magic of his historic tour to celebrate the milestone. The performance, recorded live at The Colonial Theatre in Pittsfield, MA, was also released as a film. More recently, during a short break of his Re-Generation Tour, and amid talks of heading Down Under for a series of concerts in 2019, Arlo—now in his seventies—posted on FB a message that spoke about his abiding concerns: '…I'm hoping to get to as many places as I can before the world gets too crazy, or I get too old—both seem to be happening at dizzying speed. I'm hanging in there anyway, just because I want to see how it all turns out. It would be very nice for as many people as possible to get to experience an ordinary day. A day where no one has to pay attention to the folly of others, and just enjoy family and friends wherever they are.'

4

Miles meets Marquez

A deadline is a deadline, the otherwise friendly features editor reminds me and turns the other way. September 1991, I am about four years into journalism and she has just asked me to write an obituary of Miles Davis for the Sunday pages of *The Telegraph*. What? Me and Miles? I may have heard a couple of tunes and watched some videos, but that hardly qualifies for writing on *The Man With The Horn*.

That was typical *Telegraph*. You are thrown in the deep end to swim or sink. I manage, to swim I guess, and 'A Last Post for the Man with the Horn'[1] is published on Sunday, October 6, a pretty straight-forward, factual piece sans the erudition, an obituary one of the most influential musicians of all time deserved to have had. The piece incorporated, as it surely had to, quotes from some of Miles's most notable proteges, gleaned from the pages of American newspapers and magazines courtesy the College Street centre of the American University Library at Chowringhee.

'My debt to him is huge. If it wasn't for him, I would play a little differently for sure,' my obit quoted John McLaughlin as saying.

'...you could learn so much from what he said through his instrument, it is another way of communicating,' admitted Billy Cobham.

'Miles could play more in a few notes than a lot of people play in a lifetime,' noted Herbie Hancock.

Now, a quarter of a century later, realisation dawns that a beginning was made. For if anyone had told me then that I would someday get to meet and spend time with the three jazz greats I quoted, I would have laughed. Yeah, sure, the chances of me talking to John McLaughlin, Billy Cobham and Herbie Hancock ever would be about the same as me keeping wickets for Andy Roberts at the Eden Gardens.

Career pit-stops in Delhi, Bangalore, Pune and Mumbai, nowhere near as nimble as in F1, would have their surprising spin-offs. But, Bangalore proved to be in the league of a Marquez-ian miracle. Col. Aureliano Buendia was reminded of the time his father took him to discover ice in Macondo many years later while facing a firing squad. Thankfully for the Dattas, all they faced was music.

My 'Fifty Years of Solitude', if there ever was one, would be, I guess, imagined thus: Not until 2017, when S.D. would get down to chronicling his musical meanderings would he realise that the shift to Bangalore in 1999 three years after living in New Delhi had been fortuitous. Rarely does life hand it down on a platter. In his case she did. He had come to the right place at the right time. As if he was meant to record first-hand four momentous years in the annals of live music in India when the greatest of them all came and played. Deep Purple, Scorpions, Roger Waters, Elton John, Rolling Stones all held concerts in the Garden City. (With sincere apologies to Gabriel Garcia Marquez).

Between the Elton John (November 2002) and the Stones gigs (April 2003) came the jazz masters, John McLaughlin in February 2003 with Remember Shakti, and Billy Cobham and Jean-Luc Ponty for the Lakshminarayana Global Music Festival, an annual concert put up by Dr L. Subramaniam in memory of his father. Herbie Hancock was in the country in early 2007, touring with students of the Thelonious Monk Institute of Jazz.

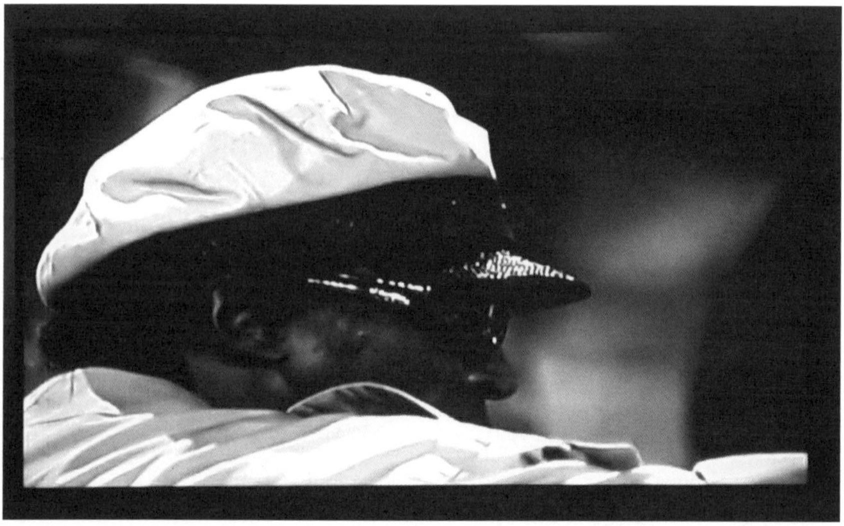

KIND OF BLUE: MILES DAVIS on television (author's personal collection)

McLaughlin was effusive while talking about Miles, saying he could go on and on for hours. 'He was the Picasso of the jazz world, a creator and innovator with far-reaching concepts. A lot of Miles' recording sessions would be organised jam sessions. He would arrive in the studio with a paper bag with some chords scribbled on it and we would have that bag in front for music,' recalled the elder statesman of jazz who is featured in some of his guru's stellar albums, *In a Silent Way* and *Bitches Brew*.

Sometime during my senior school years, while on holiday in Agra at my uncle's place, I discovered this untitled cassette, among the many that were in his collection, neatly stashed away deep inside the drawers of his book shelf, and decided to try it out. It was a live recording of guitars, played at terrific speed, so fast that I could barely get the tunes. This is the way you're supposed to play guitar is it? Somewhere towards the end, the theme from *Pink Panther* came alive reassuringly on those massive sonorous Sonodyne speakers. And I was relieved to hear something familiar. Still, I couldn't figure out who all were playing and forgot about it.

Years later, when I returned to Agra as a journalist to report on a concert by Yanni, the Greek composer and arranger who infused classical sensibilities in an orchestra of strings and keys to churn out melodious pop symphonies, I was able to make a connection. What I had heard during that holiday was the album, *Friday Night in San Francisco*, the stellar recording of the coming together of three legends on acoustic guitars—John McLaughlin, Al DiMeola and Paco De Lucia—in December 1980, a legitimate pre-recorded cassette which I possessed by the time I moved to college.

Yanni, therefore, holds a special place in my CD cabinet. If not entirely for his music, but surely for the opportunities his momentous concert near the Taj Mahal opened up. The much-publicised do had got Delhi's swish set swooning—they drove down in droves—but had also got a section of India's eco-activists worked up. They raised hell, alleging that the volume of Yanni's orchestra and the glare of his show lights would blight the Mughal-era memorial. Yanni, therefore, should be barred from sullying the environs of the pristine Yamuna riverbed.

Reporting for *The Indian Express* then, I was only too happy to be on the right side of the story, exposing the ludicrous claims of the self-styled eco-evangelists of the time. The concert happened. Lutyens Delhi got its weekend getaway with a cultural high, even if with Yanni's brand of muzak.

When I got to meet McLaughlin in Bangalore, he was happy to talk about *Friday Night in San Francisco*. Occasionally on Sundays, that night relives

itself on our Denon amp-fed Polk Audio speakers, thanks to a new-issue CD remastered by arranger and saxophonist Bob Belden. I usually close my eyes to the opening strains of *Mediterranean Sundance* to feel the effervescence of brilliance, and hear the dazzle.

A LOVE SUPREME

Mr John McLaughlin, it's been seventeen years since you visited India. How have you been? And what have you been recording?[2]

Just finished recording a CD. Commissioned by the Monte Carlo Ballet Company, it's a ballet with acoustic guitars (five) and a symphony orchestra. It's twenty-eight minutes long and is in three movements. It is called *Thieves and Poets* because all musicians are thieves, of which I am the principal, but I have poetic pretensions. Coupled with this are four of my favourite standards, a kind of personal guitar homages to different pianists including Bill Evans, Herbie Hancock, Chick Corea. Normally, they give me some money when I do these things, but this one is not about any of that. It's a labour of love.

How did you discover India?

My affection for India began long ago. Through Ramana Maharishi I discovered Indian culture first. Then came the music. And that is why Shakti is so special.

Django Reinhardt, John Coltrane and of course Bill Evans have influenced you deeply. But tell us about the great Miles Davis and how it was working with him in his albums, *In a Silent Way*, *Bitches Brew*?

I think it's quite safe to say that Miles is my guruji in every possible way. In the US, I had the opportunity to play with Tony Williams, one of the greatest drummers of the 20th century, who was himself playing with Miles. Actually, two days after I came to the US, I was in the studio with Miles recording *In a Silent Way*.

Miles was the Picasso of the jazz world. Because, it is one thing to be a good musician, but to be an innovator and creator, to have new concepts in music is very special. He was my great guru and for some reason, I could feel his affection for me.

I had the opportunity of meeting Billy Cobham, also a Miles man and your former bandmate in Mahavishnu Orchestra. He said that Miles had this uncanny ability to spot talent.

Yes, Billy was in Miles' favourite recording of Jack Johnson, which I might add, modestly, came from me. Miles had some chords scribbled on a paper bag—no time sheet, no rhythm. Well, that was Miles. And we would have this paper bag in front for music. But for this recording session, we didn't even have a paper bag. Herbie (Hancock), Billy, Michael Henderson were also

LOTUS FEET: JOHN McLAUGHLIN in Bangalore.
(Bhargavi, courtesy *The New Indian Express*)

there. For some reason, Miles went into the control room and stayed in there for quite some time. We got bored. I had an idea in my head that later became *Dance of Maya* in Mahavishnu Orchestra. I started to play the shuffle, then Billy took it up and in no time we hit a groove. It was a really good groove, upon hearing which Miles ran back into the studio and played for at least twenty minutes on that. He was soaring, truly unbelievable. A lot of Miles' recording sessions were organised jam sessions, but this was really something.

You said he had a particular affection for you.

I can't say enough about Miles. Those days I was making very little money with Tony. Sometimes, Miles would come up to me and say, 'Are you eating enough,' in that obscure, barely audible voice of his and push a $100 bill in my pocket. He really took care of me. During the day, I used to see him a lot and he used to love the guitar. He became a kind of godfather to me.

I met Jean-Luc Ponty who played with you during the Mahavishnu years. Like Cobham, he also says that playing and keeping up with you night after night was an intense, learning experience.

Well, I learnt that from Miles. He was unbelievably focused on his music.

When we first heard Mahavishnu Orchestra during our college years, it took us time to get the music. We hadn't heard anything like it before and it seemed too complicated. We knew it was something new, perhaps even great, but we had to try. But once we got into the groove, we couldn't stop listening to it.

It's commendable that you spent the time to listen to it because most people would drop it the moment they didn't like it the first time. But just to share my oneness with you, in 1964 when I got my first copy of *Love Supreme*, I had no idea what was going on. I just couldn't figure it out.

By this time I was already quite influenced by Indian thought. I had already discovered Ramana Maharishi who had a very powerful impact on me. In a way when you try to put a foot on the spiritual path, in the beginning it is quite confusing—especially with the kind of religious education I've had, which is, none at all.

On the back of *Love Supreme* there is a kind of poem and this poem really helped me. And I knew he was onto something and I used to listen to that record every day for six months. Then it's like a light going on. Hey, it's so simple, how come I didn't get it earlier.

Let me share with you a little anecdote. I was watching Miles playing in a club hall and he came down from the stage—I was standing very close to the stage—and some guy came up to him and said, 'Miles, why don't you play like you used to play?' And Miles—always the one to shift barriers—looked at the guy and asked, 'How did I play?'

That Friday night in San Francisco, did all of you—Al DiMeola and Paco De Lucia—realise that you were onto something special?

Yes, it was a landmark. And yes we knew immediately that it was special. It was a very magical night and some elements were very important. One, we all played well. Two, we stayed in tune—you know, guitar players spend half their lives tuning and the other half playing out of tune. Three, it was a good recording. Actually, prior to recording in San Francisco, we had done a European tour and I called CBS and said, 'Look, I think we should record this'. But they said, 'So what is this, three acoustic guitars? But only electric guitar sells.' They thought I was completely mad. But in the end, they took it all across North America and the record sold 1.8 million.

In fact, there was a trio before that with Larry Coryell, Paco and myself in 1978. Musically, I preferred that to the one with Al DiMeola.

We heard Larry Coryell with Shakti in Calcutta. That time you couldn't come.

Yeah, he is a very dear friend and a wonderful musician. I know him since 1967-68, but during the time ('78) he was having some personal problems. It's very regrettable that he couldn't be a part of that success.

Paco, Al and you came back in 1996 to do another album titled, *The Guitar Trio*. How was it getting back? I believe you all didn't get along that well.

I brought them together first for a tune in my album, *Promises*, which I liked. Then came the album. Yes, let's say it wasn't the most harmonious of relationships.

It doesn't show in the music though.

Of course it doesn't. We are all very serious about our music. Our lives are all dedicated to music. Paco is the same even now. Despite our differences we are all there for the music. We also did a tour of North America, Singapore, Malaysia, Japan. The recording was done in Real World Studios in England. I remember playing ping pong with Peter Gabriel every day and he could never win.

***Friday Night in San Francisco* sold 1.8 million. Do record sales matter to the John McLaughlin of today?**

In that respect, thank God I have been very lucky. I don't know for sure why but I think it's because I don't have a formula. I have never had a problem; some records will sell more than the other. Piracy is a problem which is nothing new, as I remember in 1977 record sales were down by 7 billion worldwide and sales of blank audio cassettes had risen by 7 billion. No crisis in music, rather a crisis in the way people listen to music.

I am a very curious fellow in music... continuously looking for new things. Record companies know me by now. They know what I like to do. The people who buy my records know it will be something different, though sometimes even I don't know what it will be. Still, I will continue my experiments.

Does the guitar offer any challenges after so many years?

Tremendous challenges every day. Just like life everyday is a different challenge. It's like this, you have twenty-four hours a day, how are you going to spend this time? Most spend a lot of it on work. Music is my passion. I think the concept of work gets very unpleasant connotations when you say that you work so that you can have a good time and not work. That devalues the work itself. I am a great believer in work. I know it must be hard for a person who sweeps the streets, but I believe you can sweep streets soulfully. It's difficult, I know. But who said life was easy?

In July 1964 you recorded *Heart of Stone, Some Things Just Stick in your Mind* and *(Walkin' Thru the) Sleepy City* with the Rolling Stones and the likes of Jimmy Page, John Paul Jones. Any memories?

Oh yeah, very boring. I remember hearing the Rolling Stones in an auditorium. They were out of tune then and they are still out of tune. But I like them. When the Stones were in town, Mick Jagger, Charlie Watts and Bill Wyman would come to see Tony Williams.

Wow. On that note, I shall say bye. Thank you very much for talking to me.

Thank you. Nice knowing you.

Paco de Lucia passed away at sixty-six in February 2004. McLaughlin composed *El Hombre que Sabia* (*The Man Who Knew*) in memory of the only one who was able to blend flamenco with jazz. The tune gripped everyone at intro on a November night at Dalhousie Institute in Calcutta in 2015 when he was in town with his band, 4th Dimension, comprising Etienne Mbappe, Gary Husband and Bombay boy Ranjit Barot.

It is beautiful, a ten-year-old in the audience gushed, as 'Juanito'—Paco's call-out sign for John—painted memories on a canvas of keys, bass lines and fuzzy cymbals. 'Maestro, John McLaughlin,' exclaimed Barot two-and-a-half hours later in salutation to the elder statesman of jazz, prompting the 'Mahavishnu' of guitar to spread his legs ever so slightly in mock rockstar stance and pierce out a high note on his Paul Reed Smith. He smiled in recognition of the connection 4th Dimension had just made, even if a decade after Remember Shakti.[3]

That Tuesday night would be added to DI's jazz lore. Not since Dizzy Gillespie, who with another of ours, Louiz Banks, enthralled a similarly discerning audience at the club on Jhowtala Street, had Calcutta experienced such a musical high. A fascinating reconnection with a legend that was even more inspiring since it had less to do with nostalgia. With Shakti, McLaughlin was seated, playing acoustic. Now, he is standing once again. Electric. He is climbing higher altitudes. His guitar improvising over a background of layered electronic soundscapes with characteristic ferocity and passion. Listen to *Back Light*.

NATURAL ELEMENTS: ZAKIR HUSSAIN (from left), U. SRINIVAS, JOHN McLAUGHLIN, V. SELVAGANESH. (Bhargavi, courtesy *The New Indian Express*)

Welcome to Mahavishnu Dot Next. Did we mention he is a sprightly seventy-plus?

OUTRO

Larry Coryell died in February 2017 at the age of seventy-three. Coryell, often dubbed the 'Father of Fusion', also played with Miles, among many other greats. We heard him with Shakti (Vikku Vinayakram, L. Shankar, Zakir Hussain) in the early '80s at ITF pavilion. Years later, Dr L. Subramaniam would be telling me about his collaborations with Coryell, recalling with great affection the time they recorded an album together in a church in Santa Barbara in the US.

5

Drum Machine with Heart

I found out why the best of our drummers, like Ranjit Barot and Sivamani, swear by him when Billy Cobham joined Jean-Luc Ponty and Dr L. Subramaniam for the Lakshminarayana Global Music Festival in Mumbai, Chennai and Calcutta in April 2003. Face contorted in concentration, Cobham's playing is unique. 'Like the great Tony Williams, he plays note for note, adding bits and parts with passion and subtlety to the tune you have created to improvise upon,' Dr Subramaniam explained before the Chennai concert.

Yes, as legends are wont to, Billy Cobham means much more to the world of music than what his matchless, ambidextrous skills as a drummer may seem to offer. First, let's pay homage to his career with jazz greats Miles Davis, Tony Williams, Jerry Goodman, George Duke, to name only a few. And remember, it was his advanced technique—the set-up of two bass drums and an array of toms—that shook the world during his years with Mahavishnu. Then came several pop and jazz rock projects with Peter Gabriel, Jack Bruce, Bob Weir and even James Brown, all adding up to over 300 albums as a sideman and twenty-five as a leader, including the classic, *Spectrum*.

What according to you is the role of a drummer?[1]

As a drummer, you have full control of the tempo. You can either be a metronome or play musically with feeling. Even today, I am faced with some very fundamental challenges. That's why I tell every drummer, 'Play the bass drum consistently in relationship with the music, with feeling'. That's the toughest.

Miles knew about 'feeling', right?

We were all in awe of him. Miles had this incredible ability, a kind of sixth sense to choose people—all legendary players would come out of the woodwork and play for him. Joe Henderson, Herbie Hancock, John Coltrane and many more. So, to be associated with him in several records means a lot.

Mahavishnu with John McLaughlin must have been intense.

Yes, at least 220 days of touring a year for two years. I recall certain things were bothering me about my playing. I had speed but could not pace myself. I spoke to John and he said, 'Don't try too hard. Learn to breathe and let the playing reflect that.' He helped me with yoga.

When you released *Spectrum*, that went on to be described as one of fusion's most influential albums, your playing seemed to have a hyper-strong funk/ R&B edge?

I thought I was just doing a job.

It must have been pretty amazing to be among the greats of the time?

During those days in America, there were many accomplished musicians who were past hungry like, say, Wayne Shorter, Chick Corea, Herbie Hancock, Keith Jarret, Bill Evans. All were blessed with an unrivalled repertoire. Even then, if you were to hand out music (in one key) and ask them to play it down a minor third, they could look at it and transpose it to a minor third while playing. That was the talent of the time.

SPECTRUM: BILLY COBHAM in Bangalore. (Bhargavi, courtesy *The New Indian Express*)

So respectful is Cobham of the musical talents of the time that he was almost apologetic to be spoken of in the same league. He needed to be coaxed into sharing details of his projects.

At the time, he was on a roll with Jazz is Dead, a supergroup that played jazz-tinged arrangements of the Grateful Dead. Before that, he had been on tour with Stanley Clarke and Larry Carlton. Then he joined Larry Coryell to revisit his Spaces material. And in between, when not teaching jazz drum to kids under the aegis of UNICEF, he spent time with his own groups—a German fusion trio Paradox and one with Randy Brecker and Gary Husband.

Many like to identify Cobham with Miles Davis' *Bitches Brew* and *Tribute to Jack Johnson*. Or better still, the only drummer who could match the speed and virtuosity of McLaughlin's guitar in Mahavishnu Orchestra circa 1971. For me though, Cobham is the drum machine with a beating heart.

6

Two of a Kind

They played *Cantaloupe*, an apt representation of Herbie Hancock's electro-funk infused jazz compositions that night in Mumbai in January 2007. He played with them, a bunch of young musicians from the Thelonious Monk Institute of Jazz in Los Angeles. So did Wayne Shorter.

I was there, naturally. I had heard Joe Zawinul in Delhi earlier and Shorter would complete the puzzle of Weather Report, the '70s jazz rock outfit we discovered while at Presidency College, Calcutta. Once upon a time, *Black Market*, the only album of theirs I could lay my hands on in Calcutta, used to be perpetually stuck on the turntable. It was electric, esoteric but firmly grounded in the slapping bass of Jaco Pastorius. *Barbary Coast* was our favourite track.

Back in 1964, the year I was born, when Shorter joined the Miles Davis quartet, Hancock was already there. Together with Miles, they changed the world of jazz forever. Consider *ESP*, *Nefertiti*, *Sorcerer*, *In A Silent Way* and *Bitches Brew*. Listen. They are there.

It was meant to be a strict fifteen-minute tete-a-tete on the morning before the concert, but went on for a little less than an hour. The two spoke about their music, inspirations and shared anecdotes about *The Man with the Horn*.

One goes like this. Miles, we know, had this incredible ear for talent. So one time when a greenhorn playing at a night club mustered the courage to go up to him and reverentially ask what he thought of his playing, Miles drew him close and whispered in that rasping voice of his: 'Do you talk like that to your girlfriend?'

PALETTE OF POSSIBILITIES

You are among few jazz musicians who have enjoyed both critical acclaim as well as commercial success. Your thoughts.[1]

Herbie Hancock: A lot of it has to do with being at the right place at the right time—that includes having an encounter or a collaboration with the right people at the right time. That alone won't do it. I had the great fortune

IDEA-ANCHOR: WAYNE SHORTER and HERBIE HANCOCK in Mumbai.
(Neeraj Priyadarshi, courtesy *The Indian Express*)

of working with Miles Davis when I was in my twenties and that experience has changed me forever. It has been a major influence on my foundation in a very positive way. A lot of things have helped me. For instance, I have always felt hopeful about the future, about my choices. I have also tried to be very open about looking at the lay of the land. Looking at a broader perspective than in the past.

(The) result is that the palette of choices for me is large. And I have constantly tried to encourage others to look at a large palette instead of the palette that has been given to you—you shouldn't be limited by what has been given to you.

That's a Miles legacy. While talking of how Miles used to take really good care of his band members—he would slip money in his pocket, asking, 'are you eating enough?'—John McLaughlin described him beautifully to me: 'Miles is the Picasso of the jazz world.'

Wayne Shorter: Oh, John said that? I remember I was late one time to Newport. Coming from Stockholm, the plane had trouble, landed late. Singer Maxim Sullivan and myself... we were walking up the stairs to the bandstand. And Miles was coming down. We shook hands and there was money in his hand. And he left the money in my hand and he kept going... Then, he said, 'I know.'

Hancock: Oh my (laughing). I had an experience like that too. One time, I had the flu. We played at The Adam's West, which used to be a Japanese theatre in LA. There was a girl in a trio who was performing before us. But I was there early to hear her. It was Aretha Franklin. She started playing some funky piano but when she started to sing, it was unbelievable. Then Miles's band came on to play, by which time I was almost delirious with the flu and I couldn't do very much (on stage). I felt so handicapped. We finished around 2 o'clock and we went back to the hotel. And Miles would call every hour. 'How are you feeling,' he would ask. 'Need some soup?'

He would give the shirt off his back for the musicians who worked in his band.

Shorter: My horn was stolen one time from a locked limousine. They stole it and re-locked it! Miles came, looked at everything and declared: 'Professionals.' He took out his wallet and gave me some money. 'Get a new horn,' he said. Three or four programmes later when I had the money, I walked up to him to pay him back and he went: 'Uh, uh?'

You have worked with a number of Indian musicians, right?

Hancock: I have had the chance to work with some Indian musicians like L. Shankar, Dr Subramaniam and even did a record with him. Every once in a while, he calls me about a project that he's working on. But I haven't been able to get together on any. Once in a while he would call me for an Indian meal at his house.

Shorter: I have had dinner at his house too...

We got hooked to Weather Report while in college. Jazz rock was new, invigorating and enjoyable, especially Jaco Pastorius's bass. How did the band come about?

Shorter: Joe Zawinul was leaving Canonball (Aderly) and I had left Miles. So, we were talking on the phone about starting our new bands when we said why not do something together. We had some rehearsals and we started.

And Jaco?

Shorter: He came later. We went to hear him play in Florida. Then when we were leaving the theatre, he was running down the street behind us saying: 'I heard you guys were looking for me?'

You Jaco Pastorius, we asked. And he went: 'I am the greatest bass player in the world!' So we said yeah, you must be bad!

***Possibilities*, your latest collaboration with many in the pop and rock world, reminded me of a Miles concert video I saw: Live in Paris. There he plays Michael Jackson's *Human Nature* and takes a solo for around twenty–twenty-five minutes. It's mind blowing. It also unravels unimaginable 'possibilities' that lie hidden within a pop hit.**

Hancock: Well, thank you. In *Possibilities*, I wanted to do something that was an example of using a collaborative project to encourage working out of the box. I believe that when people are encouraged to not be afraid of taking chances that they can come up with some creative solutions that show the multi-dimensionality of their own personalities. And that was really the motivation behind doing that project. Because people often consider themselves to be one dimensional: either a doctor, physician, teacher or journalist. And they think that's what they are. The truth is that's not what they are. That's what they do. And what they are—are human beings—and human beings aren't one dimensional.

Shorter: As Miles said, 'I am not what I do. I do what I am'.

Hancock: Yeah, right. That's the key. I chose to work with vocalists because I hadn't done a record with vocalists before. I have done a lot of records but rarely have there been any vocalists in my records and certainly nothing like *Possibilities* where every track has one. So I made a list of people. Some are established artistes, some new and some even brand new so that we had a spectrum. There's African influence in some, Latin influence in some… it's multicultural. The whole idea was to give each other the opportunity to really collaborate—not just do over-dubs. Collaborate from the very beginning, i.e. decide on what songs to do and how to do them. That way we would both be able to work out of the box.

The album *Phantom Navigator* had four keyboards and an array of drum machines. An extension of the Weather Report sound?

Shorter: I wanted to get certain harmonic experiences that you don't get to hear every day on record—even though I knew this record would not be marketed all over the world. I knew we would at least get these documented... a kind of harmonic mosaic. Like Beethoven's Neapolitan sixth chord! It's another matter that when the pop musicians get hold of a new chord, they run that to the ground. You hear it in 15,000 records! So *Phantom Navigator* was about that. I said I don't care about record sales, but let's just document it.

What inspires you both these days?

Hancock: Wayne reads a lot.

Shorter: The uncertainty of the present day as it unfolds.

Thank you. It's been a privilege.

Hancock, Shorter: Thank you.

The Miles enigma was slowly unravelling, having spent some time with four of his key proteges who were a part of his many transitions: Shorter's 'elliptically elegant' improvisations that pushed him to the 'borders of freedom', Hancock's infusion of electronics for his forays into 'cyclical pop rhythms' and McLaughlin's 'brash guitar' that foregrounded his rock intonations.[2]

In *Miles, The Autobiography*,[3] co-written with Quincy Troupe, he is candid about their abilities and what they meant to him.

'If I was the inspiration and wisdom and the link for this band, Tony (Williams) was the fire, the creative spark; Wayne (Shorter) was the idea person, the conceptualizer of a whole lot of musical ideas we did; and Ron (Carter) and Herbie (Hancock) were the anchors. I was just the leader who put us all together. Those were all young guys and although they were learning from me, I was learning from them too, about the new thing, the free thing.'

About McLaughlin he remembers the time he wanted him to join. 'I heard him (John McLaughlin) with Tony up at Count Basie's and he was a mother****** so I asked him to make the date. He told me he had been listening to me for a long time and that he might be nervous going into the studio with one of his idols. So I told him, "Just relax and play like you did up at Count Basie's and everything will be alright." And he did.'

For me jazz had come full circle. The journey began at the American University Jazz Club, with evenings spent in the company of music by stalwarts such as these. Now, there was a clearer path to follow. Just like the tune on the trumpet. You get it almost instantly, sway, nod your head or, maybe, tap your feet gently. It says something to you. And then the soloist begins his search, for matching notes, phrases and pauses, for the odd one that doesn't match, the jab that hurts, the pinch that teases. The tune is lost, hidden beneath the waves in an ocean of emotions. And then, just when you are sailing, the tune returns. It's the closing bars and you wish it didn't end. Why did he stop?

In September 2018, five years after his *Without a Net* album, Wayne Shorter released *Emanon*, a three-disc collection of studio and live recordings of his quartet, made up of Danilo Perez (piano), John Patitucci (bass) and Brian Blade (drums), and the 34-piece Orpheus Chamber Orchestra. The music leads up to a graphic novel that Shorter envisioned with Monica Sly and illustrator Randy DeBurke. Released together by Blue Note Records, the theme of the collaboration is central to the 'multiverse theory, on the idea that the universe we inhabit is one of an infinite number that all exist in parallel realities'—very much in line, as Sly notes, with the 'improvisational, everything-exists-in-the-moment aspect of jazz'. *Emanon*, or 'no name' spelled backwards, was inspired by a '40s Dizzy Gillespie tune of the same name. As a kid back then, 'no name' hit Shorter as something that meant a 'whole lot more' about the eternal quest for originality. Working with an orchestra was, to him, like walking across the street and talking to a neighbour whom one hadn't spoken to in ten years. 'It's the thing the world needs now: joining forces'.[4]

The 1940-born Hancock is doing just that, with Kamasi Washington, the modern-day (1981-born) American sax sensation. Of *Fist of Fury*-fame, the composer-arranger joined Hancock's band (Vinnie Colaiuta, James Genus, Lionel Loueke, Terrace Martin) for a couple of concerts in the US in August 2019. Last heard, Hancock and his troupe were touring Europe.

What is he telling us? Keep playing. Keep listening.

OUTRO

Of the handful of jazz albums I've managed to collect over the years, here's a selection we play often; and whenever we do they talk to me: keep those doors open, walk don't run.

- *A Kind of Blue:* Miles Davis
- *The Essential Miles Davis*

- *What a Wonderful World:* Louis Armstrong
- *Ella Fitzgerald Premier Collection*
- *Groovin' High:* With Dizzy Gillespie
- *The Girl from Ipanema:* Stan Getz Plays Jobim
- *The Song is You, Best of the Verve Songbooks:* Oscar Peterson
- *The Black Box of Jazz*
- *Twelve Moons:* Jan Garbarek Group
- *Word of Mouth:* Jaco Pastorious
- *Greatest Hits of Hugh Masakela*
- *Jazz Moods Hot:* George Benson
- *Two of a Kind:* Earl Klugh and Bob James
- *Seven Seas:* Avishai Cohen

7

Highway Stars

It's rare to return to a classic rock band one had let lie in the farthest crevices of the musical mind via a new song. Yet *Time For Bedlam* prompted just that.

Right from the ashes of life I learnt to behave
What to believe, what not to say, from cradle to grave
Ah… like a good little slave… I surrender to fate
No pity, no pity
Don't want no pity for me in this filthy cell
I'll see you in hell

The play-off between pile-diver guitar and symphonic keys in one of Deep Purple's latest tunes jolts you into believing that maybe someone is listening again. The year is 2017 and the world is in turmoil and simmering discontent has led us to this deafening roar. Yet, strangely enough, it has fallen on this rock band of yore, whose youngest member is in his early sixties, to hold up a mirror. See you in hell, they say. Why, aren't we there already?

It is gratifying, and exciting, to see that Messrs Ian Paice, Ian Gillan, Roger Glover, Steve Morse and Don Airey haven't confined themselves to the studio recording *inFinite*, their 20th album featuring Bob Ezrin (Kiss, Pink Floyd) as producer. They went around Europe and the US belting out the old and the new to live audiences, sharing stage with Alice Cooper in a tour titled, fittingly, The Long Goodbye.

Bedlam's beginning is eerie and haunting, the Gregorian chant-like opening lines delivered by Gillan with a sense of foreboding, making sure it is a perfect lead-up to the high-octane play-off between Airey's shimmering keyboards and Morse's textured lead. In a sense, that's where the old purple meets up with today's deep. The bonus track is *Roadhouse Blues* with an edgy harmonica, an addition fuelled by Paice's experience[1] of one night when the Doors' immortal classic

DEEP PURPLE: ROGER GLOVER (from left), IAN PAICE and IAN GILLAN performing in Bangalore. (Bhargavi, courtesy *The New Indian Express*)

followed naturally after singing *Black Night* during a jam session with a tribute band, something he would do during off-tour months to keep his chops up.

That song was an instant throwback to April Fool's Day, Bangalore 2001, when, amid the gloom the techies of the Silicon Plateau of India were facing because of an economic slowdown in the US, Deep Purple had come to play. Jon Lord was there too. At Palace Grounds, we heard them loud. A *Highway Star* met up with a *Strange Kind of Woman* in a *Black Night*, but before there was *Smoke on the Water*, the band surprised us all with a medley that included Led Zeppelin's *Stairway to Heaven* and the Beatles' *Day Tripper*. We were 25,000 of us basking under thousands of watts of nostalgia, a classic rock act doffing their hats to the legends of music and having fun.

'I am very happy you are enjoying the new music,' Paice emailed via the band's managers in between concerts in Europe in the summer of 2017 and went on to explain the sustainability of their oeuvre.

> **# 'In my opinion, the reasons for the band's longevity are, fortitude to keep the band in existence through the difficult times....'**
>
> Their first hit, *Rush*, happened in 1968. That makes Deep Purple a band that has completed half a century of music-making. In between, they've

had personnel hiccups and several line-up changes with Gillan, Glover and Ritchie Blackmore, all taking turns to leave and rejoin. Blackmore has stayed away though. His guitar was the signature sound of Purple songs. He didn't believe in exploring on stage. He knew where he wanted to go with a tune and went there fast and straight. Jon Lord provided the halo, the cushion of sound that made the guitar sound even better. After Lord's passing Don Airey of Ozzy Osborne lineage took over. Not many will recall his baroque, synth-meets pipe-organ intro to Ozzy's *Mr Crowley.*[2] Airey is as much respectful of Jon as he is of the Purple legacy. 'I do play Jon's solo from *Highway Star* note for note simply because English Heritage slapped a preservation order on it. Seriously, how could you improve it?' he says in a 2013 interview.[3] When I asked Morse about Airey's contribution to post-Jon Lord Purple, he kept it brief: 'There is only one guy that could replace the irreplaceable Jon Lord, and we thankfully have him.'

 # 'Honesty to, and respect for, our fans... Always to try to give the best performance we can every night for those fans.'

We saw that in 1995 in Bombay and New Delhi, the first time they were in India, and in 2001 in Bangalore. They did not smash guitars, as Ritchie Blackmore would often do a la Hendrix. They were then in their gentlemanly fifties, the golden grey hair either neatly ponytailed (Lord) or a languorous hang-loose till the shoulders (Morse). Sure, Gillan was a dash paler than the Prince of Wails we've known him to be, but he was screaming those high notes all right. As for Paice, he still drummed at the speed of light, thank you very much. Five years later, Deep Purple would return to Bangalore again in 2006. Thanks to DNA Networks, I was there too.

 # 'Musicianship of the highest order, which allows us...'

Deep Purple was always about being direct, a straight from the heart approach that came from the gut. Perhaps that is what enabled them to reach out to diverse sections of music lovers. Even those who couldn't care less about the uneven temper of rock music found themselves buying a couple of Purple albums that they went on to cherish lifelong. Jon Lord's solo infused a kind of classical lyricism to the otherwise screeching directness of Blackmore's guitar. Now with Morse, there is an added melodic dynamism in that department. I discovered this while listening to *Original Album Classics*, a 1996 compilation. *Loosen My Strings* and *Sometimes I Feel Like Screaming*, two songs (Album: *Perpendicular*) in which guitars jab you in the heart.

 # '...to improvise and create unique "musical moments", which both we, and the audience really enjoy.'

Deep Purple was our constant companion in late school and through college. Trying out those chord changes of *Smoke on The Water* at rock fests was a given for all aspiring rock bands of Calcutta. No one could be as merrily bland as them while singing about a *Strange Kind of Woman.*

Her name was Nancy, her face was nothing fancy
She left a trail of happiness and misery
I loved her, everybody loved her
She loved everyone and gave them a good return...
I want you, I need you, I gotta be near you
Ooh I got a strange kind of woman

 # 'A few very successful songs. And not least—luck!'

Over the years, Deep Purple songs assumed new complexities. *What Now?* and *inFinite*, boasting a visually impacting cover picture of a ship cutting through an icy sea to mark out the band's initials, bear testimony to that. Talking of luck, I got invited to a post-concert party, hosted by primary sponsors BPL, after the 2001 show in Bangalore. Paice spoke of his single-minded determination to do the 'job (of playing)', Glover about how he loved to tour, but Morse was worried and dying to get back to the US. His home in Florida had just been battered by a storm and it had suffered severe damage. The good thing was that his family was safe.

Morse, we heard later, is often at the receiving end, in jest for sure, in this otherwise very British rock ensemble whose members love everything English, including the annual Premier League. I had mailed him about it too.

'Yes, of course, all they talk about is soccer. In fact, when Don joined, I was one step ahead of him in seniority, having had about eight more years than he. However, the minute he started with the English football league, I was back in last place.'

OUTRO

The next three years in Bangalore would be heaven, a blast for lovers of music. Amid the recurring stories of corruption in politics that would occasionally drown out the gains being reaped by the Infosys and Wipros of the town, a stellar cast of performers would descend: Bryan Adams, Scorpions, Roger Waters, Elton John and Rolling Stones, all thanks to Venkat Vardhan's DNA Networks.

ROCK OF AGES: At a media interaction a day before the Bangalore concert.
JON LORD (from left), ROGER GLOVER, IAN GILLAN, STEVE MORSE, IAN PAICE
(Bhargavi, courtesy *The New Indian Express*)

8

Delicate Sound of Thunder

Roger Waters met us in London. It was just like any other London afternoon: cloudy, rainy. With me were Alan Mendonca of *The Times of India* and Venkat Vardhan of DNA Networks, the promoter of the Roger Waters concerts in India. Venkat had taken us there, keen that *TOI* and *The New Indian Express*, write a curtain-raiser to the April 2002 performances. Before being led into his suite, a man we assumed was from Roger Waters' management ticked us off. 'From India? Fifteen minutes max. There are many others waiting.'

My heart sank. So, *TOI* and *NIE* had to sit-in together. The conversation went on for over an hour. That man from Roger Waters management had come in thrice, I remember, to try and get his boss to stop. He didn't succeed.

Roger talked that day, opening up about the 'happiest days of our lives', Pink Floyd's Syd Barrett years, and the eternal search for the answer to that one question that has always been haunting him.

'On the evidence that we have now do we feel that the human race is capable of evolving to a point where we recognise what it is in life that gives us joy, and what is in life that gives us pain? Is the human race evolving towards a place where it is likely to choose more joy and less pain?'

This question has stayed with me ever since. As if a poster embedded in the inner reaches of my brain, written in Helvetica Bold unwrapping itself whenever I find myself at odds with what's going on around me. Syria, Afghanistan, Kashmir, and the patriotism posers we are being bombarded with everyday make Waters' question timeless, answers to which, as poet laureate Bob Dylan had prophesied way back in the '60s, are *Blowing in the Wind*.

Waters has been an old hand at stirring the pot and at celebrating when the broth has been cooked. He performed *The Wall* in new Germany on July 21, 1990 at the fall of the Berlin Wall. Not surprisingly, he was there at that stellar gathering of rock legends at a California desert, essentially asking the same question when he sang *Pigs* (from Pink Floyd's 1997 album) and let off giant inflated replicas across the venue to rip apart Donald Trump—then not yet elected President—with not-so-subtle slogans flashing on a giant plasma screen spanning the width of the stage.

These days, he is doing the same, if even more forcefully, during his Us +Them tour.

Big man, pig man, ha ha charade you are.
You well-heeled big wheel, ha ha charade you are.
And when your hand is on your heart,
You're nearly a good laugh,
Almost a joker,
With your head down in the pig bin,
Saying 'Keep on digging'

So, here I was face-to-face with the cerebral section of the ensemble known as Pink Floyd whose songs we would sing—no shout out—while in the school hostel shower before PT on cold winter mornings. We embraced the sheer defiance of *We don't need no education* even though we did not then, I am quite sure, grasp the real essence of *Another Brick in The Wall.*

COMFORTABLE, NOT NUMB

India at last?

Waters: I have never been to India, even on holiday. I never did the Maharishi thing. Though I have a daughter who has spent a lot of time in India, she loves the country. But I am really looking forward to it.[1]

Pink Floyd is huge in India. We've grown up singing, *We don't need no education.*

Really? Oh yes, I can see you've brought along your record. It's pretty old, more than twenty years, maybe?

Yes.

This record, *The Wall*, and *The Dark Side of the Moon*, and to a lesser extent, *Wish You Were Here*, successive generations seem to discover it when they hit puberty and start searching around for ways at disentanglement during their journey to becoming adults... and the stuff that they find in here seems to have a resonance. I did a tour of the United States in 2000 and another one in 1999, and I suspect the average age of the audience was about twenty-five, a pretty young audience.

Your decision to return to performing and touring was the result of an impromptu concert with Don Henley (Eagles) in 1992. How did that happen?

It was one concert and it was for charity. He was trying to raise money to buy and protect the literary tradition of a place in the northeast called Walden Woods where Henry David Thoreau did a lot of his writing. So he asked me if I could play a few songs at an evening in LA. He also asked John Fogerty (Credence Clearwater Revival) and Neil Young. So John, Neil, me and Don did a set of songs each. I didn't have any show, no quadrophonic sound, just Don's band and me on the guitar. I remember playing *Mother* and I can remember feeling this extraordinary wave of love from the audience. There I was singing this song which they all knew, and they all seemed so happy. And in that moment it rekindled the performer in me; I realised it was something I needed to get back to again.

Do you see yourself now as having come full circle from the time when you were so disgusted with the touring circus that you even spat at an unruly fan trying to climb up the stage?

Very much so. That incident happened in 1977. I remember it well as that was at the heart of the spark that started me writing this piece (*The Wall*). Yes, I have come a long way since then.

Is Roger Waters at peace now?

I am a lot more at peace now than I was twenty-five years ago. And I think I am beginning to operate from a more adult place than I have ever done in my whole life. You know, the abandoned child component of my personality has remained pretty powerful through most of my adult life. It's only through some of the recent events in my life that I have come to understand it, and started consciously to deal with it. I am fifty-eight years old and I guess what I am saying is that it's never too late to grow up.

What is so compelling in the world today that is forcing you to write again?

A lot of my writing is rooted in an empathy I feel for other human beings, based upon my own feelings of despair and alienation I feel from the things of my life—most famously the loss of my father. It's funny you ask me that, for I ran into Nick Mason on holiday a few weeks ago and we arranged to have dinner.

Floyd-mate with whom you use to share a deep friendship?

Yes, we were very close and we got estranged when Floyd split up.

Isn't he godfather to your son?

Yes, my elder son. So we were having dinner, Nick and I, and we were talking. In the light of everything that's going on now in the world, I find myself still trying to find answers to the unanswerable question. I was just focusing on this sitting in the cab last night, and the question that came up in a flash was: On the evidence that we have now, do we feel that the human race is capable of evolving to a point where we recognise what it is in life that gives us joy and what it is in life that gives us pain? Is the human race evolving towards a place where it is likely to choose more joy and less pain? And I find that to be a very difficult question to answer. However, the one thing that I am optimistic about is the fact that because of the explosion of information technology, I feel we increasingly have a better chance to at least pose the questions for ourselves.

How do you relate to your once angst-ridden songs of yore?

The songs are authentic. They authentically express the feelings I had then. So I can still identify with those feelings. So when I am in the song the whole thing comes back. When I sing *Wish You Were Here* now, for me it's fresh, a revisiting of the feelings. And the anxiety or angst never goes away. There's a new song I am performing this time. It's called *Flickering Flame*. It's partly about part of the journey that I have made towards the freedom of contentment. I had bookends and it starts like this:

When my neurons conspire to direct my thoughts
Away from divorce to competitive sports
Back to the place where all rivers run to the sea
Then I should be free...
My synapses pause in my quest for applause
When my ego lets go of my end of the bone
To focus instead on the love that is precious to me
Then I shall be free.

Then in the middle of the song is a piece about a friend of mine who died a few years ago. His name is Phily Constantine. He worked for a record company in Paris. We were very close...

On an African plane on a thorn tree,
My old friend Phily sits waiting for me
Surpass surpass whatever will be will be
When a friend dies and the tears rise

From that deep well that never runs dry
And women break their bracelets
And the men take their whiskey outside

I get chills even saying this now. I am transported back to the time when my friend (was around), which was five, six years ago.

We never get over loss. Loss is deeply important to me. In some ways, in experiencing loss, to some extent, it defines our humanity. I don't know... I'm rambling—but that's my work, it is kind of rambling. That's what I do. That's how I work. I try to arrive at a state where I am open to experiencing an emotion and then allow the words to come.

Do you write first and then put a tune to it?

No, it's usually together.

***Each Small Candle* is about the individual, about how one candle can light up a dark corner.**

The genesis of that song lay with lyrics that were sent to me by an Italian journalist. The first verse is written by a South American and a victim of torture. I don't know who he is. I have been trying to find that journalist. Apart from anything else I owe him royalty. If I never find him, I'll have to give his royalty to Amnesty, I guess that would be a good choice.

Will you be performing this song?

Yes, I will. Actually, I have been doing it as the last song. And a lot of people have said, 'No, you can't do that. You've got to leave people on a high'. And there's a case to be made for that. But it kind of smacks of rabble-rousing to me. (Laughs).

Maybe that's what Pink Floyd would do in the '70s.

Maybe. You do a very well-known song in the end and everybody goes, 'Oh, that one!' But I kind of like the fact that, 'Okay, now we are going to do a song you've never heard before and it is quite a difficult song, too. It's about personal responsibility.' So they then go away slightly confused—and I am quite happy with that idea.

During his last tour with the E Street Band, Bruce Springsteen ends with a new song, *41 Shots*, and before he begins it he says: 'I want some quiet in here.'

It sounds like (mine is) a similar idea.

Tell me something about Syd. What was he like?

I play *Shine On* every night when I am doing concerts. So the memory of him is very much there in that song. Actually, I have images of him on the screen as well as a tribute. But I also experience the loss of a friend that I experienced in '68 when he became schizophrenic.

I never see him. He doesn't like any contact with any of that part of his life. There was a documentary made about him on British television. It's quite informative, I learnt some stuff. Particularly about this painter called Duggie Fields with whom he shared a flat. And I began to understand certain very important things about Syd.

For instance, Syd used to spend an awful lot of time after he became ill in bed. And Duggie felt that… as long as he was in bed doing nothing he had the potential to do anything. But as soon as he got up it became apparent that he wasn't doing anything—so this potential fulfilment that he could feel in his life went away and so he would spend more and more time in bed. And I found a kind of romance in that idea somewhere and I know it was a manifestation of his illness. But it's an interesting idea for us all in a strange way: If we don't open ourselves up to the possibility of discovering where our limits are, we never do anything. And in some ways it's easier to do nothing than to try and do something.

When you look back, which were the best Pink Floyd shows in terms of stagecraft?

I think *The Wall* was pretty special. It was very well crafted. In all, it was a good show, well put together.

Yes, the animations were particularly spectacular. Who can forget the march of the hammers.

Yes, that was Jerry Scarf. I had identified the idea in the lyric. But hammer as you know is a potent symbol of oppression and Jerry came up with the drawings.

There will be some of that animation in my show this time. We are actually projecting the video—it was still projectors in America then—and so, it means we can show some film this time.

Last question, this one I have to ask. How is your relationship with David Gilmour now?

David and I haven't spoken since 1985.

But the title of Floyd's latest compilation, *Echoes*, was yours, isn't it? Apparently, Gilmour suggested *Sum of the Parts*, which you didn't like.

Yes, I must say that it was pretty poor.

That's all, I guess. Thank you very much for your time.

Thank you, it was a pleasure talking to you.

What was meant to be a strict fifteen-minute tete-a-tete with two blokes from India, went on for an hour. Alan asked his questions, I mine. For we worked out an arrangement then and there. We were to write each other's pieces using Roger's responses to our respective questions. In the end, Roger signed my *Wall* album. He even clicked pictures with us.

Once we were back in Bangalore, we were kind of celebs ourselves. Those 'lucky b*******' who got to meet Roger Waters', people said. AIR FM interviewed us about our interview, published about a week before the April 13, 2002 concert. If Pink Floyd were the prophets of psychedelia, one of the prophets stood before us, 40,000 of us, that Saturday night. Arms spread wide, bass guitar slanting at an angle, Roger Waters sang: *So, ya thought ya might like to go to the show?*

ECHOES: ROGER WATERS in concert in Mumbai five years after his Bangalore show (Neeraj Priyadarshi, courtesy *The Indian Express*)

IN THE FLESH

It was a long wait. From his militant anti-militarism to the evocation of those Dickensian sadists bent on extracting the last spark of creativity from their hapless victims, we identified with every word that Roger Waters sang. We sang along, kept time, and soaked in the visuals. We were in a trance. Time stood still.[2]

In the Flesh: Stunning, as if a dream.

The Happiest Days of Our Lives: We hug our friends beside us. No, it's real!

Another Brick in the Wall: The anthem of our school daze. Awesome.

Mother: Mother, do you think they will drop the bomb? A moment of introspection. The contemporariness of the 1979 song is eerie.

Get Your Filthy Hands off my Desert, Southampton Dock: Maggie, what have you done? Back in college, we used to love Floyd/Waters' Thatcher-bashing politics. The giant screen beams, BRING THE BOYS BACK HOME, and then turns into a field of flowers.

Pigs on the Wings, Dogs: The extended version of *Animals* is vintage Floyd. The band members break off for a game of cards rear stage while synthesiser chords fill the skies. Very Floyd. Impassive, but totally connected to the music.

Welcome to the Machine: A Chaplinesque critique of a modern, mechanised world.

Wish You Were Here, Shine On You Crazy Diamond: Songs about loss and longing. A rush of memories. Some wipe a tear (hey, that's okay).

Set the Controls for the Heart of the Sun: Oriental magic, the highest of all the high points. The giant screen flashes black-and-white stills of Roger Waters, Rick Wright, David Gilmour and Nick Mason. Syd Barrett comes out of the dissolves too. These are Pink Floyd's happiest days. Fooling around on the beach with the mannequin of Arnold Layne's fetish, we are offered a glimpse of the sunny days that preceded the rancour and internecine feud leading Waters and Gilmour to part ways. Today, the bitterness has gone, but the sadness remains. This is Roger Waters saying thank you.

Breathe: Finally, the *Dark Side of the Moon*, one of rock music's stellar creations. We are truly blessed to be alive, breathe.

Time: The old enemy ticks away. Every word hits us. We rediscover reality. *'And then one day you find ten years have got behind you, no one told you when to run, you missed the starting gun.'*

Money: It's a hit! Brilliant visuals and sounds, a spinning turntable amid the all-familiar ring of cash registers. *Time* and *Money*, the two spoilers. Floyd/ Waters motif for all time.

Pros and Cons of Hitchhiking: Roger Waters' solo album. For fans, a welcome bonus.

Perfect Sense: A frontal assault on the machinery of war.

It's a Miracle, Amused to Death: Great songs. The sarcasm-laced ode to the supermarket lifestyle is scathing.

Brain Damage: A refreshing acoustic lilt to an old song. Very surprising since it's about mad people.

Comfortably Numb: The tour de force. Encapsulates the concept behind the In the Flesh tour as it seems to say much more than what it did all those years ago.

Flickering Flame: A brand new song of hope. Roger Waters has graduated from the pain of time and money.

Back at their hotel after the show, Waters and his bandmates enjoyed a huge South Indian spread listening to the Beatles. They were, I was told, overwhelmed by the response. We were too. Drunk on Floyd's 'saucer full of secrets', all of us were emotionally drained and cerebrally recharged. Yet, it was a warm feeling. Thank you, Pink Floyd. Thank you, Roger Waters.

Waters would return to India during his 2007 Dark Side of the Moon tour. We heard him again in Mumbai, then our home, on February 18. More than a decade later, he would be touring the world with his LP that, once again, asks the same question, *Is This the Life We Want,*[1] holding forth on drone wars, terrorism, children being separated from their parents—basically our primetime news headlines.

The title track from this 12-song dystopian album is bit of a conversational rant really. Set amid a haunting backdrop, he lays bare certain home truths of our time when it is not enough that we succeed, but still need others to fail. He warns us about how fear is being used as a tool of submission and jabs us with a finality that is as brutal as the crimes we all seem to so willingly condone. He spells out our world of today where a student is 'run over by a tank', a girl's life is 'casually spent' and journalists are 'left to rot in jail'; and then reminds us coldly about the dangers of the new normal.

So every time the curtain falls on some forgotten life[3]
It is because we all stood by silent and indifferent
It's normal!

9

Beyond Boundaries

He is a man of medicine and music. He studied both, but by the time he received his Master's in western classical music in California, he had found his calling. He gave up the scalpel and took up the bow, the kind that glides on strings, and dedicated his life to healing the soul.

His journey to becoming 'Violin Chakravarty' L. Subramaniam has been chequered. From fleeing the 1958 anti-Tamil pogrom in Sri Lanka as an eleven-year-old with little more than his brothers' violins to storming the stages of South India, under the tutelage of his father, to be a part of what is even today admiringly recalled as the Violin Trio, this bowman's life has been a treasure-trove of stories. Stories he tells in tunes born out of four strings, stories about how two more were added to the repertoire and how today, the Indian violin is so much a part of the world.

It was meant to be a press conference with Dr L.S. and fellow bowman and friend Jean-Luc Ponty at a five-star near the old Bangalore airport to announce a series of concerts. Bangalore had not become Bengaluru then. Work on the Metro hadn't started and traffic was navigable. Best part, she still retained a bit part of that famed 'air-conditioned' weather. So, if it was sunny and a wee bit humid towards noon, she couldn't take it for long. By 4 p.m., the skies would open up to light drizzle followed by a bout of rain. That would do it. Cool.

It was January 2003, by when Bangalore had graduated itself to becoming the Silicon Capital of India. Although many a naysayer would squirm at that epithet, I remember distinctly how the world had, by then, been quite taken up with the city of Infosys and Wipro. At Brussels, during a trip to the European Parliament to commemorate the French Presidency of the EU, a journalist leapt from his seat once I handed him my visiting card.

Bangalore, eh? The Silicon Capital of India, welcome to the EU.

A few of us were there for the PC a bit early, waiting for the duo. Suddenly, in comes this elegant, small-built gentleman with a dark brown beard. He is escorted in and made to take a seat behind a long table. He was alone. Dr L.S., his host, hadn't arrived yet. The PR lady looked embarrassed. She brought out a piece of paper, looked at it and announced, 'Mr Ponty, the violinist is here. Dr Subramaniam is on his way. Flights, you know.'

Some of us shuffled a bit. My hands started to sweat. It was JLP, the man with the five-string electric violin! The man whose music we would listen to, at one point in our college days, through the night at a friend's place on Ironside Road opposite CCFC in Calcutta. *Mirage*, I thought.

No one was talking. Ponty sat there bewildered. The silence seemed like an eternity. I looked around and sheepishly introduced myself and started to talk. 'I have been listening to your music since I was in college.' There seemed to be a hint of a smile on Ponty's face, although in hindsight I may have been imagining it, followed by surprise.

'Is that so,' he asked.

That would be the beginning of a conversation which would continue till the next day.

Dr Subramaniam arrived about forty minutes later and filled us in with his plans. At the time, he had been touring with a host of top-draw musicians, including JLP and Billy Cobham, for the Lakshminarayana Global Music Festival held in memory of his father who was credited with a number of innovations that revolutionised violin playing in India.

Thiruvananthapuram and Mumbai were done, while Delhi and Calcutta were to follow. What was to unfold in the coming days, first in Bangalore and then in Chennai, was history. The concerts were among the best jazz and jazz-rock dos I have ever attended. In Bangalore, they did not play Ponty's *Mirage*, the hauntingly illuminating track where JLP's violin soars amid a landscape of sophisticated phrasings on the keys accompanied by some gently slapping bass. Yet, the duo more than made up for it with *Conversations*, a duet Dr L.S. premiered in an eponymous album with another maestro, Stephane Grappelli. On the album, the track sets itself up for a sawal-jawab marked by two distinctive solos. One a trifle intense, busy even; while the other a plaintive exposition aimed at the heart. The duo soar, all the while remaining beholden to the tune that you willingly submit to.

Exactly fifteen years later, in the January of 2018, when Calcutta's mild winter is at its peak, Dr Subramaniam was in my home city, that I had returned to a decade earlier, to perform an all-nighter at the iconic Dover Lane Music Festival, an annual fixation for connoisseurs of Indian classical music, along with son Ambi. I met him again to pay my respects and renew, if I could, the earlier acquaintance. We got talking.

How did the Lakshminarayana Global Music Festival start?

It started as a tribute to Prof. Lakshminarayana, my father and guru, who changed the violin scenario on the world platform. In Carnatic music, violin was always an accompanying instrument. You played it with somebody, a vocalist, or someone playing the veena or flute. It never had that prime spot as a solo instrument. Even some of the greatest violinists of that period, and those before them, primarily played accompaniment. Once in a while, they played solos.

And Prof. Lakshminarayana did not approve of that?

My father was a virtuoso kind of player. But he was having problems of his own. While accompanying someone, if you play more than what the primary artiste expects you to, and if the public gets enthralled by your performance, then you won't be called (to play) ever again. The main artistes did not want the limelight to be shared. That was the kind of attitude that had developed in those days. He did not see any future in that kind of playing where there was nothing to fall back on.

He went to Sri Lanka in the 1930s and developed playing techniques. Like for instance, the veena technique and plucking, so much so, that if you heard him play, it might have seemed that two or more people were playing. His idea was that we should be performing globally and that the West should respect the Indian violin as one of the greatest classical traditions of music and not treat it as an instrument to be played sitting on the floor as accompaniment to ethnic or folk music. He was very bothered about this and said that we should work towards making the Indian violin a solo mainstream instrument, like, say, Lord Yehudi Menuhin, Jascha Heifetz and David Oistrakh, some of the greatest violinists of all time, were doing.

He was calling for a change in attitude and culture.

Absolutely. In those days, Indian music concerts were being held in basements and small halls with potluck dinner for accompaniment. My father was against this approach. He wanted to play in proper venues and wanted us to develop techniques to earn the respect we were seeking.

Looking back, I now realise that part of the problem was the way the violin playing technique had developed. Basically, it was to accompany someone. That meant, that someone sings or plays (a veena or flute perhaps) within one and half octaves and you play within that range. So, a virtuoso kind of technique was never developed for the violin. And we seem to have been satisfied with that—they sing or play for five minutes and then we play three minutes and fill-in here and there while the main instrumentalist gets a break. The attitude was something like this: I have finished my alaap, so you also do something so that I can rest my vocal chords a bit.

The family fled Sri Lanka during the 1958 riots. Is it true you all left with as little as the clothes you were wearing and three violins?

We fled but could never believe we could be in that situation. Our house was targeted. But our neighbour, a Sri Lankan lady, was very close to my mother, who, I remember, would always send sweets and savouries during festivals. So, this lady came over and started crying. She told us that we should leave immediately as our lives were in danger. 'If you don't leave now, believe me, you will see all your children being killed in front of you. And then they will

> also kill both of you,' she told my parents. She also told us that our well had been poisoned, and hence, we should not drink water from there.
>
> Initially, my parents did not believe the threat was so serious. So, my father called his cab driver, the one who always used to ferry him to concerts to, for instance, Jaffna, 250 km from where we were. My father had financed his car and he would be there whenever he wanted him. But this time, when my father called him, he said he could not come, saying he would also be killed if he did.
>
> That shook my father. Then he called a friend, another Mr Subramaniam, whom we used to call uncle. He advised us not to go anywhere but move to the next house.
>
> So we left, I think with my brother's violin and whatever we were wearing, and waited in an adjoining house. Subramaniam uncle sent a jeep with security men and we went over to his place, which was guarded heavily because it was a mill. My father wanted to go back to the house to collect our belongings, and to the bank to withdraw money. But, Subramaniam uncle advised us against it. He said a lot of people were waiting outside banks to rob, and then kill, people like us. So, we never went back. Later, we heard that our house was ransacked.

After 1958, by when the family had returned to India, Prof. Lakshminarayana thought of a way out. He formed a trio comprising his sons, L. Vaidyanathan, L. Subramaniam and L. Shankar (the double violinist of Shakti). Under his tutelage, the brothers excelled themselves. They demolished conventions and broke all rules with impunity. The result was a dramatic transformation in the way the violin was heard in South India. And the Violin Trio was born. 'Our playing was very intense,' Dr Subramaniam recalled of the time he was ten and his brother a year older. 'So, when people saw us, three kids playing ferociously, they were taken aback. We were playing varnam compositions in multiple beats which no one had done before. We played in multiple speeds, swaras and different sub-divisions. We used very complex rhythmic structures. My father was very strong in mathematics and these were all his ideas.'

That changed the story of the violin in India. From an accompanying instrument, it became the instrument to be heard. The Violin Trio was being noticed by the likes of Palghat Mani, regarded as one of the foremost exponents of the mridangam, who sent word that he wanted to play with them. The trio started touring. Playing to packed audiences was becoming the norm. Prof. Lakshminarayana's dream was being fulfilled, if not in entirety, at least 50 per cent in 1958, noted Dr Subramaniam.

The Violin Trio was a game changer. Yet, you all did not continue.

On the home front, my father was struggling to raise six children by teaching—a lot of his students went on to become very big like, say, Ilaiyaraaja. And I went on to study medicine. While I was in my second year, a German violinist, who had heard me, told my father that I was very good and that I had great potential. He asked my father to allow me to join him for further work on the violin. He even promised me a scholarship. My father was thrilled and agreed. He always wanted the violin to be globally recognised as a solo instrument and finally, here was an opportunity. But when he broke the news at home, my mother said, 'No, nothing doing.' She wanted me to finish my MBBS first which I did.

In 1974, you toured with Ravi Shankar. Ultimately that became *Ravi Shankar and Friends*, the album. How did that come about?

After I finished my medicine course, my mother allowed me to study music. I sent my tapes to the California Institute of Arts where they also had an Indian music department. They offered me a scholarship and a teaching assistantship. So, I decided to go there. This was in 1973. At the time, Ravi Shankar asked my father if he would allow me to come with him on a tour which was being put together by George Harrison. Raviji said several Indian musicians would be joining him, including the likes of Allahrakha, Hariji,

Shivji and Sultan Khan. My father called me to say that I should join them. But I had just joined the institute. So I took permission and joined the tour.

We played in Europe, London, and practised there. At some of the venues George played in the second half to ensure crowds. Subsequently, we travelled to LA and recorded the album there. That was followed by another album. George was fascinated by the Indian violin.

We also played at Royal Albert Hall, where Ravi Shankar did a solo piece and I too had a solo segment. Later, we all joined in as an ensemble. It was a very memorable interaction, among the earliest between North and South Indian classical music.

During the tour, L.S. went on to meet several musicians, including Emile Richards, who used to play with Frank Sinatra, and ended up doing an album together titled, *Fantasy Without Limits*. It was produced by Richard Bock, who had also worked with Ravi Shankar, Ali Akbar, Jean-Luc Ponty and George Duke. Bock went on to sign L.S. for five more albums. That led to *Spanish Wave*, *Indian Express*, *Conversations*, and *Mani and Company* (with Merhut Ferguson and the legendary Tony Williams). Soon, everyone wanted to play with 'Mani', the affectionate title bestowed on him by friends and collaborators, the list of which reads like an encyclopaedia of musicians and genres spanning rock, jazz and contemporary to classical. From Lord Yehudi Menuhin and Stephane Grappelli to Larry Coryell, George Duke, Stanley Clarke and Herbie Hancock, in addition to the New York Philharmonic Orchestra.

How did you get to play with Stephane Grappelli?

Grappelli came to hear me play at a concert in Paris. The concert was sold out. When I heard that he had come to hear me, I arranged a seat for him. There, he told me he would be in Los Angeles soon and that he wanted to do something with me. He gave me his manager's number.

But, I realised soon enough that his manager did not want this (project) to go through. He kept telling me how busy Grappelli was and that he would never find the time for a collaboration. So, I kept quiet. Then, all of a sudden, Grappelli calls me and says, 'What happened Mani, aren't you interested to perform with me?' I was taken aback. I told him that I had called his manager a couple of times and that he kept telling me how busy you were, etc. Then Grappelli asked me to come over to his Beverly Hills hotel immediately. There, as we got talking over a cup of tea, he realised that his manager wasn't telling him everything.

Then he said, 'Are you free tomorrow? If so, let us record.' So, I started writing pieces because I wasn't prepared and we had to do a full album.

You mean *Conversations* was written the night before it was recorded?

Yes, and I called it *Conversations* because that was the first thing that came to mind, a conversation between two musicians. Even after finishing three pieces, we were short by five to six minutes (to complete the album). So, Grappelli sat on the piano and started to play and improvise. I didn't know he could play the piano so well. So, I asked him if I could use his piece in the album. He went on playing and called it *Tribute to Mani*. But, we were still short by two-three minutes. So, I played the *Paganini Caprice* only to complete the album. In the end, the whole thing became interesting.

Did that open more windows?

Subsequently, major orchestras started to call for collaborations. When the New York Philharmonic Orchestra called, my mother had just died. They wanted me to write a new piece. It was to be a big concert and we were to play for four days with the entire orchestra. But I told them that I had already written a new piece, a double concerto with violin and flute with Hubert

Loss, the legendary jazz player who was also classically trained. But they insisted on a new piece, me playing solo. But given my frame of mind at the time, I didn't feel like doing it, and I told my father that.

But he said, 'Think back. All our life, we wanted the Indian violin to be recognised and accepted as a solo instrument. And now we are moving on to the next level. An orchestra that usually backs a western soloist will be backing you. And you will write an Indian piece. This is a victory for Carnatic music and the Indian violin. So, you should do it. I will be there.'

That is how *Fantasy on Vedic Chants* happened.

Yes, it went on to become a huge hit. The following year, when President Venkataraman was going to Russia we were asked to perform *Fantasy*. Even recently, we played the piece with the London Symphony Orchestra.

***Beyond the Flames* with Larry Coryell was recorded in a church. I find it to be a deeply melancholic, yet uplifting piece.**

I started recording a series of classical albums (*Saraswati, Kalyani*) in an old church in Santa Barbara, courtesy Water Lilly Acoustics, a production company. Church acoustics are usually very good. We used to play at night. The downside was that suddenly a motorbike would speed past and we would have to record all over again. Those days, it used to be one take, start to finish. Then, the company asked me to do something different and I expressed my wish to do something with Larry Coryell, just acoustic violin and guitar without any percussion.

Larry was a very lively person, and a very versatile player, comfortable with rock, pop, blues and jazz; a true crossover musician. I remember telling him that what I had in mind wasn't classical music, neither Indian nor Western. It was just music. We'd be taking a few notes from ragas, try to see the emotion in the notes. 'You do what you can, I'll do what I can,' I remember telling him. He was all for it. I had lost both parents by then. Maybe that explains the melancholy you spoke of.

In the album *Indian Express* you used a violin synthesiser.

Yes, there was a guy who had made this Zeta Violin. It was his concept to use electronics. He approached me and presented me with one with the request that I use it. He had given it to others too. At the time I was doing a series of five albums for a label, Milestone, in the West Coast. I worked on it as I had to get used to it. I remember playing *Flight of the Humble Bee* with it. It had created quite a stir for its frenetic pace. I now realise that a beginning was made with *Indian Express*, and many players went on to take up the solid-bodied electronic violin after that, adding accessories like a foot pedal for distortions and so on.

Jean-Luc Ponty told me about Barcus Berry violins.

Barcus Berry had come up with his special five-string electric-acoustic violin. You could play it without hooking it up to an amp. The other advantage was that when we were playing in a large open-air venue or with an orchestra, there was no feedback. (With a microphone, after a certain volume there is feedback). Barcus had also given one to Grappelli. But Grappelli told him that if there was anyone who could make good use of it, it would be me! The vice president of the company came home and offered me three. I asked for two five-strings (the tuning for these would be different) and one four-string (because I was playing a lot of Western classical then).

At that time, I was premiering *Vedic Chants* with the New York Philharmonic. And they asked me if I could use one of the five string violins. I said I would try, because the technique had to be different. One, there were five strings, the curve of the bridge was different, and I had to change the tuning to ours as opposed to the Western tuning. It was a totally new experiment. I had to practise on it, because some of the techniques I had developed on a four-string, I had to now specifically develop on the five-string; like, for instance, I could pluck the outer two (strings) and play the middle strings simultaneously. I worked on it and then, we premiered it with the NY Philharmonic. Subsequently, five string violins became very popular. Now, a lot of people, even in India, are using five-string violins.

Apparently, you had a problem with the colour of some of the models?

They had given me two that were of the regular colour. One was shiny blue and spray-painted. I remember playing it at the Hollywood Bowl once, but somehow, every time I looked at it, I found it to be too intimidating a colour. When I told the VP of Barcus Berry about it, he gave me another one in regular colour.

Your father's dream was coming alive.

Things had gone way beyond my father's dreams. All I wanted was to see my Indian violin being played in international arenas, like Royal Albert Hall and Lincoln Centre. I am very grateful to my parents and some of the saintly people whom I was fortunate enough to have come across. There has to be

JUGALBANDHI: L.S. with son AMBI at Dover Lane Music Conference in Calcutta (Sanjoy Chattopadhyay, courtesy *The Telegraph*)

some spiritual guidance and blessings. Otherwise, you can't end up doing things you didn't even know you were capable of.

Of late, I have been thinking about my father a lot. I was in Sri Lanka last week (on 17.1.2018) to commemorate seventy years of India-Lanka relations at the Bandaranaike Auditorium. I had played at the same auditorium in 1999 when I was approached by the Bandaranaike family to come back and perform there. I had told them that I would play on January 11, my father's birth anniversary. At that concert, we had M.S. Subbalakshmi singing the prayer song. Hence, the Lakshminarayana Music Festival started as a one-off tribute to him there. Today, it has become a global celebration.

L.S. has some serious concerns about the future though. One that there is a vacuum of the kind of musicians who come once in a century, the kind that make a difference; the likes of say, Palghat Mani Iyer, M.S. Subbalakshmi, Bismillah Khan Saab. Maybe rooted to that is the trend of instrumental music being relegated to second place primarily in the South unlike in the North where instrumental music has always been very strong, like Ali Akbar Khan and Ravi Shankar, both of whom have played a stellar role in propagating Indian classical music in the West.

'The danger,' feels L.S., 'is that in the South vocal music is being pushed to the extent that instrumental music is becoming secondary. Ten years down the road, whenever there is a world music festival, instrumental representation from the South will dwindle. The advantage in the South is that classical music is very well structured. There are 72 parent scales, the maximum number in any tradition; and millions of scales derived from them. In terms of rhythm cycles, there are 175 basic talas, and another group of 108 talas, chhapu talas and other talas where you can play in multiples, say, 21 and 3 quarters and so on. This kind of scientifically developed system can be projected easily to the West without a language barrier. So, by promoting only vocals, this representation will slowly disappear. This is dangerous. I feel both vocal and instrumental should co-exist.'

Yet, L.S. observes that the West is a lot more serious about Indian classical music today. Decades after the Beatles and Ravi Shankar were able to generate that curiosity, the West no longer views it as another aspect of world music. 'The West respects it as another classical music tradition which is exemplified by the growing number of people who want to learn Indian classical music. A lot many are turning up at Indian classical music concerts. Things have changed.'

At the Dover Lane Music festival, the father-son duo started early at 3 a.m., when it was still dark, and played till dawn broke at Nazrul Manch, once upon a time OAT (open air theatre) where rock concerts and theatre thrived side by side. They played Kambhoj Varnam, Ragam Tanam Pallavi in Chandrapriya and an extended encore of Raga Bhairavi.

'Calcutta is always special. It is a place of culture. People sit all night to listen to classical music, which is something beautiful and satisfying. I wish other places were like this,' the maestro told me hours before he took the stage. What will he be playing this time, I blurted out. 'I haven't thought about it,' he said, at which son Ambi smiled as though he was half expecting the question. 'It's all about the moment,' said the twenty-six-year-old disciple, also a piano player. 'Sometimes, he even announces a piece and then proceeds to play something entirely different. It is hard to keep up.'

But then that is exactly what L.S. is all about. Spontaneity. Firmly embedded in classical traditions, he is equally at ease with both Malkauns and jazz. 'An inner voice guides you… and then the music becomes a part of you,' he explained. No wonder L.S. is never shy of foraying beyond boundaries.

10

Cosmic Messenger

In the early days, when drummers saw him, he was just another violin player on the fringes of the Paris jazz scene circa 1960. They would take out their brushes as they would for the leading light of the time, Stephane Grappelli, and start playing softly—for otherwise the violin would be drowned. But once they heard him, felt his energy and punch, they'd drop the brushes and switch back to sticks—for otherwise, the drums would be drowned. This is the legend of Jean-Luc Ponty, the man who electrified his violin to compete with hard blowing brass players and went on to unleash a raga-like improvisation style that broke barriers. He blazed a trail in jazz fusion that others have since followed.

'I can tell you that the violin is a lot more accepted today than it was when I started in 1962-64,' said the bearded professor-like Frenchman, a wee bit overwhelmed at the recognition and the collection of album covers I had placed before him to autograph, but eased up soon enough when I said that we've been listening to him since college.

In India for the first time to receive the Lakshminarayana International Award and perform at the annual Lakshminarayana Global Music Festival, this 'Cosmic Messenger' was part of an ensemble of world musicians who had been brought together by Dr L. Subramaniam to honour the memory of his father.

Dr L.S. and Ponty have been friends for long, not just because they share a penchant for that extra fifth string in their violins. 'Mani and I jammed for a television documentary in 2001. He came to my house and we just improvised. That was the first time. In September 2002, I recorded one track for his upcoming album.'

Throughout his career, Ponty's collaborations have all been stupendous successes. In 1967, his performance at the Monterey Jazz Festival led to a US recording contract resulting in albums like *Electric Connection* with Gerald Wilson Big Band and *Jean-Luc Ponty Experience* with the George Duke Trio.

Two years hence, he had the 'bizarre and eccentric' Frank Zappa composing music for his famous *King Kong* solo album, and soon found himself touring with The Mothers. Ponty then joined the second edition of John McLaughlin's Mahavishnu Orchestra and his spark is evident in the two albums *Apocalypse* and *Visions of the Emerald Beyond*.

Ponty's music has gone on to encapsulate the same astral soundscapes, mystical backdrops and jazz fusion he has been synonymous with. Moving ahead by cutting down on technology and incorporating West African rhythms (consider the 1991 *Tchokola* and the 2002 *Live at Semper Opera*), his fiddle still makes statements that have the sweep and swoop of a hawk searching for its prey. Only, Ponty aims for the heart and touches the mind.

'I think I convinced a lot of people. My approach was to change the sound of the instrument to adapt it to modern music,' he told me in conversations held over two days, the last time when he returned my call to his hotel for some clarifications. 'Oh, you still have more questions?' he blurted out, laughing at the other end of the BSNL landline.

ELECTRIC CONNECTION: JEAN-LUC PONTY in Bangalore (author's personal collection)

How did this tour with Dr L. Subramaniam come about?

We met in 2001 in New Jersey and began talking about coming to India as I had been wanting to do that for a very long time. We jammed for a television documentary done for him two years ago. He came to my house and we improvised. That was the first time. Last September (2002), I recorded a track for his upcoming album. So one of the goals of this tour is to play together.

You have quite a fan following here.

Is that so? I have not come with my band but I have my bass player of the last eleven years with me. Guy Nsangue Akwa, whom I met in Paris in 1991 during the recording of *Tchokola*. Here, we are playing with local musicians, a keyboardist and a guitarist. Instead of drums, we have Indian percussionists. For me, this is an introduction to India, a contact point with Indian musicians.

Tell us something about your latest album, *Live at Semper Opera*.

This is the first live album I have done with this band with whom I am playing for the last eleven years. There is no guitar, it's been replaced by African percussion. It started with the project I did with West African music in 1991 called *Tchokola*, which was a great experience. And two of the musicians also played jazz and other types of music apart from their native music. That's why Guy and Moustapha Cisse, the percussion player, are in my band.

When I play my music, the rhythmic arrangements are now more African than American. That is the essential difference. It's more acoustic, though bits of electronics are still there. Maybe it is closer to jazz with more improvisation, more than I used to do in the '80s which was closer to rock. This latest live album was done in an opera house in Dresden, Germany, where the audience is a lot more reserved than the Americans. The acoustics were fantastic and the audience was a mix of opera lovers, bourgeois Germans and the screaming jazz crowds who were my fans. But by the end of the concert everybody was standing up and clapping. The concert was not supposed to have been recorded for an album, but since the recording turned out to be good and the band played so well, I decided to release it as a live album.

Unfortunately, Dresden in Eastern Germany was devastated by rainstorms last summer (2002). The Opera House, which is on the second floor, is still there, but the building suffered a lot of damage—the first floor and all the musical instruments were ruined.

Hence, your plans for a benefit concert?

Yes.

How did you find yourself playing with John McLaughlin and his Mahavishnu Orchestra?

Billy Cobham was part of the first band. And I was with the second edition. In fact, John and Billy wanted me for the first band but I couldn't join as I was living in France then and it was very difficult for me with immigration and the musicians' unions in those days. So they had Jerry Goodman who did a fantastic job with the band because of his different style, more like funk jazz.

Once I moved to America in 1973, John called me for what would be the second band. I had a good affinity with his music. We were of the same age, same generation, and we went through the same experience as we grew musically from classical music to jazz to blues to rock. So we had a lot in common and it was a great musical experience. I was with the band for one year and we did two albums. But a year later, I realised there was no room for me to write music. He was the only one to write for the band and I decided to go on my own.

How was the experience?

For me the Mahavishnu experience was challenging because his music, although electric and jazz fusion, was very much influenced by Indian music in the meters, like 7-11, and was very fast. So, I had to adapt to that. And he is such a strong player that you had to work hard every night to match that level of intensity. It was a great education.

But your earlier collaboration with Frank Zappa wasn't enjoyable?

There were two projects. The first one was when I signed my first contract with an American record company, World Pacific Jazz. And the producer of that label wanted me to record outside of the jazz idiom. And he introduced me to Frank Zappa and asked him to write and arrange the music for my solo album. That was *King Kong*, which was a very pleasant experience. I was the sole artiste and Zappa was the arranger and composer. In fact, he was the producer, he chose the studio, etc., but because he was on contract with Warner, he couldn't be credited with that.

After that in 1973, Zappa invited me to tour with his band, The Mothers, and the first few months were really great as he was writing some very interesting instrumental music. And he called George Duke and me because he wanted very good jazz soloists who could also read music and play anything even if it was very difficult.

But the problem was that he was a prisoner of his image as a bizarre rockstar with this huge audience—we were playing in stadiums. But the majority of his fans came for the satire and the funny lyrics and not for deep instrumental music which went over their heads.

After about a few months, he realised that although he was proud to have put together one of the world's best bands, he was losing touch with his followers. So he began cutting down the instrumental part and after six months we were mostly doing songs and I was playing background. I did not want to do that and since I was not happy with the situation, I left the band. He was not happy about that because nobody ever dared leave Zappa's band. What was worse is that a few months later I started playing in the Mahavishnu Orchestra and that really upset him. We didn't talk after that. But I don't have any grudge against him. It was more musical than anything else. Just too bad he died so young.

You brought in a number of changes to the instrument itself, by adding a fifth, and at times, even a sixth string.

I don't use the six-string (violin) much. I love the five-string. And that's another thing in common with Mani (Subramaniam). Barcus Berry, the violin-maker, came up with the fifth string. And because we were in California those days we got the same instrument. But I used that plus electronics.

It's true that initially, the classical instrument did not give me the sound I was looking for. I was looking for a bigger sound and I wanted to play with percussionists and drummers, which means you need a certain level of volume which is not there with the acoustic instrument. So that's how I started to use the electric violin, only out of necessity. But I realised that the sound was very different and instead of trying to reproduce a very classical, traditional sound I went the other way round and said, 'Let's try something else'.

So I used a lot of devices because I was in California and in the late '60s and '70s a lot of young electronic engineers were coming up with new, more user-friendly sound devices for us to use on stage. I was then playing with Zappa and his band, The Mothers, and everybody was coming to him when they were inventing a new pedal or phase-shifter or a new distortion device. I would try them too as I had an electric instrument. However, I use less of sound alterations now because I finally have what I think is a very good electric violin. And I use it direct and pure as it is, because it is already a gutsy violin sound. I think we need more violinists like L. Subramaniam and myself to improve the role of the violin in modern music.

Have you then grown out of electronics?

(Now) I prefer the challenge of playing the pure instrument. I think that's the most important thing. But for a long time, I did not really consider myself a violin player who had to be the star of the evening and show off. The day I became a composer and a band leader I used myself like the other musicians in the band, one voice in the band. What was important was the musical result.

How was it in the early days, being a violinist in the jazz scene?

I can tell you that it is a lot more accepted today than it was when I started in 1962-64. Those days there was a big prejudice against the violin in jazz or rock. But I think I convinced a lot of people—after all they were hearing me, even in those days. My approach was to change the sound of the instrument to adapt it to modern music. Stephane Grappelli did it the other way, he adapted the music to the instrument, keeping the European Gypsy sound which is great too. I am not saying my approach is better, but just that it is different. I love Grappelli very much, but I was from a different generation and I had other ideas about what to do with the instrument. And I think it helped generations of jazz and rock fans to accept the instrument.

You used to jam with Django Reinhardt's son Babik?

That was in 1960, when I was eighteen. I was going around smaller jazz clubs of Paris as I did not have the courage to go to the bigger professional clubs. We met in one of those clubs. He was drawn to me instantly as a violinist in that circuit was a rarity. He took me to the outskirts of Paris where his whole family of cousins were living in about eight to ten caravans. The most beautiful caravan belonged to Django Reinhardt's widow. And I would jam with him and other Gypsy musicians. I remember he played me an album by Clifford Brown, a great American bebop trumpet player, who died early but had a great impact on me.

And Stephane Grappelli?

Babik was still in touch with Grappelli and it was he who told him about me, this crazy eighteen-year-old guy who played bebop on the electric violin. He introduced me to Grappelli and we soon became friends. Grappelli heard me play and said that I was talented and that I should go on. He asked me to visit him in his apartment and when I did we would talk mostly. I never became his student though and when we would jam, he would play piano.

In the album, *The Rite of Strings*, you were part of an acoustic trio with Al Di Meola and Stanley Clarke. Tell us about your experience.

In fact, I had never recorded a completely acoustic album like that before. Al Di Meola, whom I met during my days with Mahavishnu in NY—you know, Chic Corea and Return to Forever and all the others were there those days—had been trying for long to do something with me. In the '90s, he called me and asked how I felt about doing an acoustic trio with Stanley Clarke.

When we started, it was very challenging. Without drums and a rhythm section, I had to play background on violin for other soloists which I had never done before. It was a new situation which was very stimulating. But it was not easy as sometimes we would argue a lot—three band leaders used to having their way, it wasn't easy. But when the energy of the three musicians were in tune, the sum of it would lead us to summits rarely attainable by any other band.

It is a great album. Stanley Clarke is so good on bass the drums aren't missed.

Thanks. Yes, Stanley is a very solid bass player. I love him. And he doesn't really play bass all the time. He plays a lot of electric guitar and writes a lot of music for film. But even without practising he comes, picks up the bass and plays. Incredible!

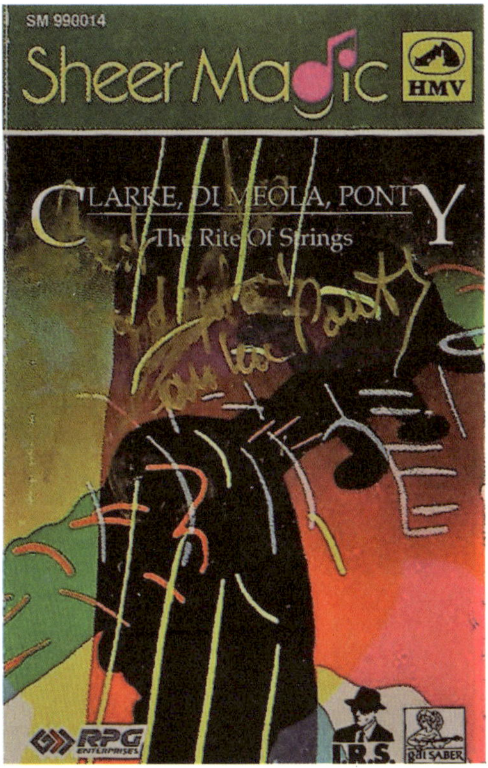

Who are playing good fusion these days?

Yellow Jacket, that's a very good band. Then, you've heard Pat Matheny and Joe Zawinul. But fusion has now been recycled by some young bands, though not in the way we were doing. It is not a movement as it was during our time.

For the record, what other instruments do you play? I know you play the clarinet and saxophone too.

Piano is a very good second instrument. I learnt violin from my father and piano from my mother, who was a piano teacher. Till eleven, I studied both instruments and then I was made to choose one. I chose violin, but I never dropped the piano completely. When I decided to start writing and arranging music for my band, my knowledge of piano came in handy.

In fact, that's the key to my whole work—not only as a violin player but a combination of both—the music writing and the colours of sound that I got from different keyboards. Clarinet and saxophone came after the piano, but once I decided to play the violin in jazz, I decided to give up the two as it was difficult to carry on with so many instruments.

Thank you very much.

It was very nice talking to you.

OUTRO

At the Lakshminarayana Global Music Festival fifteen–sixteen years ago, my regret at L.S. and Jean-Luc Ponty not playing *Mirage* in the Bangalore concert was short-lived. I decided to go to Chennai for their show days later. There, they did play it, one of the favourite tracks of my Presidency years. There was a bit of history in there too. Billy Cobham joined them on drums, much to the delight of everyone, particularly Ponty.

11

Cricket, Stones and Calcutta

The Beatles want to hold your hand. The Stones want to burn your house down. The word was out, Bangalore and Mumbai would have to guard their homes, lest Tom Wolfe's pithy observation came true. So when Venkat Vardhan of DNA Networks confided in me early in 2003 that the Rolling Stones were indeed coming to India, I couldn't believe it. But they did come. They did play, Bangalore on April 4 and Mumbai on April 7. And when that happened, it represented the coming together of three things that I hold dear to my heart: Calcutta, cricket and the Beatles.

Venkat, the promoter, is from Bangalore. But the man who hooked him up with Messrs Mick Jagger & Co. was Dilip Doshi, the left arm orthodox spinner who used to play in Calcutta even though he is from Gujarat. We rejoiced his belated inclusion in the Indian Test squad—why not, he was a '*Kolkata-r chheley*' after all—in 1979 against Australia in Madras (Chennai) where he ended up scalping 8/167 in the match. Yet unknown to us then, his other passion was the Rolling Stones. Writing about it in *The Telegraph* (London) in August 2006, Doshi recounts how at his request the enterprising owner of Calcutta Gramophone Stores on Lindsay Street would have Stones records shipped to him from Decca Records, England, in the mid-'60s. A serious pursuit of cricket led Doshi to England where, lo and behold, he got to meet Jagger in the '70s while playing county.

Suffice to say the India leg of the Forty Licks tour would not have happened, but for Dilip Doshi. 'I first met Mick (Jagger) when I was playing for Nottingham in the '70s. Both he and Charlie Watts had come to watch England play,' he told us in Mumbai at a meet-the-Press to announce the India concerts. Soon they became friends. Good enough to practise together at the nets at Lords on several occasions.

Doshi revealed he had long been discussing with Jagger the possibility of a Stones gig in India. It all fell into place once Venkat agreed to produce and manage the shows in India.

START ME UP: DNA Networks founder VENKAT VARDHAN (from left), DILIP DOSHI and Sony TV's KUNAL DASGUPTA (courtesy *The New Indian Express*)

Exactly thirteen years later, in October 2016, the Rolling Stones would be playing on two consecutive weekends at a desert in California. They did a bluesy cover of *Come Together*, a song Jagger nonchalantly described as being penned by an 'unknown beat group.'

Reading about it first and then watching a recording of the performance on YouTube, I was transported back in time and reminded of what Keith Richards had told me during a telephone conversation barely twenty-four hours before their Bangalore concert, the first time the Rolling Stones would be performing in India.

Yet, I can't forget how the India tour may not have happened at all. China, the Stones stopover prior to India, had imposed certain conditions. The Stones were asked not to play certain songs because of, I presume, the sentiments they seemed to encourage. As bizarre as it may sound now, the Stones agreed.

Thank you for not calling off the India tour.

Keith: Yes, the band can't wait to get to India. That mechanical failure (the aircraft snag) just held up things. But we are here. By the way, I love your carpets.

You called off the China tour because of the South Asian health scare over SARS (Severe Acute Respiratory Syndrome). The fans there must be a disappointed?

We are very disappointed. Personally, it was okay with me, you know, but when you are talking about the lives of hundreds of people you've got to take a call. The idea is to enjoy the concert; when that isn't going to happen, there's no point to it. But we'll go back there for sure, once things get cool.

China had banned the Stones from playing *Brown Sugar, Let's Spend the Night Together.* I thought you guys would be the last to agree to censorship.

It's kind of weird to be told what to play and what not to. It's only a love song. But we respect the sensitivities of other countries. And since I have no political axe to grind, I say, 'You don't want us to play it, okay we won't. I don't give a damn'.

On to music. You have said that the only place that instils a sense of peace in you is the stage. Explain that.

That's the only place where we don't have to answer phones and no one is asking us questions. You are alone at peace with the music. I think the other guys in the band will share my feelings.

LET'S SPEND THE NIGHT TOGETHER: MICK JAGGER (right) and KEITH RICHARDS during the Bangalore concert (courtesy *The New Indian Express*)

How do you inspire yourself to play *Satisfaction* a zillion times?

Satisfaction is a dream. I know it in my dream. When I play *Satisfaction* it's like living a dream. And who doesn't like to live his dreams?

Do you still feel that Scotty More's solo on Elvis' *I'm Left, You're Right, She's Gone* is the best thing to happen to music and you?

I can't believe you know this. Yes, Scotty is great and believe me I still can't play that solo (laughs).

The Rolling Stones vs the Beatles. How was it like in those days? You know, John (Lennon) and George (Harrison) were particularly fond of the Stones.

John was a very dear friend of mine. I miss him dearly. I think the Beatles learnt and took quite a lot from us just as we did from them. Often, we used to say we should have all been in the same band. Now, John and George are not with us—nothing in the world is perfect. You know that don't you?

That night Bangalore got itself another introduction—the city that kicked off the India edition of the Rolling Stones' Forty Licks tour. 'This is a good place to start our gigs in India. It's good to be here,' screamed Jagger.

True to reputation, the *Brown Sugar* opening left us in a daze, the booming bass drowning all but Charlie Watt's drums. Ron Wood seemed to be looking askance towards Richards, while Jagger couldn't hear what was going on. And it was not until we had rolled over *It's Only Rock 'n' Roll* and *Start Me Up*, that the sound system warmed up and we all settled down to experiencing history.

Then it started to rain and we weren't the only ones to get wet and muddy. Richards and Wood took turns out into the side extensions of the stage, and Jagger performed what seemed like a cross between Bharatnatyam and breakdance on the smaller front extension. Occasionally, we tapped our neighbours, as if to confirm that it was all real, while the giant screen at the back beamed startling close-ups of the men in action, alternating with frisky caricatures of the Stones' trade-mark lascivious tongue.

If memories are personal, this one night would be special for many. For some, it would be the sheer size of the performance, the gadgetry and the unbelievable rockstar act of the inimitable Stones' frontman, Mick Jagger, mouthing every lyric as if his sixty-year-old life depended on it. From the romantic *Angie* to the pulse-pounding *Sympathy for the Devil* in an illuminated jacket, and the pile-diver encore, *Jumpin' Jack Flash*, he was the master showman playing us to his tune.

For others it would be about raindrops looking like snowflakes in a night sky lit up by powerful spotlights as Richards sang *Slipping Away*—'dripping away,' he joked. I know of at least two friends from New Delhi who admitted they did shed a tear. As for that unfussy little boy perched atop his dad's shoulder right in front of us, it will surely also be about the rain and protection from it in the form of an empty popcorn packet later replaced by a windcheater on loan from a generous fan.

'The Rolling Stones has sunk so deep into our blood that we may even be able, by now, to pass the knowledge on genetically to our children,' wrote Salman

Rushdie.[1] I kind of agreed. Days after the show, we kept talking about how perhaps the only other band that could stake claim to such life-inspiring fame is the Beatles. Yet the crucial difference is existential in nature. The Stones are still on a roll, their story having transcended their age-old tales of notoriety. During the Forty Licks tour, they were being celebrated in magazine covers as the billion dollar band, a partnership of four linked to a tax haven offering aspiring business management graduates a lesson in corporatising entertainment.

In hindsight, many of us didn't quite agree with the way the essentially anti-establishment Stones capitulated to censorship. Otherwise, why would they even consider playing in China when the land of the Forbidden City banned them from playing two of their all-time hits. But hey, the Stones are against war—thank God. Inscribed in bold on the back of Keith's jacket was: Make peace not war.

My own thoughts were simple. Here we were in Bangalore, in 2003, and who would have ever imagined Forty Licks live in our backyard? What was it about the Rolling Stones that did it for so many generations? Most of the twenty-odd songs they played were older than many of us, but there we were celebrating them over and over again as though they were new.

The answers, I imagine, could well lie with that little boy, the boy on his father's shoulders, getting wet with all of us. He must be a decade and a half wiser today. Keith Richards spoke of the joys of playing *Satisfaction*, what if for the zillionth time, describing the process as 'living a dream'. That night we all got to live ours.

12

Calling Elvis

I never got to know for sure why at 27B Rashbehari Avenue in South Calcutta, electricity was an uninterrupted 24/7 luxury even during the years of load-shedding through the '70s and '80s. The house belonged to one of my aunts and I had heard my mother discuss with her sisters how the three-storey corner plot building beside a park near the local gurdwara was perhaps linked to the same grid that powered the electric crematorium at Keoratola, barely a kilometre away. And since the bereaved could not be made to wait to conduct the last rites of the dead, power supply had to be continuous. Yet, only 27B and a few other adjacent houses seemed to enjoy such a perk.

So, when it was known that Doordarshan would telecast a segment of Live Aid, the sixteen-hour music marathon that was to take place simultaneously in the UK and US on July 13, 1985, I decided to spend the night there so as not to miss it.

That evening I saw Dire Straits perform live for the first time, on black-and-white television. The first song they did was *Money for Nothing*, along with Sting; and then they performed the iconic *Sultans of Swing*, the number that got the music world hooked to the band and Mark Knopfler's unique finger-picking guitar style and lazy J.J. Cale-like vocals.

The feeling was heady, I recall even today. For one, the concerts were momentous by sheer scale. If George Harrison's Concert For Bangladesh for victims of famine in 1971 was ambitious at the time with Ravi Shankar, Ali Akbar Khan and Allahrakha helping propel Indian classical music into the collective consciousness of a generation in the West, Bob Geldof's Live Aid for the benefit of Africa was a reshaping of the concert-for-a-cause template with epic proportions.

For Live Aid, two simultaneous concerts, one at the Wembley Stadium in London and the other at Philadelphia's JFK Stadium, were beamed live across the world using thirteen satellites. Over a billion people in 110 countries saw performances by Queen, Elton John, Madonna, Santana, Tom Petty and David Bowie among many others. Phil Collins performed at both dos, using the Concorde to fly out of London after his set. 'I was in England this afternoon. Funny old world, aint it?' he told the audience from the stage at JFK before sitting in on drums with Led Zeppelin, the first time they would be playing after the 1980 death of their drummer John Bonham.

Knopfler's concert in Mumbai in 2005 brought back all of these memories, and more. Right to the time I bought my first Dire Straits record from Symphony in New Market (Calcutta).

Sultans of Swing, the first track of the self-titled album with a hazy photograph of a woman on the cover, would jump once or twice at the beginning, during the opening bars. I changed the record at least twice. But, it didn't help. It turns out all those who had bought the album in Calcutta, if not across India, at the time had to live with those jumps, a familiar feature of vinyls. It was only when I got myself a Dire Straits compilation CD that I got to hear the opening guitar phrases uninterrupted.

Knopfler's Live Aid performance of the song was an extended version of the original, a slow interlude of keys working itself up to a sax solo. That was something he would characteristically do with his other masterpieces whenever performing live.

When I met Mark in Mumbai at a Press meet in February 2005 to announce his India concerts in Mumbai (March 5) and Bangalore (March 7), *Boom, Like That* was his latest hit from the album, *Shangri-La*.

I realised immediately he was a man of few words.

'Why are your songs so short these days?'

'I guess I have less to say...'

Nevertheless, he did end up telling me a lot over email, about his music, collaborations with Bob Dylan, horsing around with Eric Clapton and why every time Newscastle United scores a goal, they all hum *Local Hero*.

Welcome to India, but why so late?

You must pose that question to Venkat. (T. Venkat Vardhan, MD of DNA Networks). I was touring in the vicinity of your great country and so it became possible. I am on a world concert tour to promote *Shangri-La* and was scheduled to play in Dubai on March 3. So my manager asked, why not India? After Mumbai and Bangalore I'm off to Australia, New Zealand and Europe.[1]

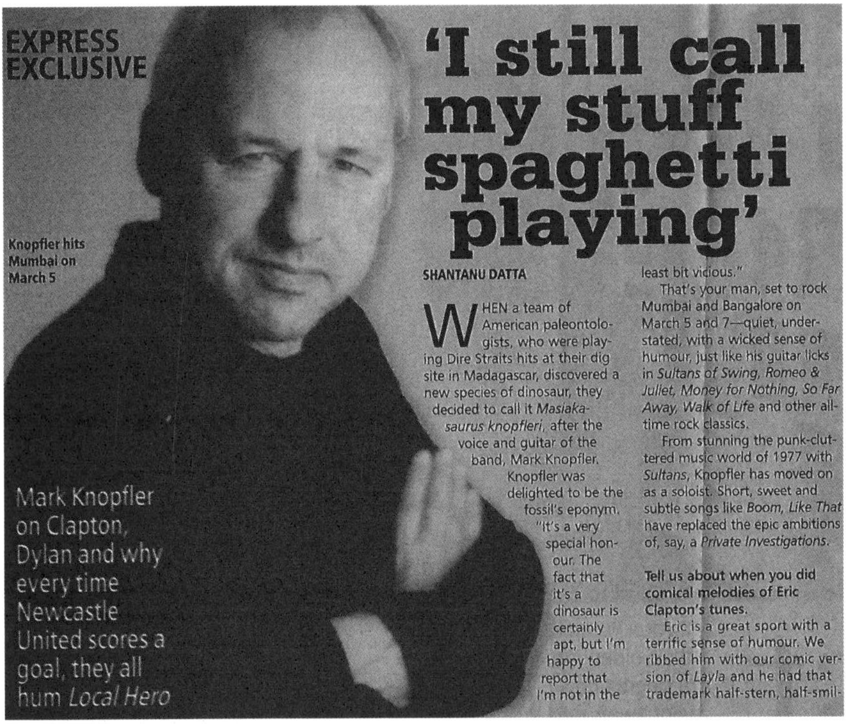

EXPRESS EXCLUSIVE

Knopfler hits Mumbai on March 5

'I still call my stuff spaghetti playing'

Mark Knopfler on Clapton, Dylan and why every time Newcastle United scores a goal, they all hum *Local Hero*

SHANTANU DATTA

WHEN a team of American paleontologists, who were playing Dire Straits hits at their dig site in Madagascar, discovered a new species of dinosaur, they decided to call it *Masiakasaurus knopfleri*, after the voice and guitar of the band, Mark Knopfler.

Knopfler was delighted to be the fossil's eponym. "It's a very special honour. The fact that it's a dinosaur is certainly apt, but I'm happy to report that I'm not in the least bit vicious."

That's your man, set to rock Mumbai and Bangalore on March 5 and 7—quiet, understated, with a wicked sense of humour, just like his guitar licks in *Sultans of Swing*, *Romeo & Juliet*, *Money for Nothing*, *So Far Away*, *Walk of Life* and other all-time rock classics.

From stunning the punk-cluttered music world of 1977 with *Sultans*, Knopfler has moved on as a soloist. Short, sweet and subtle songs like *Boom*, *Like That* have replaced the epic ambitions of, say, a *Private Investigations*.

Tell us about when you did comical melodies of Eric Clapton's tunes.

Eric is a great sport with a terrific sense of humour. We ribbed him with our comic version of *Layla* and he had that trademark half-stern, half-smil-

BACK ON THE DANCE FLOOR: The MARK KNOPFLER interview published in *The Indian Express*

To start off with your Dire Straits days, tell us about the time Eric Clapton used to visit (as guest performer) your concerts and you guys had done a parody of his *Layla*, *White Room* and more.

Eric is such a great sport with a terrific sense of humour. We ribbed him with our comic version of *Layla* and he still wore that look which is between half-stern, half-smiling. Those were terrific days.

How is it when a great guitarist whom you have idolised comes around and does a cover of one of your songs like *Setting Me Up*?

The idol is placed on a higher pedestal in the mind and in the heart.

Didn't you ever feel the need to do a cover of a song you love? Or is it that you give vent to such impulses by teaming up with the artiste himself, like you have with Chet Aktins, Van Morrison, Emmylou Harris?

When I team up with an artist, I believe the song gets a magical edge, for one adds one's emotions to that of the creator.

Your album with the Notting Hillbillies was excellent… crispy fresh, cool and homely. How did it happen?

It was 1987 and I was sitting with Dire Straits manager Ed Bicknell, who also happens to be a terrific drummer, at a meal in a Notting Hill wine bar and I said, 'Okay, Ed, we've formed a band and you're the drummer.' Of course, I had thought about this for a while. So I got Brendan Croker, Steve Phillips, Guy Fletcher and backing musicians Paul Franklin, Marcus Cliff and we recorded the album, *Missing… Presumed Having A Good Time.* It became a multi-platinum hit and we toured a while (with it) in the '90s.

I *have* to ask you about Bob Dylan and your recording experience with him on *Slow Train Coming.*

Bob Dylan had discovered his core spirituality in the late '70s. *Slow Train Coming* was a mellow, masterful offering that we recorded at the famous Muscle Shoals Sound Studio in Alabama. He asked me to accompany him on *Gotta Serve Somebody* and I gave it all I could. I believe the album is a work of amazing strength and the only reason it is underrated is because of its Christian theme. I have produced some albums with Dylan and also played with him. Have you heard *Jokerman* from *Infidels*? He is such a genius and so easy to work with. He explains his song, how he wants it to sound. He hums, he sings and we work out the passages.

Are you into classical music seriously? For, Sir George Martin is known to have commented during the recording sessions of *On Every Street* that some of the parts reminded him about Bela Bartok compositions.

I do listen to classical music, perhaps have even been influenced by it. You should be able to discern that.

Of all your film projects (*Local Hero, Last Exit to Brooklyn, Wag the Dog*), which ones were you most satisfied with and why?

That's tough. I don't really know if I have done them well. There are obviously other people better equipped than me. The way I do film music is sit down with the director and do a little session discussing where he wants the music to go and I write down where those bits are. With a film I tend to circle it from a distance and then think about a couple of general themes so I can close in on it. With *Local Hero* I had created the theme already, but at the request of my friend David Puttnam, the producer (*Chariots of Fire*), I added a lot of energy to it. That subsequently became the theme to Newcastle United, which is a lot of fun when you're up there at St James' Park.

Wag the Dog was a dark, more cynical film, but real fun to do. You just have to try and find something in yourself which reflects what's going on. I sit down with an image and play the guitar till the ideas converge. I think about the script, the film, the music and then all three together and it happens. You know as a teenager, I liked the spaghetti Western music of Ennio Morricone. I think his influence has come through in my music. I still call my stuff spaghetti playing. I always enjoy the music of the movies a great deal.

Martin Barre of Jethro Tull spoke very highly of you when I had the occasion of meeting him years ago in Mumbai. I believe you had once called him up about his guitar sound?

Yeah Martin Barre, I love his guitar work. Ian Anderson acknowledged on more than one occasion that there would be no Jethro Tull minus Martin. He plays rock with a blues and heavy metal influence. A lot of his lead is played in minor pentatonic and he plays technical riffs in harmony with Ian's flute which is fantastic. I learnt he had studied jazz and classical music and it shows.

Lastly, as a one-time journalist yourself, will you spare a thought for a fellow hack and Dire Straits fan and make sure you answer all my questions?

I hope I have.

Mark Knopfler, it was reported in those days, believes ordinary people have good taste. And I latched on to a story that corroborated that.

Once not so long ago, a consortium of paleontologists from the State University of New York at Stony Brook and the University of Utah were apparently playing Dire Straits hits like *Sultans of Swing* and *Money for Nothing* while at work at a dig site in Madagascar. When they discovered a new species of dinosaur with dangerously protruding teeth that walked the earth some 70 million years ago, they decided to call it 'Masiakasaurus knopfleri' to doff their hat to the band's frontman. On his part, Knopfler was said to have been delighted to be the fossil's eponym. 'It's a very special honour. The fact that it's a dinosaur is certainly apt, but I'm happy to report that I'm not in the least bit vicious,' he reportedly said.

I will remember Knopfler as quiet and understated. Just like his later songs, say, *Postcards from Paraguay*, a story about an over-reaching banker on the run in the album *Shangri-La*. There was more in *Sailing to Philadelphia*, stories about life in *What It Is?* and the Mason-Dixon Line of the title track. In 2015's *Tracker*, Knopfler is also doffing his hat to people, writers, poets and musicians.

'You're also tracking back in time, and to me the question of time is much more important as I've got older,' he says in the Timeline section of his official website.[2] The lead single, *Beryl*, a definite throwback to his *Sultans of Swing* days, is about one of his favourite authors, Beryl Bainbridge; *Basil* is about poet Basil Bunting whom a fifteen-year-old Knopfler had met while serving as copy boy at the *Evening Chronicle* every Saturday afternoon. And *Broken Bones* is my favourite, a rough-hewn tribute to J.J. Cale whose music has had a profound impact on Knopfler's playing.

Knopfler would go on to be among a chosen set of musicians—alongside Tom Petty and John Mayer—invited by Eric Clapton to play on *Breeze*, an album he recorded in appreciation of the minimalist master that was Cale.

'It was an honour to play on *The Breeze* that Eric Clapton just made. When Eric asked if I would play on a couple of those things, that was very nice to be able to do that. J.J. was playing in our rented rooms a lot in those early days, as were a lot of other artists. So, you look back on those records with a lot of affection. The sounds that you grow up with, they're just there all the time. That music is very important,' noted Knopfler.

Local Hero, the 1983 indie film written and directed by Bill Forsyth for which Knopfler had composed the soundtrack, is now a full-fledged musical. The play, with lyrics and new music by Knopfler, premiered in March 2019 at the Royal Lyceum Theatre, Edinburgh, Scotland. In November 2018, Knopfler released his ninth studio album, *Down the Road Wherever*. The songs are vintage Knopfler laced with jazz and funk. I latched on to *Back on the Dance Floor* immediately, just as I had done with *Calling Elvis*, the opening song of the Dire Straits album of the '90s, *On Every Street*, even though for entirely different reasons.

Back on the Dance Floor, a snapshot of a group of high-rollers, spoke to aging dinosaurs directly, egging us on with a message that it's never too late for a comeback. The hope is always that '... we'll be the toast of every knocked out boogie shack' as we strut our way in.

Such straight-from-the-heart story-poems had long replaced the epic ambitions, and prolonged guitar conversations of, say, a *Private Investigations*, *Romeo & Juliet* and *Telegraph Road*. I never did mind the shift in gears. For I embraced *Calling Elvis* as being about music's higher calling, being anchored to your roots and respecting the past. It articulated sentiments that all great artistes try not to lose connection with.

'Calling Elvis' would also become the title of a music column that I went on to pen for *The Indian Express* for a few months.

Well tell him I was calling
Just to wish him well
Let me leave my number
Heartbreak hotel
Oh love me tender
Baby, don't be cruel
Return to sender
Treat me like a fool

Calling Elvis
Is anybody home?

13

Englishman in India

The story goes that the first time Sting was in Bombay as the frontman of The Police, sometime in the early '80s, he took on the cops. After a few men in uniform started to hassle a young crowd, trying to pin down those who were exhaling a particularly strong hue into the breezy night, Sting screamed into the microphone: 'This is The Police telling the Bombay Police to f*** off.'

If the authenticity of that quote couldn't be verified, blame it on the air that night. But any band that could fuse reggae, rock and standout bass riffs and come up with an album titled *Zenyatta Mondatta* was capable of anything.

Much later, in 1988, yoga and 'causes' got to him and he was in New Delhi's Jawaharlal Nehru Stadium with the likes of Peter Gabriel, Bruce Springsteen and Tracy Chapman, singing Bob Marley's *Get Up, Stand Up* for Amnesty International. I was there, having scaled the 10-feet steel mesh wall to get on the ground from our seats in the stands (Rs 300) to be closer to the mammoth stage that had been erected. The JN stadium gig was one of twenty concerts held across the world over six weeks to raise awareness about the Universal Declaration of Human Rights on its 40th anniversary and the work of Amnesty. It was sponsored in part by Reebok Foundation and presented in India by *The Times of India*. And with a line-up such as that, who could resist a trip to Delhi.

Peter Gabriel sang *Biko*, his eulogy to anti-apartheid activist Steve who died in police custody, and *Games Without Frontiers*, a critique about belligerent nationalism, with stage lights on cranes that seemed to follow him obsessively. Bruce 'The Boss' Springsteen played everything, from *Dancing in the Dark*, *The River*, *I'm On Fire* and of course *Born in the USA*, his set running into more than two hours and bringing the curtains down at 3 a.m. on what was the largest-ever conglomeration of rock stars on a single night in India.

'It's nice to be back in India,' screamed Sting and over 50,000 of us screamed back. Springsteen joined him in his rendition of *Every Breath You Take* that he once described as a 'cool, seductive song about the ill-effects of being possessed

BRING ON THE NIGHT: STING at Jawaharlal Nehru Stadium in Delhi for the Amnesty International concert (author's personal collection)

by someone you love.' He opened his set with *If You Love Somebody*, the antithesis of *Every Breath...* celebrating the very essence of love, which is, as the song goes, *Free, free, set them free. If you love somebody set them free.*

This was among his earlier post-Police tunes that were played with a carefully chosen band of jazz musicians like Kenny Kirkland (keys), Branford Marsalis (sax), Darryl Jones (bass) and Omar Hakim (drums). Naturally, his music acquired an elevated sophistication. It took on various shades, becoming a wholesome experience that was all the more richer with his lyrics, encompassing everything from the deeply personal to the overtly political.

Unfortunately, I did not get to meet Sting in 1988. Nor did he have time for interviews when he was in Delhi later to perform at a music award show. Finally, I managed to hook up with him over email in 2006, when he was visiting India yet again. It was a short exchange in which Sting shared his thoughts on writing, friendship with Mark Knopfler and why George Michael was one of his favourite singers.

Finally, *Desert Rose* in India, live. How did that song happen?

I spent a lot of time in dance clubs in Paris during this recording. I heard this amazing hybrid sound and became very interested in it. When I met Cheb

Mami, one of the most famous singers of Rai music, I decided that I would write an Arabesque song and try to get him to do a duet with me. That's what happened. I'm happy it's a huge hit.

How different is your last album *Sacred Love*?

I like to think there's some kind of evolution taking place. My intention is to be a better musician than four years ago—a better arranger, songwriter and performer. Whether I succeed or not is up to the listener to decide.

In the film, *Bring on the Night,* you speak of a very humbling moment in your life when you heard a window cleaner singing *Roxanne.*

I enjoy hearing people humming my tunes unconsciously. I see them on the street, in a restaurant, in a factory, I see people singing my song. I find that comforting and sweet. A song I made up in the privacy of my home becomes so recognised. I love it.

Do you like George Michael's version of *Roxanne*?

George is one of my favourite singers. I thought the song was ultimately successful, different from mine. I did my version of his *Wake Me Up,* but nobody liked it.

How did you team up with Dire Straits frontman Mark Knopfler in *Money for Nothing?*

I have been Mark's friend for a long time. We both come from Newcastle. I was on holiday on the island of Monserrat. He was recording *Brothers in Arms*. He asked me to come over to the studio and play a few notes. That was it.

Broken Music* is your memoir. But, you hint of being afraid to write another one in your song *Book of My Life.

Well, I approach the first part of my life in the book because I have introspected on it; I can recognise the landmarks. I can give it some narrative shape. I am really close to the subsequent twenty-five years of my life and I can't really see the wood for the trees yet. I may be able to. At the moment, it is too confusing and I am a bit afraid.

How does literature influence your songwriting? Like *Moon Over Bourbon Street* was inspired by Anne Rice's *Interview with a Vampire.*

I read a lot. I think that has some influence on the level of literacy in my songs. I want them to mean something. I want the words to be beautiful. I want people to appreciate them.

In the Michael Apted-directed documentary, *Bring on The Night*, that follows Sting and his band rehearsing for a major public concert, he talks about how, sometimes, it is for the better when an overtly political song is rendered irrelevant over time. Like for instance, *Russians*, featured in his 1985 debut solo album, *The Dream of the Blue Turtles*:

In Europe and America there's a growing feeling of hysteria.
Conditioned to respond to all the threats
In the rhetorical speeches of the Soviets.
Mister Krushchev said, 'We will bury you.'
I don't subscribe to this point of view.
It'd be such an ignorant thing to do
If the Russians love their children too.

Yet, over three decades later, we're back to living under a Cold War shadow with evidence of Vladimir Putin's Russia meddling in the US elections that saw Donald Trump becoming President. Human rights is in deep focus back home

with the world looking at India on two counts—its response on the humanitarian crisis involving over four lakh Rohingya refugees from Myanmar and the events in Kashmir.

Sting's songs are, therefore, a throwback to history repeating itself. They are also about his life's defining moments. In *Don't Stand So Close to Me*, he cries out about his days as a school teacher, inspired by Nobokov's *Lolita*, and then moves on to becoming a tea-sipping *Englishman in New York* only to remind us how *Fragile* we all are. In between he's celebrating friendship in *It's Probably Me*, an infectious slow burn with a star line-up of Eric Clapton, David Sandborn (sax) and Steve Gadd, that was featured in the film, *Lethal Weapon 3*. He is also telling the story of a gambler in *Shape of My Heart*, one who plays not to win but to find some sense in life's game of chance. It's the kind of stuff that may have been going through the head of that thirteen-year-old orphaned girl (played by a young Natalie Portman) as she is walking away from Leon (Jean Reno), her protector who is about to die, in that consummate Luc Besson film of the same name in which we hear the song play out while the end credits roll.

And every time he sings these songs in that high-pitched rock 'n roll voice of his, teasing one note and bending another, it seems Sting will never hit the high note he is trying to reach. But he always does.

14

In Guitar Heaven

One of the Santana songs our college band Hipgnosis would often play was *Let Me Inside*, a slow, reggae number with a sharp guitar lick. Its progression of minor chords on the keys were doable on the guitar and the fairly steady drum pattern, that worked well with the intricate, but manageable, bass line, ultimately emboldened us to attempt it at a gig at Bengal Club. We were the support act that December 31 night, and I remember the song going off well, given its suitability as an early evening dance track that helped usher in the mood. No one remembers the song these days, much like the way we moved on too. Hipgnosis's tenure was short-lived and my *Shango* LP, the album that featured the track, gradually stopped getting play time on our turntable.

Decades later, the memories of *Let Me Inside* came back while hearing Carlos Santana live in Bangalore. No, he didn't play the song, having perhaps let it go just like his fans had.

Let me inside
Open up your heart, come on
Let me inside

The first time we saw Carlos playing with his band Santana was during our college years. It was a grainy VHS recording of him playing at Woodstock over two decades earlier in 1969. *Evil Ways* and an incredible drum solo by Michael Shrieve on *Soul Sacrifice* were my takeaways. They were in their twenties then and would go on to become the signature sound of a new kind of rock music, a heady mix of Latin rhythms and distinctive guitar solos. *Evil Ways*, in addition to *Black Magic Woman, Jingo* and *Oye Como Va*, became hits soon after, when Carlos signed up with Columbia Records, at the time helmed by Clive Davis.

The two joined hands again in the 1990s. By then Davis, who had left Columbia and formed Arista Records, was supervising careers of pop music sensations. And Santana, well, was looking for a way to connect with a new

SHAPE SHIFTER: CARLOS SANTANA in Bangalore (courtesy *The Telegraph*)

audience, the bulk of which belonged to the download generation. Carlos signed up with Arista and *Supernatural* was born.

It was Davis's idea to have him team up with contemporary musicians, the likes of Dave Mathews, Rob Thomas and Wyclef Jean, who collaborated with the guitar wiz and came up with songs like *Smooth*, *(Da le) Yaleo*, *Corazon Espinado*. The album was an instant hit with its pumped up horn section and Santana's signature guitar sound. We were in Pune then, and I remember hearing *Smooth* the first time on our car radio and being instantly hooked. *Supernatural* reconnected old fans to Santana again and earned him a new legion of followers. Santana was back with the album going on to sell 25 million copies in ten years, prompting the release of *Supernatural (Legacy Edition)* in 2009–10.

'My role was to complement the music and to be gracious, patient, and trusting. In fact, that became my mantra as Clive Davis, the visionary, began to hook me up with all those wonderful and different musicians. And once we started, just about every song was done in one take!' Carlos said when asked to look back, the *Legacy Edition*'s liner notes of Hal Miller inform us.

Two years later, Santana was in India, playing concerts in Bangalore and Delhi. At the time, he was out with yet another Clive Davis offering, *Guitar Heaven*, that re-invented rock classics like *Riders On The Storm* (Doors), *Sunshine of Your Love* (Cream), *Smoke on the Water* (Deep Purple), *Little Wing* (Hendrix) and *While My Guitar Gently Weeps* (Beatles) with a stellar cast of notables like Chris Cornell, Rob Thomas (again!), India Arie & Yoyo Ma, Chester Bennington and Ray Manzarek. The Yesterday Generation was in raptures with this modern day celebration of rock music, in no time reaching out for their records and cassettes. Carlos Santana was so very back, again.

I was able to have a phone conversation with Carlos Santana a week before his Bangalore concert. The legend was soft-spoken, almost embarrassed by the adulatory references to his past.

Thank you for coming to India. Your first time, is it?

Namaste. And yes, it will be my first time. I am indeed very honoured and privileged to be able to go to India.

What will you be playing for us?

It's 'Yesterday, Today and Tomorrow'. We play close to three hours.

Olivia Harrison said you and George had an 'invisible connection'. And you have maintained that you are a very visual person even when it comes to a song. What do you see when you are playing *While My Guitar Gently Weeps*?

Thank you for saying that. I see George, Ravi Shankar and Yo-Yo Ma (the Grammy-award-winning cellist featured alongside vocalist India Arie in the album *Guitar Heaven*).

Judging by the success of *Supernatural*, where you team up with younger musicians of today, you get on very well with the current generation of stars. How do you do that?

I am sixty-five now. But I feel that it's not impossible to connect with the songs by say, Lady Gaga, Justin Bieber, Adele or any other of the Grammy sensations. You only need to choose the right song.

Woodstock was incredible. I was five years old and nowhere near the place. But I heard stories about that day, it was supposed to rain, but the sun shone when you and your band came on to play.

It rained alright. But yes, the sun started to shine when we were on stage.

So many years later, you still rock. How do you manage?

I think you need to be focused if you want to learn. Anybody who is anybody, like Albert Einstein, Shri Aurobindo and Leonardo Da Vinci, they all did that. If you have to accomplish anything you have be focussed. Focus. Focus. Focus. That's all there is.

How has your playing changed over the years?

Well... It's very naked. I know a bit more now, I think.

Tell us something about your partnerships with jazz-rock masters John McLaughlin and Wayne Shorter.

Thank you for talking about them. They are two of my favourite musicians. When I am around them, I feel I know nothing. And I am happy to know nothing! And that's a nice place to be in—the purity of innocence.

Your latest album, *Shape Shifter*, is a collection of original instrumentals. Why did you choose to keep out songs?

There are songs in it all right. But, only I am not singing. My guitar is.

Thank you, it was a pleasure.

Thank you.

I realised soon enough how singularly daft I was not to have slipped in a question about *Let Me Inside*. How did the song happen? Why did he let go of it or, more important, how difficult is it to let go of a song? Nevertheless, I took along the album, *Shango*, to Bangalore, in the hope of meeting him at the concert venue on the outskirts of the Silicon Plateau of India.

It was a night of magic and a love supreme. The two and a quarter hour-concert left the oldies in thrall and the youngsters jiving on what was a distinctly pleasant evening offering a blast from the past, soul-stirred with the present, and hints of what the future might throw up.

With shifting images of the Vidhana Soudha and Mysore Palace on the giant screen as homage to the host city of his first-ever concert in India, Carlos Santana and his band were on fire, belting out classics and the latest with the kind of gusto and finesse only legendary performers of his ilk are capable of. So, a crowd that seemed to keep growing—last count 12,000—got to see, and hear, the guitar god whipping up a heady concoction of his trade mark, Latin rhythm-infused rock which meant that his contemporary hit, *Smooth* got itself a Cuban jazz ending, while *Maria Maria* had more of that sexy swagger of the original.

The surprise package came in the form of *Corazon Espinado* with his wife Cindy Blackman sitting behind the lion-painted drum kit and churning out a ten-minute solo that included a jugalbandhi with bassist Benjamin Reitvelt who thumped, plucked and beat up his five-string as if there was no tomorrow.

Black Magic Woman and later *Jingo* had the percussionists on overdrive, while Santana's guitar talked, teased, wailed, sang and shrieked. On *Samba Pa Ti*, he just sat on the sound monitors and played, gently probing, questioning and then ferreting out the answers from within.

Awesome.

At times, he addressed the audience that hung onto his every word. 'Just as Lennon and Bob Marley spoke of one world, one family, we are here to celebrate love and unity.' Were there any takers for such Utopian ideals in these cynical times? During those two hours, we were all ready to believe anything.

SETLIST

- *Stopover in Bangalore/Yaleo*
- *Love Is You Love Is Me*
- *Black Magic Woman/Gypsy Queen*
- *Oye Como Va*
- *Maria Maria*
- *Foo Foo*
- *Corazon Espinado*
- *Jingo*
- *Samba Pa Ti*
- *Batuka/No one to Depend On*
- *Taboo/Everybody's Everything*
- *Se A Cabo*
- *Europa*
- *Evil Ways/A Love Supreme*
- *Smooth/Dame Tu Amor*
- *Encore: Soul Sacrifice*

Days after that mesmerising performance, I remember thinking what it was for a sixty-five-year-old man, a musician all his life, to be able to bring so much energy and passion to a craft he seems to rediscover all over again, night after night. When you churn out thirty-odd albums (and still counting), sell over 100 million records and bag as many as ten Grammys in a career that's won over generations, what else do you strive for?

Maybe the answer lies in his openness, something that's reflected in the ambience the Santana band is able to create while playing their signature songs. During the Bangalore performance, Woodstock footage beaming on the giant screen behind them, Carlos took us back to a time when he was in his twenties, a lanky, dark-haired fellow with his face contorted, unveiling himself to a world that did not know who he was. Or what he would ultimately become. That day, *Soul Sacrifice* ended with a drum solo by Michael Shrieve. In Bangalore, there were bits of a Doors lead riff and George Harrison's *While My Guitar Gently Weeps* that he infused into the song.

'God, please help me stay in time and play in tune... I promise never to do this again,' Santana reminisced about their Woodstock performance in a BBC documentary that went behind the scenes to reveal that the band, awaiting their turn, had tripped on stuff thinking they would go on stage much later. But scheduling went awry and they had to get on almost immediately. And so the guitar neck felt like a slithering snake and he was, in effect, making all those faces to ensure it stayed straight.

Decades later, we find Carlos Santana in India, saying thank you all over again, slipping in bits and pieces from masters like John Coltrane and the rest.

'What can I say, the man has been around and we have been following his music for so long,' gushed Subir Chatterjee, a guitarist of distinction who had come for the concert from Mumbai. 'It was great to watch him, especially from

backstage where I made it a point to go and see his playing,' said the former Calcutta resident who made his mark playing with High along with founding members Dilip Balakrishnan, Lew Hilt and Nondon Bagchi.

Anjum Katyal, a blues singer of repute, also from Calcutta, had booked her tickets within half an hour of the show's announcement. 'Beyond the thrill of seeing him on stage, it was a very warm and genuine performance. He is a master at changing the dynamics of a show. From the soft rendition of *Europa* and *Samba Pa Ti*, he could instantly change over to the Afro-Cuban groove that kept us moving. That's where his magic lies. Even his little homilies on peace came from the heart,' she summed up.

As for me, I did manage to meet Santana prior to his performance and show him my *Shango* vinyl that I was carrying. Love, peace, he wrote on the cover as he signed the album. Hearing him live, talking to him and then finally meeting him was a singular privilege.

15

Sound of a Thousand Drums

What's that, asked the elderly gentleman in a bush shirt behind an old wooden desk at Braganza's, a quaint, no-frills shop that was home to everything musical on Marquis Street, opposite Jamuna cinema in Calcutta. I had gone there as a seventeen-year-old in the hope of hiring a drum kit and his surprise, bordering on irritation, was in response to my revelation that I lived in Salt Lake in the eastern fringes of the city then connected only by a few buses and taxis that refused to ply there after sundown.

Braganza & Co. was founded as early as 1942 by Francis and Thomas Braganza and was the first to sell imported pianos and drum kits in a city where sub-par replicas had become the order of the day. For anyone harbouring ambitions of learning an instrument, a western music instrument at that, Braganza's was the only hope. Why even the likes of S.D. Burman and R.D. Burman were regulars there, as was Satyajit Ray, a pianist himself.

What school do you go to? That was the follow-up question posed to me by one of the two Braganza elders—they were always there at the shop.

La Martiniere, I mumbled, but fairly sure that the name would ring a bell.

Ah! Who is your music teacher?

Mr Tony Menezes.

Get him to write a letter introducing you and the drum set is yours. Rs 40 a month.

So began my tryst with the drums, the kit made up of a green coloured floor tom-tom, a single smaller tom-tom on the bass drum that sported a smart black border. In those days, the drums had animal skin, as opposed to the synthetic variety of modern times, and these would waver with the weather. So, if it was cloudy and rainy outside, my strokes on the snare drum to Johnny Wakelin's *Black Superman* playing on our Garrard record changer would sound as flat as a kick on a deflated football. But when it was nice and sunny, I was as good as Ringo on *Hard Day's Night*. Well, kind of.

EVERYTHING MUSICAL: Braganza & Co. on Marquis Street, Calcutta (courtesy *The Telegraph*)

My neighbours at Vidyasagar Niketan were indulgent, thankfully. And I was quite the toast of my local friends, many of whom were already playing tabla under the tutelage of Tarun Ganguly, who with his wife Krishna, used to run a music and dance school where Suchitra Mitra, one of the stalwarts of Rabindrasangeet, would, at one point in time, come to teach. Ganguly's son was part of our gang too and with him in the lead we mustered the courage to approach him.

Would Tarun 'kaku' help us form a drums orchestra?

Talobadyam was the title of the soiree we went on to perform that Puja for residents of Vidyasagar Niketan in the early '80s. The tabla taranga, an arc of serially tuned tablas on centrestage, accompanied by a host of percussion instruments like the dhol, packhawaj, congas, bongo, cymbals and a huge gong struck to meticulous time by one of our most rhythmically challenged friends. My 'jaaj set' was part of the ensemble too.

Tarun kaku had worked out several compositions so that none of us felt left out. '*Dha tere kete tako, dhere dhere kete tako*', a friend, now in Moscow, remembers playing. *Gram Chhara Oi Ranga Matir Poth*, a Baul song composed by Rabindranath Tagore in 1909 in celebration of the meandering village road,

TABLA TARANGA: TARUN GANGULY at a performance (courtesy Bhaskar Ganguly)

was played on the tabla taranga by Tarun kaku's son, he reminds me on Whatsapp from the US. It was particularly well received by an indulgent audience of friendly faces, our parents and other residents of the housing estate.

I may have picked up a couple of guitar chords later on in life, but the drums was my first love. Ringo Starr was the first in a list of heroes that has, over the years, grown to include Jim Keltner, Ian Paice, Barriemore Barlow, John Bonham, Steve Gadd, Billy Cobham and Omar Hakim. Growing up in Calcutta, our local heroes were Nondon Bagchi and Jeffrey Rikh; and then one day, I heard Ranjit Barot, who had come down to play at a rock festival organised at the OAT with his band. Man, he was good, just like Barriemore Barlow, I remember thinking that sunny afternoon.

One of the first assignments I volunteered for in Delhi in the August of 1996 was to interview Sivamani, that wondrous drummer from Madras who was playing at the Maurya Sheraton on the occasion of the fourth anniversary of the hotel's exclusive Jazz Bar. I had not heard him play till then. But it would be more than two decades later when I would get to hook up with Barot—a telephone conversation initially intended as a short tete-a-tete on the music of guitarist Amyt Datta with whom he had played, but that went on for about an hour discussing his amazing journey that began at home in Varanasi in a family rooted in classical traditions.

When I did get to hear Sivamani, it was as though a thousand drums were playing. Anyone who was there at the Jazz Bar that night when Siva played with the Louiz Banks quintet would tell you he moves at the speed of light and how his one-to-ones with the bass would make everyone forget their drink. His technique is mind-blowing, his innovations stunning. Not many in his clan end a tune with a sharp smack on his bloated cheek. 'Pop'.

DREAM BEATS

Did-dig-dig, tum-tee-tum, shuwe…eep.[1]

That's the beat to which I entered the Jazz Bar that Sunday morning. The hangover of the night before hadn't been cleared off the tables, but Sivamani was there. Fresh in his well-groomed ponytail. Ón the drums, jamming.

If Siva's inspiration came from his mother, his idol was his father. A drummer of repute himself, S.P. Anandan was sure about one thing: Siva would not play the drums. So, when papa was working at the studio, young Siva would bang away to glory at home. Right?

'I used to create a lot of noise, but amma never said anything.'

That was only the beginning. Siva was soon bunking school to hide in the studio and watch his father play. Noel Grant, another famous drummer in the Madras of the '70s, was the one a young Siva worshipped. 'His riding on the cymbals (hitting the stick to the cymbal gently, continuously) was amazing.'

Dig-dig-dig, tum-tee-tum, shuwe…eep…

Thrust on to stage suddenly one evening in 1974 to play R.D. Burman's hip swinger from *Sholay*, young Siva excelled himself. Yes, it was *Mehbooba*, one of R.D. Burman's biggest hits which we later came to know was 'inspired' by *Say You Love Me* by Demis Roussos. In any case, S.P. Balasubramanium loved Siva's playing that day. Soon, he was a permanent fixture in S.P.'s troupe. With extended drum solos at every performance, the big time beckoned him.

But Siva got tired of film music after a while. And in came Frank Dubier, who played the hotel circuit.

'Just when I was looking for other avenues, Frank introduced me to jazz sometime in the '80s. And boy, I was dazed and confused. The only thing I can now remember is that I thought, "Man, what a beat."'

Dig-dig-dig, tum-tee-tum, shuwe…eep…

There was no looking back ever since. Although Siva knew nothing of the genre, he surprised everyone by his perseverance. He often played alongside a track he hadn't heard before. And since jazz is all about improvisation, he had no problems. Seniors said he had the touch.

It was not long before tabla wizard Zakir Hussain spotted him. No one had introduced them. No one needed to. Their music did the talking. In passing Siva spoke of his idols and mentioned the legendary Billy Cobham. 'My dream would be to touch his feet one day, I had told Zakir casually,' he recalled. April 24, 1990 turned out to be a red-letter day. Zakir would be playing with Billy Cobham in Bombay, and Siva was invited. Others in the band were Vikku Vinayakram (we heard him with Shakti) on the ghatam and father Anandan. They set Rang Bhavan on fire.

Dig-dig-dig, tum-tee-tum, shuwe…eep…

Billy, they say, was zapped. He invited Siva to the Munich Jazz Festival. France, Switzerland and the US followed as did fairly regular appearances at the annual Frankfurt Jazz Fest. It was there that Siva joined the ranks of other great drummers when Zildjian, one of the world's most sought-after cymbal manufacturers, asked him to endorse their range.

But Siva stayed grounded. The collaborations with Billy Cobham and Zakir Hussain, gigs and jam sessions with Grover Washington Jr and George Benson were only the beginning. He is still open to popular film music and works regularly with friend A.R. Rahman among many others.

But if passion truly has a colour, it is the shiny golden hue of his drum kit. He loves to play.

Dig-dig-dig, tum-tee-tum, shuwe…eep…!

At a live concert, Zakir Hussain once introduced Siva as a 'phenomenon that walks the planet but once in a century'. These days, he surely straddles the music world, both at home and abroad. From IPL opening shows (2008, 2010) to films (think *Anima Nambi, Kavithan* as composer, *Roja*, *Rang De Basanti*, *Dil Se* where he played), Siva is a first-name recall among music lovers. His collaborations, Asia Electric with pianist Louiz Banks and sitar virtuoso Niladri Kumar, and Siraha Trio with pianist Harmeet Manseta and U. Rajesh (younger brother of U. Srinivas) on mandolin, are a happy mix of ragas, western harmonies and orchestration. His work with New Life, that includes vocalist Runa Rizvi, keyboard and harmonium player Vishal Dhumal and Ojas Adhiya on tablas blend ghazals, sufi and folk music. Constantly exploring, he stops at nothing, creating tunes from Limca bottles to drumming up a rhythm with biryani handis of various sizes. Why, he was in Calcutta in January 2018, playing with guitarists Amyt Datta and Pandit Vishnu Mohan Bhatt, prior to a solo tour of the US between April and May. Siva just keeps going.

Zakir Hussain, on his part, would pluck out another young drummer, this time from Bombay. Ranjit Barot, already a wee bit tired playing original music best described as progressive rock, was running his own studio then. One gig led to another and suddenly there was a man called John McLaughlin on the horizon.

MADRAS COMBO: SIVAMANI (courtesy *The Indian Express*)

KONNAKOL KING

In April-May 2017, Ranjit Barot and a host of accomplished musicians were performing in Varanasi for the Sur Ganga Mahotsav, a 43-day music festival to commemorate its designation as 'The Creative City of Music' by UNESCO two years earlier.

I got to talk to Ranjit Barot one afternoon and he opened up about his journey; growing up in a home frequented by classical musicians, his conversations with his mother, a classical dancer of repute, and how he had stopped playing for fifteen years when this Ustad came and pushed him to the deep end.

I remember hearing you for the first time sometime in the '80s at Gol Park's Open Air Theatre in Calcutta where a day-long festival of music

was being held. You blew our minds. Your drumming reminded us of Barriemore Barlow!

Yes, I remember playing at the OAT.

It's no longer 'open air' though.

That time I was with a band called Waterfront in 1976. Essentially, Waterfront was a jazz/blues-oriented progressive rock band. I sort of honed my skills in it.

How did you get involved with music?

I have been fortunate because I got this very inquisitive spirit from my mother Sitara Devi (Kathak dancer from Varanasi). I think she fostered a very open cultural atmosphere in the house. Visitors to our house were predominantly Indian classical musicians. When she saw that I was into rock 'n roll and into Bach and jazz, she was extremely positive and encouraging. Sometimes, we would sit and listen to songs together and she would be very encouraging and, sometimes, very amazed at how the western world was evolving musically. So, that sort of atmosphere was very conducive.

BADA BOOM: RANJIT BAROT (Twitter)

You used to run your music studio in Mumbai.

We had to close it down because we were underneath a bridge and the bridge was going in for repairs. My life has come full circle. I started off playing drums, and then went into production as I had no work as a drummer. And just when I had done enough of that, like sitting in front of a computer recording other people, my life went back to playing drums.

Now, my principal travelling and recording work is with John McLaughlin and A.R. Rahman, whose band I manage. They keep me busy pretty much half the year, either performing with them or preparing for these tours and interactions.

How did you get back to playing?

It was all because of Ustad Zakir Hussain. He just pulled me up and said, 'We are playing tonight and I want you to come, not to watch the concert but to play'. I ended up playing at the Millennium Concert he did in December 1999. He sort of pushed me to the deep end. I hadn't been playing and my chops weren't all right. Then one thing went to another and I toured the United States with Zakir bhai. Then I met John McLaughlin in 2006.

And your album?

Yes, I was working on *Bada Boom*, which released in 2010 and John was a part of that along with U. Srinivas (mandolin)... I was on fire, you know, in my mind.

How did you end up joining John McLaughlin's band, 4th Dimension?

John called me in 2011 and asked me to join the band. From then, it was full-time on the drums because I had to focus on taking my playing back to an international standard. Remember, I had been away from my drum set for fifteen years or maybe more. I had to go back and practise, listen to what young drummers were doing, because the language and vocabulary had changed, the approaches had changed. It was no longer the same thing.

In fact, John says you 'just had to be in the band'.

Yes, this is what he tells me, that it was meant to be... that we were to be linked by our music. This is very flattering to me because he is my guru along with Ustad Zakir Hussain, the two great mentors in my life. This is our seventh year together and it (4th Dimension) is the longest band he's (McLaughlin) ever had. We are going to release a double album which is a live recording at Ronnie Scots Club in London. So, I am very fortunate.

How do you manage to straddle so many genres of music? You used to be this flamboyant rock drummer and now you play modern jazz and also arrange music that is put out in the popular domain.

We like so many kinds of music. Like you said, we like Jethro Tull, I like John Coltrane, Bach and Indian classical music. Well, if I like all these things, I want to inform myself about these things. I want to spend time listening to them. And if I spend time listening to them, I will be informed enough to tell my body and the facility that I have to chase that sound because it gives me joy. I have a way of playing drums and I have to steer this technique to evoke different sonic identities. When I am playing jazz, I fall back to the vast library in my mind of people I grew up listening to like Elvin Jones, Tony Williams, Billy Cobham, Billy Joe Jones, so many of them... I have observed the spirit of these people and that manifests itself on my playing.

And when you play rock?

I tap into Mitch Mitchel (Jimi Hendrix), Ian Paice and John Bonham. I don't have to work hard. I have listened to so much music in my lifetime. I think your musical diet should be varied. But some people stick to one kind of music which is okay. I mean I love Michael Jackson, Christopher Cross, Steely Dan and A.R. Rahman. So, there's good quality music and there's good quality music of which I want to be a part of. I am greedy that way.

Greedy?

Yes. I learnt this from the masters, from Ustad Zakir Hussain and John McLaughlin who live and breathe to play music. Unless you make this the driving force in your life, I don't know any other way to be. I don't want to sound clichéd. From the moment I wake up till the moment I go to sleep—maybe even in my sleep—I am in music land. I am a musician; this is what I was born to do and I consider it a privilege and an honour. I don't take it lightly and I want to be worthy of the muse and of the life that has been given to me. It's beyond my wildest dreams that I can support my family doing this.

Musicians like you work very hard. Yet sometimes there's not much coming back from the audience.

Working hard for a musician is a given. It's a discipline like any other. One has to work very hard to gain a musical voice. I think there are Indian musicians who could rise to this challenge and be internationally worthy if they just worked hard and don't take audiences here (India) as a reference point. Don't be defined or defeated by the audience's inability to listen to a higher music.

It's up to you, really. If you are good at what you do find the 500,000 people you want to play for. And the other 100,000 people that don't come to hear you are fine because you're not playing for them anyway.

We tend to peg performance against attendance. I agree some of that has to be paid attention to because eventually we are musicians trying to make a living. I also believe that music reflects the times we live in, and if you are paying attention to people who are around you, and music that is being made globally, you will find elements of what's out there already exist in you. You'll then have to hold that and present it to people with your DNA on it. It's a process.

Your final thoughts on being a musician?

Being a musician is a multi-layered existence. It is not just the ability to play an instrument, it's a way of life. We have to treat each other with respect and compassion; and if we are in possession of a certain truth and knowledge about music, it's our responsibility to share this, either through the songs we write or through the personal encounters with other musicians that we meet. I am very fortunate. And I pray that every lifetime I must be given this gift. This is all I can ask for because it is truly a wonderful state of mind.

Ever since that conversation with Barot, the one enduring image that I keep playing back in my mind is that of a mother and son, sitting together and enjoying music. The young boy playing his favourite tune, maybe an Elvis Presley song or a Bach concerto, at times drumming his restless fingers to a beat, while his mother listens with rapt attention, as if dissecting each note, looking for, and discovering, nuanced similarities between eastern and western traditions of classical music or the sheer defiance of rock n' roll.

It says something about the all-encompassing richness of Indian music that it allows individuals the freedom to explore, empowering them with an almost natural impulse to try out other forms of music. Consider the lives of Ranjit Barot or Zakir Hussain, Ravi Shankar and Ananda Shankar, all of whom have grown up in a milieu of essentially Indian musical values rooted in riyaz and the guru-shishya parampara. Yet, all have branched out to the other side. They have crossed over to genres such as rock and jazz where improvisation hold the key.

Ananda Shankar, who was born in Varanasi but spent a large part of his life in Calcutta, thought it was most natural to strum *Jumpin' Jack Flash* on the sitar. His uncle Ravi Shankar and Ali Akbar Khan had the audacity to play Indian compositions while opening the Concert for Bangladesh at Madison Square

Garden alongside rock legends George Harrison, Eric Clapton and Leon Russel to name a few, way back in 1971. Lord Yehudi Menuhin chose L. Subramaniam to play with at the UN. Now, Ranjit Barot is with John McLaughlin's 4th Dimension, relishing bouts of Konnakol (the South Indian tradition of performing percussion syllables vocally, akin to bol in Hindustani music) as he plays out complex rhythms on the drums while the elder statesman of jazz explores the outer reaches of a tune on his electric guitar—think Dalhousie Institute, Calcutta, 2016.

From Calcutta to Graceland and the Big Apple, from Varanasi to Ronnie Scots Club in London, music has done a back-and-forth of the seven seas a million times. Yet self-appointed culture vultures of the day keep prying, their avowed mission to protect our Indian-ness and save our cultural heritage. What are they trying to protect when nothing is in danger? What are they trying to save when nothing has been lost? What are they trying to purify when nothing has been sullied?

Tony Menezes, my first music teacher at school, is no more. Tarun kaku has passed away, his daughter running their school at Vidyasagar Niketan now. The single-screen Jamuna cinema, where we got to see *Jaws* as kids since the management was a bit lax in enforcing entry curbs during screenings of A-certified movies, is now a mall. Braganza's, where I got my first drum kit, is still there. It looks neater and is comfortably air-conditioned. Most of Calcutta's musically inclined families still go there, or to their new outlet on Free School Street, for that first violin, guitar, or piano books prescribed by ABSRM (Associated Board of the Royal Schools of Music) or Trinity College London. Tony and Dicky, sons of the Braganza seniors, run the shops stocked with an infinitely better choice of equipment. Yamaha pianos, Zildjian cymbals, Fender guitars are all available across the counter—why, a Tamạ drum set is there for hiring for concerts and college festivals. At home we have a Chappel (London) piano from Braganza's for a young student who simply loves its tone. The piano, Tony tells me, is over a hundred years old. Yet, it is pitch-perfect. So is the one at the home of the late Satyajit Ray on Bishop Lefroy Road. That one, Dicky tells me, is from Braganza's too.

I am thinking Ray films. I try and imagine this tall man with a baritone, working the keys of that piano, fleshing out a tune for Goopy and Bagha to play. Their songs will stay with us forever.

Dekho re nayan mele, jagater ki bahar...

16

Rite of Strings

It's nice and breezy at Swabhoomi, an East Calcutta culture hub of tasteful architecture. The Amyt Datta quartet, the fourth musical act of the evening, is playing *Dance Acoustica*, a sparkling guitar track that is kind of bouncy in a measured way. The bass holds it together, the percussions infuse minimalist frills while a second guitar embellishes the chords. The underlying theme pretty apparent from the early notes, *Acoustica* is a fantastic opening track, the kind that makes it easy for you to choose your poison for the night. Tequila with Blue Curacao, perhaps?

I have visions of a quaint open-sky café in, say, Valencia, where patrons sip vino (wine), listen to the music and talk in hushed tones only in between tracks.

Amyt is a master of such atmospheric wonders. The kind that sets you on imagined journeys to places where only jazz can take you. *Pulse*, the fourth track he plays, is, by contrast, busy and intricate, more demanding. *Electric Insanity* is bloody intense, layered as the other tunes, but aggressive. It is based on a 5-note scale devised by John Coltrane, he informs the disciplined audience by then deep into the music. *Camellia* is meant to soothe the nerves. It's a slow, soulful and mysterious piece about 'secrets'—very Al Di Meola with shades of *Cielo e Terra*.

'Yes, my music is very Mediterranean-ish,' Amyt tells me two weeks later at his apartment in South Calcutta, and I remember thinking it was exactly sixteen years since I heard him at Vidya Mandir playing with the likes of Lew Hilt, Nondon Bagchi and Subir Chatterjee to celebrate Dilip Balakrishnan's music. He was Amit then and sported a shoulder-length rockstar mane. Now, he is Amyt, having shed his locks for a daring close crop, a pair of shades adding to the cool quotient. His music has crossed the seven seas and beyond. Complex and sophisticated, there's something deeply personal—as all good music is—about his guitar playing.

Jazz.

'But, it also has this undercurrent of certain Indian-isms,' he points out. 'Mind you, not Indian music per se, as I know nothing of Indian music. I just use the smell of it.' To Amyt, the Indian and Mediterranean mix, however tenuous it may seem to some, is as natural as, say, the samba-jazz fusion of Bossa Nova. 'A lot depends on how you are wired. Indian doesn't have to be in the notes. It could be in the breathing, the feel. You play a flurry of notes and you slow down. There's contrast. And I get that from watching life very closely.'

If creativity revolves around life, then Amyt is wise enough at a sprightly fifty-six to know that nothing comes without dedication and perseverance. 'You will have to do the riyaz and the wood-shedding,' he insists, laughing while pointing out that he has been without the guitar only for the first twelve years of his life. From then on, practising has been a part of his days and nights, his mother often chiding him for not devoting enough time to the instrument.

'My mother is from the family of R.C. Boral (considered to be the father of Hindi film music). For her, music is too dear, too sacred not to pursue just because it comes with inherent career risks. I said, "I will try..." One can only try. But I am very honest. If I am awake, I am with the guitar. I practise.'

Those who know him well enough say his reaction to anything and everything is the guitar. Amyt doesn't disagree. 'If I am angry, I storm into my room and pick up the guitar. If I am happy, the joy pulls me to the guitar.'

When he is not? 'I listen to the everyday sounds the city offers.' And Miles Davis, Charlie 'Bird' Parker and other legends of jazz. 'Miles is my all-time philosopher. Just as John Coltrane is a master of his craft with the mind of a supercomputer. Consider *Giant Steps*.'

And McLaughlin?

'John McLaughlin is my absolute favourite. He has the romance of Spain, the complexities and sophistication of jazz and the divinity of Indian music.'

Amyt loves Laurindo Almeida too, for his 'most beautiful chord voicings behind Stan Getz's free-flowing lyricism', Al Di Meola for bringing 'Mediterranean music to the mainstream', Jean-Luc Ponty for 'doing wonders with the electric violin' and of course Jimi Hendrix, Carlos Santana and Ritchie Blackmore.

Sometime in the late '80s, Amyt and his brother Monojit 'Kochu' Datta, an accomplished drummer and percussionist with a penchant for Latin rhythms, joined Airwave, a band fronted by Gyan Singh with his wife Jayshree on vocals. One of Airwave's most memorable gigs was at Dalhousie Institute featuring Louiz Banks on the keys. Hanging around with them backstage later, I remember Amyt telling us how Louiz had called the band members 'masters of memory',

NEVER BLACK & WHITE: AMYT DATTA in performance (*Prosanto Mohato*)

complementing their musicianship even though they weren't proficient in reading notations.

'True. At the time, Mr Louiz Banks came over to Calcutta for three days, stayed at Jayshree's house. We used to practise from 10 a.m. through the day. It was thrilling to have him in the house. That's how we got close.'

These days, Amyt is able to instantly write down tunes that come to his head, something he admits happens most often when he is on 'The Throne'. He usually grabs a mobile and hums the bare-bones tune, 'even though I am embarrassingly bad at it'. His approach to music is philosophical. With emotions at its core, the tunes are almost always about the 'various shades of grey in between black and white'. Once ready, he loves to hold up the sheet of music and marvel at the notes, represented calligraphically by crotchets, minims and quavers, a delightful visual of the ideas that led him to the tune.

'But learning the craft of writing a tune is quite a heavy task. It's just the notes of course. But then, I realise, it's not the notes that we recognise as a song. Travelling from one note to the other is the key, both in terms of intervals and time and space,' he explains.

Growing up in '70s Calcutta of divided loyalties, between the Bengali film industry and those pursuing so-called western music, Amyt's 'haateykhori (initiation)' happened courtesy Khokon Mukherjee, who used to then play with

Hemanta Mukhopadhyay. Later, lessons from the late Carlton Kitto helped open a window to the world of jazz and improvisation.

Among the earliest bands Amyt remembers playing in was New Blues Connexion, a quartet that included brother Kochu. They played at Anglo-Indian weddings, school competitions, fests, pubs and even small-time club gigs, loving every bit of it. Subsequently, with Gyan and Jayshree at Airwave, they did songs by Pointer Sisters, En Vogue, Nona Hendryx, Sade, Steely Dan, Doobie Brothers, Deborah Berg and many more, imbibing nuances of pop sensibilities and, in the process, acquiring a sense of discipline that comes with playing in a covers band. They practised everyday firm in the belief that the more they played, the more gigs would come their way.

'Jayshree would explain to me what a four-minute pop tune should contain or how to say what one has to say within a thirty second guitar solo. Taking a keyboard player's approach would be more fitting and the fact that I had to "play" to the "song" was what I learnt from her,' recalls Amyt.

By the mid-'80s, the siblings started playing and touring with other set-ups, primarily Shiva, another of Calcutta's signature bands, helmed by P.C. Mukherjee. In 1988, the duo were back with Gyan and Jayshree, this time also playing originals, in various formations, most notably Pop Secret, Skinny Alley and Pinknoise.

But the good times didn't last. A series of tragedies struck. Gyan Singh passed away, and Jayshree was diagnosed with cancer. Then suddenly, in October 2017, Kochu died. Now, Jayshree is no more. 'I did not know how to look at life. With anger? Or with hopelessness? I was in a vacuum and my music became silent. Dead were my notes,' he wrote in *The Telegraph*.

But Amyt has soldiered on, vowing to himself to carry the torch. He has stayed on in Calcutta even though his music could have taken him anywhere he chose to go. 'Luckily, for me, I don't think too far ahead. But yes, questions do arise. Should I have gone to New York? These days, when I go there, although not as frequently as before, I realise it's no longer what we used to think, that every American musician was better than us. Some of us have managed to go over to the other side.'

Here's how. Amyt's first three albums, *Ambience de Danse*, *Pietra Dura* and *Amino Acid*, were composed between 2008 and 2011. Now he's working on *Amygdala*, which Googles to 'an almond shaped part of the temporal lobe of the brain involved in emotions of fear and aggression'. Amyt describes *Amygdala* as a 'surgical inquisition of the guitar,' for which he'll be resorting to OTX, or octave tuning experiment. That means, he will be altering the order of the guitar strings from the conventional E, B, G, D, A, E. 'There are about twenty ways one can do this, I have zeroed in on one.' But before that he wants to record an album of seven tracks, tentatively titled, *Roja Planta.*

Both pianist-composer Louiz Banks and drummer Ranjit Barot are effusive about Amyt's playing. Banks ranks him in the top bracket, easily among the ten best guitarists of the country. 'I have always been amazed at his creativity, grasp of various genres, vision, dexterity and technical brilliance. Amyt has the amazing ability to play music of all genres with deep conviction and ease. He does not profess to be a jazz musician but given a jazz tune he can come up with incredible solos,' he says.

For Barot, Amyt is a sensational guitar player. 'I think he is an excellent rock and blues guitar player, probably among the best we have... We have played a couple of times together. He has also recorded on some of my compositions. He is constantly exploring.'

Reclusive singer-songwriter Bertie DaSilva, who has played with Amyt, believes he's in perfect groove when he is playing the blues. 'The tones, the bite, the edginess. There is an expressiveness in Amyt's playing that goes beyond virtuosity,' says the professor by day and poet-musician by night in an article for *The Telegraph*, explaining how it is only natural for an intelligent talent like Amyt to 'break down notes, take structures out of familiar contexts, shape, trace, erode the margins and erase the boundaries.'

Essentially, Amyt's mission has been to make guitar playing a dignified way of life in Calcutta. 'Maybe I am mad... I realise that. In fact, chief minister Mamata Banerjee presented me with an award, recognising me as a guitar player. I am grateful that such things have started to happen.'

The truth is Amyt is mighty miffed to see people using the guitar as prop to up the cool quotient. 'I understand its popularity. When you carry the guitar to play it makes you look better than you are. But, there are those who are doing it to adopt a 'rockstar' image without realising that investing one's blood, sweat and tears for decades is not enough to master the instrument.'

Yet it warms the cockles of his heart to say that a generation of serious Indian guitar players, from Tripura to Bengal to the South, were his students at some point of time in the three decades he has been mentoring. 'I didn't realise this till recently, but most of those playing publicly are my students.'

'Amytda taught us to break things down to the last note... to learn the rules well enough to know when to break them,' says Bodhisattwa Ghosh of The Bodhisattwa Trio that performed before Amyt at Swabhoomi that evening. Rohan Ganguly and Rishav describe him as their 'God and mentor', a kind of go-to elder for advice on everything beginning with the guitar and encompassing all else there is to life. 'The best part of Amytda is that he never tells you what you should do. He will give you three-four options and let you choose. He taught us to think on our own,' says Rohan, who is wrapping up a final master of his first jazz album. Rishav remembers the Wednesday he joined Amyt's classes. It was December 2011. Since then, he hasn't missed a single lesson. 'Amytda gave me the courage to try and become a professional musician,' says the blues-rock guitarist. 'He tells us about "Mr Music" and that we must all play to serve Him, a living idea that has character and myriad personalities.'

Today's students are as loving and reverential. One sheepishly gives Amyt a bar of chocolate as he sets up his gear, including a new BOSS guitar effects processor. Another has just arrived from Dhaka. Handing over a copy of Bob Dylan's *Chronicles*, he settles down to record on his iPhone the music lesson that follows.

'This interest and energy must find an outlet,' says Amyt, pointing to the Sunday morning gathering that is spilling over to the corridor of his apartment.

The day's exposition is on triads, the three notes that make up a chord. Amyt wants them to work on A and G chords. Using the 'Cadbury boy's' Fender, he plays the A triad and puts it on loop on his processor. He then plays A and G triads over that to illustrate improvisation limited to a set of notes. 'If you can sound decent using only these six notes, imagine what you can do when there are no curbs,' he explains and asks them to try one by one. Most do but make mistakes. Yet, Amyt is reassuring.

'You played well, but that's not what I was asking you to do,' he tells one of the younger students of the day, answering in excruciating detail the questions about scales and harmonies that invariably follow. They end the day with the 12-bar blues. Amyt puts the typical three-chord progression on loop and plays. His fingers pluck, pinch and tease out notes at a leisurely pace, his solo gentle and joyous, the pauses apt.

His guitar is on song.

No, this isn't Friday night at Buddy Guy's Legends in downtown Chicago. It's Sunday afternoon at 71C, Hazra Road, Calcutta.

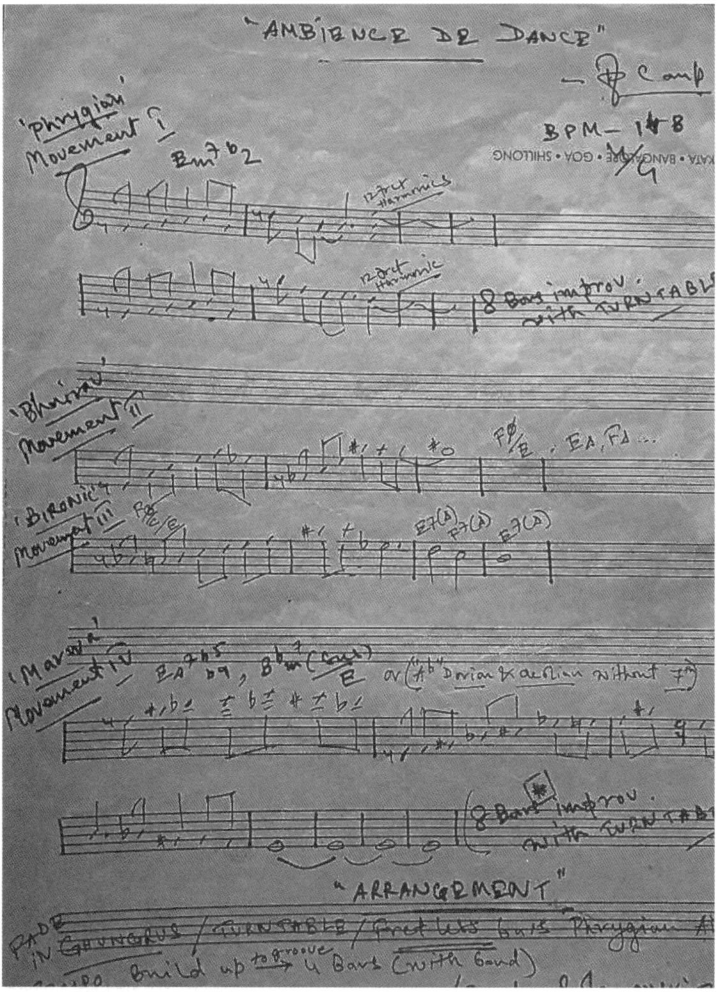

SO IT SHALL BE WRITTEN: The sheet music for *Ambience de Danse*

17

Dizzy with Louiz

My earliest memory of 'jazz' is the word itself, seeing it written with gold dust in elegant calligraphy, on specially crafted cloth-bound wooden music stands, the ones used by musicians to place their book of notations while playing. These were lying around on the south side of La Martiniere For Boys. They were there, grouped together on one side of the steps leading to the field. On one long weekend, our school grounds would be the venue for JazzYatra, an annual concert of musicians from India and abroad that used to be a fairly regular affair well into the early '80s in Calcutta before lack of sponsors forced it to fade out and come alive occasionally in Bombay or Pune or Delhi.

What is this jazz?

Oh, music. Then I must listen. For, the word has a cool ring to it. Can we come for the concerts?

No. It's music for grown-ups.

That was school. While in college, AUC Jazz Club became our tutor. It was easy to get hooked. And then Dizzy Gillespie happened. Dalhousie Institute, around the mid-1980s. Louiz Banks was on piano. Midway into the concert, strains of azaan came floating in from the nearby mosque. Dizzy smiled. He listened for a while, picked up his signature bent trumpet and played along; joining, instinctively as it were, the call to prayer. We were blessed. That night they also played *A Night in Tunisia*. Dizzy's horn was soaring, in technicolour; exploring the outer reaches of brilliance and beyond. It was magical, but real.

A WhatsApp message from Louiz Banks in the summer of 2018, accompanied by a picture of him that he said was the cover of his forthcoming album of jazz standards, was the memory trigger. A rash of images, seen, experienced and heard of, flashed before me. DI, a gig at the Maurya Sheraton Jazz Bar in Delhi, and...

Anyway, when the man whose name has been synonymous with jazz in India says he's working on an album of jazz standards, you take note. Note for note. But why? Because the book of standards, he tells me, is the Bible for jazz musicians, and so, it's incumbent on us music lovers in India to once again turn back and reconnect with past gems. After all, what better way to move forward than to look back. 'I always wanted to do a couple of albums on my favourite songs, giving it a twist of my own,' he tells me during a conversation held over days on email and telephone. 'You got to know these (songs) and you need to play them often and put your own stamp on it in terms of approach and styling. I want our up and coming jazz musicians to know this and not to neglect, or avoid, playing standards. There is so much joy in this... an integral part of a jazz musician's vocabulary.'

The selection, invisibly packaged in downloads, USB cards and pen drives, includes *Bye Bye Blackbird, More Than You Know, Skylark, Summertime* and *Chopin's Prelude: Opus 24 No. 4* 'for its exquisite melody and harmonic structure'. That's how twisty Mr Banks wants to get but confesses that this album—he has six solo and countless collaboratives—is a tribute to the style of Herbie Hancock. 'I love Herbie and he is my biggest influence in piano playing and thinking... Many avid listeners will find these interpretations similar to his approach to styling.'

More of that later, I think, because that memory trigger is firing away.

NOTE FOR NOTE: At his seventy-fifth birthday celebrations (courtesy Louiz Banks)

My memory of you is watching you play with Dizzy Gillespie at Dalhousie Institute in Calcutta. It was an evening of magic. How did that come about?

To cut a long story short, I was vacationing in Washington and staying with my dear friend Sam Cambata, who passed away—God bless his soul. And Sam asked if I would like to go and listen to Dizzy Gillespie at the Blues Alley Club. I said, 'Sure', and we landed at the club and took a table and waited for Dizzy to start the music. After a while, Dizzy came down with the band and apologised for the missing pianist who could not make the gig.[1] He then went on to play a fantastic first set, took a break and went upstairs to the band room. Sam then asked me if I would like to meet Dizzy. I jumped at the idea and we went upstairs where my friend introduced me to Dizzy saying, 'This is Louiz Banks and he is a jazz pianist from India.' Dizzy looked at me and said, 'Jazz pianist from India. They play jazz over there?' And I said, 'Yes we do.' Dizzy could not believe it but nodded his head. We chatted for a while and came down and waited for him to play the second set.

The band came down and Dizzy went up to the mike and said, 'I believe we have a jazz pianist from India in the house and I would like to invite him

GROOVIN' HIGH: With DIZZY GILLESPIE during the India tour (courtesy Louiz Banks)

to sit in with the band.' My knees started to tremble, my heart was beating fast, but mustering some strange inner strength I stood up and went to the stage amidst applause. Dizzy smiled and said, 'Let's play *Stella by Starlight*.' He looked at me and I nodded. (Thank God I knew the tune.) God is great!

The night turned out great. We played, and Dizzy nodded to indicate his approval. After that he played some of his tunes which I knew. Dizzy was happy, the band was happy and I was relieved, but ecstatic!

The following year Dizzy was brought to India for a series of concerts by another friend of mine, Rajesh Jhaveri. Rajesh called me up to tell me about it and said Dizzy wanted me to play the piano with the band. Wow, what a great break for me! So, that's how I did a five-concert tour of India with Dizzy and landed up in Calcutta for a concert. It really was an unforgettable experience for me.

Stella by Starlight, a standard among jazz standards, is often described as 'haunting' and 'beautiful'. It was originally the theme of the 1944 film, *The Uninvited*, a ghost story that received rave reviews for shunning the gory and graphic for restraint. Victor Young, whose orchestra played the tune for the film, asked Ned Washington to write lyrics to it. By 1947 it had hit the pop charts, courtesy versions by Harry James and his orchestra and then Frank Sinatra.

But it was not until 1952, when Charlie Parker and a massive orchestra of strings recorded his version, that *Stella* came to be recognised as a template of jazz improvisation. Subsequently, almost all the greats did their take on the song—Stan Getz, Chet Baker, Bud Powel, Ella Fitzgerald, Tony Bennet and Larry Coryell (*Fallen Angel*).[2] Why, even Nat King Cole has an instrumental version.

In the 1958 album, *Miles Davis and John Coltrane, The Complete Columbia Recordings*, the song 'swung hardest'[2] in the hands of Miles Davis's classic sextet that also included Bill Evans and Cannonball Adderly. Two years later, in *Highlights from the Plugged Nickel*, Miles took the tune to places it had never been to, while Bill Evans's elegant version, in the 1962 album, *Conversations with Myself*,[2] saw the beginnings of his foray into overdubbing multiple piano parts, a practice that led to a furore at first but quietened down later when all agreed how tastefully he was using the technology.

I warmed up to *Stella* much later, after hearing Miles play it alongside George Coleman (tenor sax), Herbie Hancock (piano), Ron Carter (bass) and Tony Williams (drums) in the 1965 live album, *My Funny Valentine*, a recording of the quintet's 1964 performance at the Philharmonic Hall of Lincoln Centre in New York City. According to Ian Carr, Miles's biographer,[3] two albums were made from the concert recordings. *Four & More* was a compilation of the more up-tempo pieces, while *Valentine* had tunes played with 'more depth and brilliance than Miles had achieved before'.

Herbie Hancock, only twenty-three at the time, notes they all were under a lot of pressure for the concert. 'I really wanted to play good—the whole band really wanted to play good because that was the whole band's first time playing there… although Miles had played at Carnegie Hall (Philharmonic Hall) before… but it was a special concert… it was really funny… when we walked away from that concert, we were all dejected and disappointed. We thought we had really bombed… but then we listened to the record—it sounded fantastic.'[3]

Stella is also referred to as being 'rhapsodic', an epithet experts say[2] is apt since Young's compositional influence was Sergei Rachmaninov (1873–1943) whose melodies are often described similarly.

Yet *Stella*, the song that began Louiz's tryst with jazz greats, I note, isn't part of his latest album which, in effect, takes him back to where and how it all began. He started off with, would you believe it, the horn. His father, himself a trumpeter par excellence, named him after the king of them all, Louis Armstrong. For, he was quick to realise that Louiz ('z' replaced 's' in 2001, courtesy numerology) had it in him and started teaching him to play the horn in right earnest. But since George Banks also played the piano, the young boy—eldest among five siblings—was made to study classical piano too. Later, however, Louiz gave up the horn for reasons cerebral and got hooked to jazz piano for Oscar Peterson, the Canadian master of high-octane swing. 'Dad had a band in a club (Gymkhana) in Darjeeling and I got hands-on training to play with the band from the age of thirteen, playing both trumpet and piano. Guess I was developing fast as a musician. But, eventually, I gave up the trumpet because I could not think on it. I would improvise on the trumpet via the notes of the piano. It was not correct. Hence, I decided that piano would be my main instrument. I loved the piano and gradually stopped playing the trumpet completely. I guess it was my calling.'

The Gymkhana experience in the '50s proved invaluable since the repertoire was wide, from dance tunes of the day to foxtrot, waltzes, samba, cha cha cha, mambo, tango. 'The club imported a whole lot of arrangements from London and the band rehearsed these charts and played them at nights. It was a great learning experience for a teenager like me.'

Then George moved to Nepal and Louiz ended up playing similar stuff for the 'Anglicised clientele of the Soaltee at Kathmandu'. Occasionally, he would throw in some favourite jazz standards. 'I honed my jazz piano skills during these years.'

Oscar Peterson was your earliest hero. What struck you about his playing?

Once, when my dad was playing me a jazz record at home, I asked him, 'Who are the two pianists playing?' He said, 'It's only one pianist and his name is Oscar Peterson'. I was totally blown. It was a turning point for me… to get into some serious jazz piano playing. I was still in my teens. Oscar's amazing technique, the relentless swing, the blues inflections, the melodic content and of course the rapid fire and explosive right hand. Wow, I wanted to learn to play even half as good as that. And my dad said, 'Practise'. My conversion to jazz piano began right from that day.

What about other influences? Thelonious Monk (a descendant of the Harlem ticklers), Duke Ellington?

I love Thelonious Monk as a great composer. Art Tatum, Errol Garner, Ramsey Lewis and George Shearing from that era, and then Herbie Hancock, Keith Jarrett, Chick Corea, Gonzalo Rubalcaba and some of the new pianists. There's so much talent out there.

I had the opportunity of interviewing Herbie Hancock and Wayne Shorter in Mumbai in 2006 and we ended up speaking about Miles Davis a lot. To what extent has Miles been an influence?

Miles Davis remains my all-time favourite jazz musician. His lyricism blows me away, with Herbie Hancock coming a close second. I met him in the '90s when he had come with a bunch of musicians (probably from the Thelonious Monk Institute of Jazz in Los Angeles). He came to the club where I was playing and his band jammed with us. He also complimented my playing. I love Herbie. He is my biggest influence on piano playing and thinking.

WATERMELON MAN: With HERBIE HANCOCK circa 1990s (courtesy Louiz Banks)

And in the pop/rock sphere?

Stevie Wonder, Yanni, Vangelis, Alicia Keys, Harry Cornick Jr, Ray Charles. Norah Jones, Barry Manilow, Diana Krall, Nina Simone come to mind.

Louis, long before he became Louiz, was always the edgy youngster yearning for more. While at Kathmandu, a singer, Laurie Pereira, while commending his playing as 'good', remarked how in Calcutta there were at least ten other piano players who were all better than him! 'That remark spurred me and I moved to Calcutta because I wanted to be a better jazz pianist.' By 1974, he had formed the Loiuz Banks Brotherhood with Colleen Mendes, Don Saigal, Ignatious D'Souza, Carlton Kitto, James Dias, Peter Saldanha and Johnny Edmonds. 'It was one of the best bands that I have ever had. When Braz Gonsalves and Pam Crain joined me a little later the band became even better. Braz was undoubtedly the best saxophonist that India ever had. Pam Crain was the diva of divas, gorgeously beautiful and the best jazz singer India has ever had. God bless her soul. Yes, Calcutta was something else. Park Street was swinging every night with many bands playing at all the night clubs. What a great scene it was, like Broadway in New York. The unsung heroes were Benny Rosario, Eve, Anton Menezes, Jenny, and many others… my memory fails me.'

It was while playing at Blue Fox one night that a musical legend, one whose lineage can be traced to Tripura, dropped in, a chance meeting that Louiz now likes to describe as 'divine intervention'. Cut to the Shashi Kapoor-starrer *Mukti*. Listen to *Suhani Chandni Ratein*. Relive the joys of Bollywood's mellifluous past.

I am told R.D. Burman had no idea about the band that was playing that evening.

Long story, but I'll cut it short for you. One fine day R.D. Burman came into Blue Fox. He did not know who I was, and I didn't know who he was. He sat down at a table with a friend and listened to my band, clapped and all that. When we took a break, he called me over and spoke, telling me how much he enjoyed my piano playing. And then introducing himself, said, 'Would you like to play piano for a film?' I was totally blank. My world was different. I told him I have never played for a film before. He said, 'No problem. Come and play piano.' I said okay and went to Bombay for a week or so and played all the piano solos in the film. It was a unique experience for me, quite enjoyable too. In a sense, he asked me to stay back and join him. I declined saying that I had a band in Calcutta, a contract plus a family. He asked me to work it out and come to Bombay.

A year later, I packed up my Fender Rhodes piano, and with Rs 300 in my pocket, took a train and came to Bombay. My sister was there, and I stayed with her. The next day I went to see R.D. and told him that I had made the shift. He said I could join him, and I started working with the R.D. Burman film orchestra and became a part of his inner circle. My family also joined me.

I played all the piano solos in his films after 1979. R.D. Burman changed my life, and I discovered money! I started earning in a day what I used to earn in a month. My wife was happy... lots of shopping. But I continued to work with my band with Braz in Bombay during nights. I was busy as hell.

I had no idea about your involvement in Amitabh Bachchan's *Hum* until now.

Yes, I started to do background scores and *Hum* was one film. Till now, I have done background scores for over thirty films. So, I had two identities, a jazz pianist/band leader and composer of background scores for Bollywood films.

If Hindi film music, about which he knew nothing, became his bread and butter, ad jingles were the bonus. The first one, for Four Square cigarettes, was an instant hit. Then came Cadbury Dairy Milk's *Kya Swad Hai*, the very Indian *Hamara Bajaj* and the instant recall of Britannia's *Ting ting ta ting*! Eventually, the ad world is said to have anointed Loiuz with the title of 'Jingle King' for having notched up over 10,000 jingles that came with numerous awards and accolades.

With a career spanning five decades, Louiz is now an energetic seventy-seven. Bread and butter issues sorted, he still keeps busy, having recently wowed the US with Crosscurrents, an Indo-jazz fusion group comprising Zakir Hussain, Shankar Mahadevan, Dave Holland, Chris Potter and son Gino Banks. 'Yes, Crosscurrents is an incredible band. The music is exciting and fresh. The musicians are all superstars in their own fields and they come together to explore music... I am extremely proud and happy that Zakir has chosen my son Gino to play drums, and Gino is doing a great job. I contribute a lot of the music in the band's concert repertoire. The band is being received well by the American audience. The shows are sold out with standing ovations and encores everywhere. God is great!'

Louiz also fronts several other outfits (Guitar Synergy, Ganga Shakti and The Matrixx Trio) with promising young musicians of the day. And that's precisely why his interpretations of jazz classics make that much more sense. A man so much in tune with the contemporary is bound to have a fresh feel for the notes of yesteryears.

Louis Armstrong is known to have famously said: If you have to ask what jazz is, you'll never know. I stopped asking after hearing Louiz play with Dizzy Gillespie at DI that night. I remember the moment even after so many years. Louiz plays a solo piece. Dizzy is leaning on the grand piano on his elbows with palms cupping his chin and listening. He stays that way all through. The piece is over, the last note is gently, but definitively struck, and Dizzy is grinning—that trademark grin. He looks at the audience, points to Louiz and urges us to acknowledge the performance. All of us clap hard.

Jazz happened for me that night, stayed with me ever since.

VERY CALCUTTA: Dalhousie Institute is about music, quizzing and fun (courtesy dalhousieinstitute.in)

18

Fly-free Girl

She is this unusual band leader. She plays the saxophone, a huge brass one with an elegant sepia finish, and often, moves over to the wings, dancing to the riffs her co-musicians bounce off each other. The Nubya Garcia quartet has just stunned everyone into silence with her first tune, *Static*, on a Sunday at Tollygunge Club Calcutta, its first stop in a tour organised by British Council that's celebrating seventy years in India. Playing it for the first time for an audience—'global premiere,' she smiles—*Static* is explosive in the way the twenty-six-year-old hits some high notes on the sax that pierce through a shield of booming bass, intricate keys and percussive drums.

Garcia's music is jazz alright, but it's a different kind of jazz, the kind that eggs you on to the dance floor, the kind that contemporary London seems to have been nurturing, so much so that big-time DJs and independent record producers who travel the world scouring new sounds are being hit with curious queries about 'the British invasion'.

'We grew up in an era where jazz is not the only music that we love, listen to and play. When you hear so many things you don't just choose one of them. You kind of emulate,' she tells me enthusiastically after the performance, explaining why diverse cultural strains show up in her music. It helps she is from Camden, Northwest London, a counter culture hub known for its flea markets and funky clothing. From Afro-Caribbean rhythms to hip-hop and neo-soul, Garcia is part of a London scene that is liberating jazz for a wider audience and loving it. This 'new' music is played at night clubs and concert halls. Together with the likes of Moses Boyd (twenty-six, drummer), Shabaka Hutchings (thirty-three, sax, clarinet), Sheila Maurice-Grey (twenty-seven, trumpet) and Yazmin Lacey (twenty-nine, singer-songwriter), they have, *The Guardian* reports and *New York Times* notes, knocked off the snooty from jazz as we know it.

The mix is evident by the time Garcia and her bandmates—Dominic Canning (keys), Michael Shrimpling (bass) and Jake Long (drums)—are on the second

MODAL MELODY: NUBYA GARCIA at Tollygunge Club, Calcutta

tune. *Fly Free* is this spacious canvas on which Garcia lines in a beautiful tune. It is gentle and sophisticated, the bass notes setting up a mystical background she feels the need to address by playing them herself on the sax while closing.

'I wrote *Fly Free* in January 2017. I am really into the 6-8 modal figures in the kind of music I listened to when I was young. So I really wanted to experiment on modal beats,' she says about a style that is characterised by fewer chords and extended spaces for an improvising instrumentalist to fill in inventively (*So What* in Miles Davis's *A Kind of Blue* is a stellar example). Not surprising that her list of influences would pretty much fill up that little black book of all jazz aficionados.

'John Coltrane is a huge influence. And Miles Davis, obviously. And then Herbie Hancock, Wayne Shorter, Ella Fitzgerald and Billie Holiday, Charlie Parker, Cannonball Adderley,' the 2016 graduate from Trinity Laban Conservatoire of Music and Dance continues. But her eyes light up talking about Dexter Gordon, the American tenor saxophonist who had a penchant for playing his notes ever so slightly behind the beat and who was himself an influence on Coltrane. 'Dexter Gordon was the first sax player that I really, really got into. I was twelve or thirteen when I started listening to him.'

Garcia's first album with six tracks, called, *5ive*, released on vinyl and CD, was re-issued thrice. Her next, *When We Are*, is a success too, having already been re-pressed once. In early 2018, while playing at a music festival in Texas, there was a long queue of admirers, waiting to buy her EP immediately after her performance. But she was carrying only a handful with her. 'Yes, that was amazing. I am still surprised,' she notes with relish.

No wonder she's going places. Garcia has played at a do headlined by Erykah Badu, the American singer-songwriter-activist whose music I was reminded of while hearing her set—'that's wonderful because she is a huge influence too'—and at the popular Love Supreme festival at Glynde Place in East Sussex alongside the great dame of soul Mavis Staples.

When We Are has traces of gospel, neo-soul and electronics, something she learnt from Sam Shepherd, the English electronic musician/producer who works under the title Floating Points. These London scene musicians will stop at nothing. The reach of their music seems endless. If jazz is about breaking fresh ground, it's as though these guys have uprooted the picket fence around their homes, opening themselves up to anything and everything.

'It's like five people tell you five different stories and then you go and tell another story, and you've got elements of all of those bits; and make it one big story. We were just fortunate to have grown up in an age when traditional jazz was still a big part of our lives. But we also go out to hip-hop gigs, raves, garage nights. We're a product of this vast array of influences,' Garcia sums it up definitively.

For her, watching performances is a catalyst. 'Often when you see a gig and it's like, "Ah, I want to go and write something now". Sometimes it's a tune or a groove in my head that I go on to produce by working out a bass line, the chords and so on.'

There are several facets to this creativity, channelled through various outfits. For instance, the one she toured with in India (Bhubaneswar, Odisha; Itanagar, Arunachal Pradesh, for Ziro Festival of Music) isn't her own band. Only drummer Jake and she have worked together as a part of another band, the spiritual jazz-inspired Maisha, for which they've spent hours playing as a duo and then fleshing out melodies and subsequently full-on compositions.

With so much happening in the UK, are jazz musicians making enough in today's world of YouTube and livestreams? Garcia is upbeat. She believes it is better than the past specifically for jazz as there are more venues open to hosting jazz nights. 'We are not rockstars and it still isn't as good as a salary, but you do get to see the world and meet people if you are lucky. In that respect it's very enriching. I wouldn't say it makes you rich, but you can get by.'

In the words of John S. Wilson, a jazz historian, the wheel keeps turning even though 'jazz has always been a music of freedom, implicit in its improvisational nature.' Primarily a music for dancing, in the beginning it was even considered vulgar. Yet it thrived and moved across America to take on forms that typically sought to write-off the predecessor—from Big Band Jazz and Swing to Bebop, that wanted patrons to get off the dance floor and listen, to the Cool Sound, Jazz-Rock and now New Fusion of R&B, soul and electronica.

'The spirit that originally motivated it—good time music in the first two decades of the 20th century, from Storyville, New Orleans; to Memphis, St Louis, Chicago, New York—the sounds, textures, techniques, the forms change from decade to decade not because past methods are no longer valid but because jazz continues to attract adventurous minds and virtuosic talents—the Louis Armstrongs, Don Redmans, Charlie Parkers, John Coltranes, Ornette Colemans, Miles Davises. Jazz opens up possibilities for each musician to express himself or herself in his/her own terms.'[2]

The likes of Nubya Garcia in the UK, Kamasi Washington and Esperanza Spalding in the US are doing just that, not by themselves alone, but by collaborating and listening to each other. 'It's inherently a generous and cosmopolitan art form,' critic and author of *Playing Changes: Jazz for the New Century* Nate Chinen says[3] while noting that the basic attributes of jazz that its practitioners value are curiosity and a mission of cultural openness and outreach and exchange. 'It (jazz) is really a music that belongs to the world at this point.'

The key of course is originality, as Garcia agrees. 'It's about creating something that's true to you; not end up copying something that is doing well. It's what you want to do, what you want to create, who do you want to play with. It's individual and that's what makes it special,' she elaborates before winding up.

On our way out, I ask Garcia about Coltrane's *Both Directions at Once: The Lost Album* that's surfaced now, fifty-five years after it was recorded. 'Yes, I got it immediately. It's incredible that they found it. I really like it. The amazing thing (about Coltrane), is he's still giving us joy so many years later.'

Hours later, a ping on my phone; it's a tweet from Jazz at Lincoln Centre: Happy birthday to a creative genius and titan of jazz: #JohnColtrane. The Tolly Club gig was on September 23. We were discussing Coltrane but did not realise it was his 92nd birth anniversary. That's joy. Pure fly-free joy.

NUBYA'S 5IVE
NUBYA'S 5IVE

19

Folk Rocks

They started with a song from, and about, the hills because 'that's where all the trouble is these days', an obvious reference to the over 100-day shutdown between June and September 2017 in Darjeeling and the rest of North Bengal where the demand for statehood had triggered a familiar political and social impasse akin to the Gorkhaland agitation of the 1980s. So, it was perhaps in the fitness of things that the five musicians playing on a Monday evening at the DI bar were served tea, Bhoomi's beverage of choice while performing. 'Milk, sugar and the works,' declared Somu, the lead singer, percussionist and frontman as if to reinstate his Bengali roots.

On their 1,701st show, Bhoomi is belting out signature tunes of yore, the kind we have all grown up with, the ones that blend various strains—from the soulful Bhatiali to Irish folk, a bit of blues, reggae and all the intonations of Indian folk from Bihu and Lavani to Baul and everything in between.

L9 Bus is our *Penny Lane*. Think of the double-decker cruising along Southern Avenue, then Beltola Road and on to Chakraberia. Yes, we've all been on it. *Lale Laleshwari* is about the coy village bride having just bought her first 'ladies ghori (watch)' while *Aaj faguni purnima ratey, chol polaiye jai* extols the fun of, simply, running away. And then, the eternal favourite, *Sohag chand badani dhoni, nacho to dekhi.* Why don't you do a dance, you pretty little thing?

This song—unabashedly, yet delightfully, politically incorrect—had everyone up on their feet. Much like our Puja days at Vidyasagar Niketan, the earliest housing complex to come up in the early '70s at Salt Lake, Calcutta's first planned township conceptualised by former Bengal chief minister Bidhan Chandra Roy on the eastern fringes of the city, where we heard Nirmalendu Choudhury sing it with only a harmonium and tabla for accompaniment. He brought the house down. The best part? Our parents from the teaching fraternity approved.

It was strange that it took me so many years to hear Bhoomi live, having discovered them purely by chance on WorldSpace satellite radio while we were

ROOTED: SOMU (centre) with Bhoomi (courtesy the band)

in Pune circa 2004. We took an instant liking to them. Bangla songs that the daily grind of a working life outside of Bengal had simply dropped off our playlist came alive once again courtesy their albums, *Gaan Doriyay* and *Lokgeeti Local.* For the DI concert, Somu, or Soumitra Roy, was accompanied by longtime associates Abhijit Ghosh, Hemanta Goswami and Robin Lai. His son Arjyesh was on drums. Missing from the line-up was one of their signature voices, the multi-instrumentalist singer-composer Surojit Chatterjee, who had by then parted ways. Lead vocal responsibilities were therefore, solely on Soumitra's shoulders, who, I thought, did a wonderful job considering he had to play the congas too.

We spoke at length about a week after Bhoomi had performed a sellout concert to celebrate nineteen years of singing together. Old bandmates joined in and a great time was had by everyone. Quite something for a Calcutta band with over a thousand shows under their belt, including a momentous one at the United Nations headquarters.

What's with the tea before every concert?

Yes, tea before a show is our ritual. We joke around and talk a lot, but never discuss the setlist. But once we are on stage and face the audience, things fall into place; and the songs come out one by one as per the list of the day. For our anniversary show, we were joined by a number of musicians of Calcutta like Tuki, Chandrima, Lopamudra and Anindya Chattopadhyay. We followed the setlist, played twenty songs and finished exactly at 9.05 p.m. We wanted to finish by 9 p.m.

How did the idea of Bhoomi come about?

In those days, we used to have a band called Dusk, which was primarily a gig band, playing dance music. After practice, a couple of us used to sing some Bengali folk songs. I used to sing one or two on the guitar—I know only three chords—like, say, a Neil Diamond number, and at least two Bhatiali songs, *O Amar Dorodi* and *Bhobosagoro Rey*. During these sessions, my friends would tell me that these songs were sounding good with guitars and drums. I realised it too. And that is how the journey of Bhoomi started in 1997. But it was not until 1999 that we would do our first major show, at Gyan Manch.

Tell me about *Lale Laleshwari*.

When I was a boy, my cousins and I used to go to our uncle's place at Manicktola. It was actually his in-laws' place, but we used to call it our mama bari. There, the elderly lady whom we used to call didima (grandma), used to tell us this rhyme while putting us to sleep.

Tim tim haathi chole lichu baganey,
Ekta lichu pore gelo chayer dokane.
Cha dokani, cha dokani dorja kholo na
Borishaler bou eshechey, dekhtey cholo na

(Elephants trundle along to the sound of bells around their necks; a litchi drops into a tea shop; tea man, tea man, open the door; come let's go see this bride from Borishal)

We used to love it. I married some more words to the rhyme and spun a yarn around it to create *Lale Laleshwari* (This bride in red with shades and a ladies' watch going to her sasural).

Lale laleshwari, chokhe chosma pori,
haatey ladies ghori, jaabey sosur bari.

Did you guys ever think Bhoomi would be this successful?

No. We did not expect anything when we started. It's been a great journey.

It certainly has, especially for that five-year-old who recalls that his first real 'remuneration' for being part of a 'gig' was a big scoop of ice cream in 1965–

66 at Magnolia on Park Street where the family had gone for lunch when the band of the day asked him to join them on stage with bongos after they were mighty impressed with his time-keeping on the table; or when he played the bongos sitting on Uttam Kumar's lap, singing, would you believe it, *Chhoti Si Mulaqat*, that Mohammed Rafi-Asha Bhosle song where the Mahanayak dances the twist with Vyjayanthimala in the 1967 Hindi film of the same name. That performance of '*ya, ya yippie yippie*' earned little Somu his first taste of whiskey, that too from the glass of Bengali cinema's most celebrated hero. And when his mother protested, Kumar apparently retorted: *Aha ki hoechhey? Boro hoey bolte parbe* Uttam Kumar-*er kole boshe ami amar* first whiskey *kheyechhi* (Oh, don't worry. When he grows up, he can proudly say that he had had his first whiskey on Uttam Kumar's lap)!

The key to Bhoomi's longevity is best explained by V. Balsara, who guested on their album, *Lokgeeti Local*, playing the Univox, melodica and accordion on a couple of songs. He spoke of their simple lyrics and no-frills arrangements that brought out the key elements of folk music: immediacy, spontaneity and an honesty grounded in personally experienced realities. Soumitra recalls how the legendary pianist-composer spent an entire day with them recording and listening to every take and unhesitatingly opting for re-takes even for a minor tweak if he felt that would better the end result.

'It was very humbling to see such a senior musician taking so much trouble with our songs. He used to say that he liked Bhoomi for our originality. "*Tomader gaan kono din purono hobey na… tomader gaaner kotha khub sohoj aar sorol, manusher moner moddhey genthey jai. Shoja kotha sohoj bhabe bola khub kothin byapar.* (Your songs will never get old. They tug at the heartstrings. The words of your songs are simple. It is very difficult to say simple truths in simple language)."'

Essentially, Balsara was talking about re-interpretations. Old tunes and songs re-imagined in a way to re-emphasise their contemporariness. Bhoomi has been able to do that, not so much by striving to pull off a 'fusion' of forms but by going by the ear; trusting their instincts with what sounded good. Simply put, they started playing these songs on western instruments like a guitar, drums and bass and stuck to the arrangements when there was unanimity about the songs sounding refreshed.

Bhoomi's songs helped me reconnect to my growing up years at Bhawanipore and then later, at Salt Lake. At 98, Beltola Road, I would often wake up to the strains of *Sangachhadhawam sanvadadhwam*, the Vedic hymn which also served as the institutional song for the teachers' training college that was housed there, often followed by the Tagore song with a similar tune, *Anandalokay, mangalalokay.* There would be Bratachari songs too. I remember two. One was about lazy people who were always ready to eat, but never there to work on the rice fields, while the other celebrated the beauty of twin moons, the second one in glorious reflection on a river.

> *Kaiye dhaan khailo re khedaner manush nai;*
> *Khaowar bela achher manush—kamer bela nai—*
> *Kaiye dhaan khailo re* (Sari Gaan)

> *Holo mati-te chander udoy ke dekhbi ai—*
> *Amon jugol chand keu dekhish nai—dekshey nadia*
> *Tora ke dekbhi ai, tora ke dekhbi ai*
> *Amon jugol chand keu dekhish nai—dekshey nadia* (Baul Nrityer Gaan)

These are an absolute delight to sing and dance to, as are most of the other songs written by Gurusaday Dutt in the 1930s when he conceived of the movement based on a set of ideals centred around labour, physical fitness, character, knowledge, truth, unity, music and dance. The tunes were catchy, as folk songs are meant to be, and the dance forms, most often Baul and jhumur, were specified too. It is of course an equally delightful coincidence that I now get to live on a street that is an extension of the one named after the founder of the Bratachari movement.

At Vidyasagar Niketan, we grew up with all kinds of music, Hindi and Bengali songs, some from popular films of the time, and western pop and rock on the radio and on records at home. One friend, who was a 'Deadhead', had this great sounding tape deck where we would often listen to Lindisfarne, a folk group that took its name from an island off the north-east coast of England and whose music had a 'good time' vibe that led to its popularity in the college circuit in the late '60s and early '70s. Decades later, I stumbled upon a 'Best of…' album at a music store in Bangalore where the senior manager of the company, a Calcuttan, nodded in vigorous approval at our choice, going on to confide in us how he felt vindicated for having ordered the CD in spite of apprehensions of the senior management about whether it would sell. My favourite Lindisfarne song from the Vidyasagar days, *Warm Feeling*, wasn't among the sixteen classic tracks on the CD though. One line came back to me after all these years. It is about feeling 'the harmony grow' in a song of love.

> *Sittin' by the fire glow*
> *Waitin' for my girl to show*
> *Feelin' the harmony grow*

I met her just the other day
She has helped me find my way
Feelin' the harmony grow

Puja functions at Vidyasagar Niketan would showcase some of the most important Baul and folk singers of the time, in addition to renowned exponents of Rabindrasangeet like Subinoy Roy. Prahlad Brahmachari and Purna Das Baul would sing late into the night as would Utpalendu Choudhury, who had over the years taken on the mantle from his father Nirmalendu. Their repertoire would inevitably include *Gole male, gole male pirit koro naa*, a naughty take on the eccentricities of love that would have the ageing Brahmachari doing a little jig around the mike, standing, and, inevitably ending the line with a neat wink! Other all-time favourites would be *Amar jemon beni temni robey chul bhijabona* on the dilemmas of getting your feet wet; and *Menoka mathai dilo ghomta*, a funny take on the Shiva-Parvati legend, which has undergone several incarnations, one of the most brilliant ones by Jai Uttal, whose reggae take with pronounced bass lines went on to hook audiences across the US.

Many bands of today are also into revisiting traditional favourites. Ram Sampat, the jingles man who is among the young crop of most sought-after music directors of Bollywood, put out a lovely interpretation of *Sundori Komola* on MTV's Coke Studio Season 3. Juxtaposed with an old rock song of his, *Souls on Parade*, *Sundori Komola* retains all of the naughty charms of the original Bengali 'Çhatka', thanks to the nuanced singing of Usri Banerjee, even as it is re-jigged with some intricate bass played to a steady drum beat heightened by a sax interlude that helps frame the two songs neatly.

Rangabati, one of Odisha's most familiar folk tunes from Sambalpur, is also refreshingly presented by his ensemble in Coke Studio Season 4. Sung by Sona Mohapatra, who is also Sampat's wife, the song becomes a Tamil-Malayalam-Odiya sawal jawab, thanks to the infusion of some rap, ultimately climaxing in a celebration of one's roots that also happens to be the singer's home state of Odisha. Both tunes work so well, no doubt a fruition of Sampat's own upbringing in a milieu of accomplished Carnatic musicians.

Today's leading light of popular film music, Amit Trivedi, who forced discerning audiences to return to Bollywood soundtracks with the earthy effervescence of his songs for Anurag Kashyap's *Dev D* circa 2009, is less obvious in the way he falls back on his roots. Trivedi's early trysts with devotional music and Gujarati folk find an outlet in his non-filmi compositions. His *Yatra*, a symphonic exposition that blends the shehnai and South Indian classical vocal

REFUGE OF HAPPY MEMORIES: 98, Beltola Road, Calcutta

traditions to stir up an infectious song, was quite the toast of Season 2 of Coke Studio India.

Everybody grows up to music. For me, it was records, 78rpm and all, and All India Radio, especially *Mahisasuramardini*, the pre-dawn broadcast of an oratorio to welcome Goddess Durga on Mahalaya Day. It is heard traditionally in every Bengal household, every year. Scripted by Bani Kumar with the music of Pankaj Mallick, the shlokas are chanted by Birendra Krishna Bhadra. It is an all-too familiar incantation of the age-old fight between good and evil, and in spite of the Pujas acquiring ostentatious carnivalesque proportions, this particular rendering of the Chandi underscores the permanence of music in the formative years of our lives.

That Monday evening, Bhoomi ended their concert with *Dhitang dhitang boley* (Hemanta Mukhopadhay, lyrics and music by Salil Chowdhury), a song our Bengali teacher at school Mr Sinha helped us perform for a cultural evening. Most of us in the choir at La Martiniere knew it, at least the first few verses. One verse, before moving to that evergreen refrain, goes like this:

E desh tomar amar,
Ei amra bhori khamar
Aar amra gori sopon diye sonar kamona

Suddenly, it strikes me: We have been singing about our country ever since we were kids. In doing so, we would be adding to, and building on, the idea of an India, its million mutinies notwithstanding. Our hopes and individual aspirations were never in conflict with that idea. The default setting was for multiple harmonies to grow. At every para do, at every Independence Day function the staple for children would be to put up a group dance to *Dhitang dhitang boley*. We sang about an India that belonged to you, me and everybody. And had fun too.

So how did we end up forgetting who we are?

20

The Flying Horsemen

The space between the two buildings was narrow. Very narrow. Only a greenhorn like Bapi, of slender frame and boyish looks, could squeeze himself through to reach what was a three bigha plot where Monida and Co. would be waiting. Bapi was carrying rotis, about 150 of them, and daal in a container. That 'spread' was meant to be the meal for Monida and his friends, absconders all, in hiding from the police in the early '70s of a turbulent Calcutta when the youth were perceived to be either a part of, or sympathetic to, the Naxal movement launched in Bengal by the legendary Charu Majumdar. Those were the end days of the 'revolution' inspired by the peasants' uprising of April 1967 at Naxalbari. Students of Presidency College, opposite which the first posters in support of Naxalbari surfaced in Calcutta, who had gone out into the villages to preach revolution among farmers, had either been rounded up or killed for embracing the idea of 'annihilating class enemies'. But some survived.

Monida, Gautam Chattopadhyay, who was subsequently imprisoned, silently suffered the torture of taunts in jail and wrote songs about a reality centred around failure, hopelessness and dejection. Something he and his friends would have to live with the rest of their lives. In 1975, he formed Mohiner Ghoraguli, a band that would sing songs, in Bangla, of life in Calcutta, using motifs of rock music, from Beatles to Hendrix and Led Zeppelin, they had listened to as youngsters even as they devoured Hindi film hits of, say, an O.P. Nayyar. 'Baul jazz' was coined at the time to describe their music which also drew from folk. Yet their songs were brazenly contemporary, startlingly original and deeply moving. The melodies were seamless and the harmonies intricate, often lost in inferior recording technologies of the time.

They were ahead of their time, audacious enough to venture into writing rock songs in Bangla. A certain Dilip Balakrishnan, who used to bob around Calcutta's western music scene around the same time, had displayed similar chutzpah, when he formed High a year earlier to write original rock music in

MOHIN, NOW: TAPAS 'Bapi' DAS

English. Monida and Dilip may have chosen different lyrics, but their music was embedded in similar roots. What Dilip was to Lew Hilt and Nondon Bagchi and others, Monida was to Bapi, Bula and Bhanu.

Monida knew what he had in mind had not been done before. Hence, the name of the band had to be different, nonsensical even. They zeroed in on a line in 'Ghoda' (Horse), a poem in a book titled, *Shatthi Tarar Timir*, by Jibanananda Das, the modernist Bengali poet who dared to break away from a literary tradition till then beholden to Tagore. The second line of the poem, loosely translated, reads, 'Mohin's horses graze on the horizon, silhouetted in a moonlit night in autumn'. They reined it in at Mohin's horses. Hence, Mohiner Ghoraguli.

Brilliant.

The original band members were Monida's cousins, friends and fans. The line-up changed at times. Pradip 'Bula' Chattopadhyay (flute), Tapas 'Bapi' Das (lyrics, vocals, rhythm guitar), Tapesh 'Bhanu' Bandopadhyay (vocals), Biswanath 'Bishu' Chattopadhyay (drums, bass), Abraham Mazumdar (piano, violin), Pronab Sengupta (drums, filling in for Bishu) and Raja Banerjee (vocals, rhythm guitar). Monida knew classical guitar and also played a bit of saxophone. He would compose most of the songs. Ranjon Ghosal (lyrics) was the band's best man, who took care of media relations. Sangita Ghosal designed the iconic sea horse logo. Almost all of them would sing lead and harmonies. 'At times,

Monida would also play the saxophone even though he could only reach about eight notes on it. That was his idea of showmanship. Just as he forced me to play the clarinet one time. "The first note is B. You'll find your way as you move up," he told me,' recalls Tapas, who prefers being addressed as Bapida.

We are at his Thakurpukur apartment. In his early sixties now, Bapida is perched on a bed, the salt and pepper beard and longish hair resembling a certain Karl, albeit friendlier than the Marx portraits we are used to. On the walls of the room is graffiti painted by fans—lines from their songs, pithy slogans and a majestic sea horse.

The first time I had heard a Mohiner Ghoraguli song was at the Presidency College canteen, sung by some of my batchmates. It was something about liking the Beatles and Dylan, Ravi Shankar and Ali Akbar Khan and yet experiencing a void at the way things were. That song, I learnt years later, was *Hay Bhalobashi.*

Bhalobashi Piccaso Bunoyel Daante
Beatles Dylan ar Beethoven sunte
Rabishankar ar Ali Akbar sune
Bhalo lage bhore kuashay ghore phirte
Tobuo kichhui jano bhalo je lage na keno
Udahsi pother majhe mon pore thake jeno
Kothay roechhebhabi lukiey bishad tubuo

I thought of it as our song, we the 'petty bourgeoisie', the useless in-betweens that represent Marx's derogatory definition of our 'class'. Well, it still is a great song, one that many of us feel a kinship with. And no one can take that away. Not even Mr Marx.

That evening Bapida told me how he wrote the song, as a nineteen-year-old while ferrying Monida back on a boat from Sunderbans where they were in hiding. He also spoke of Behala Flying Club, then a vast expanse of six-feet-high tiger grass, their place of refuge when '*bhalo na laga*' kicked in, like one time after watching Ritwik Ghatak's *Subernarekha*; and how willpower and self-belief kept them going even though Mohiner Ghoraguli's records never really sold much. What was unsaid though was that after Monida's death in 1999—a heart attack while making a film—there were fewer places left in Calcutta to go to for refuge.

They did three EPs: *Shongbigno Pakhikul O Kolkata Bishayak* (1977), *Ajaana Udonto Bostu ba Aw-Oo Baw* (1978), *Drishyomaan Mohiner Ghoraguli* (1979). The first one cost them Rs 7,000. As much as Rs 5,000 came from friendly donations, while the remaining Rs 2,000 had to be borrowed from a 'kabuliwala' (money lender) at 14 per cent interest per day. 'Monida would often refer to "foreign funding" as the key resource behind Mohiner Ghoraguli's launch,' Bapi recalls with a hint of smile.

When *Shongbigno Pakhikul* was released, not many bought them. You were even ridiculed as 'disciples of Elvis the pelvis'. What made you stay on course?

We had loads of willpower and self-belief.

You and Monida were particularly close.

Yes. We would be spending close to thirteen to fourteen hours a day. That apart, I also knew all those who were associated with him during the time of the Naxalite movement, say, everyone from Behala to Beliaghata. Those days (1970), I used to be in college and work at a ration shop on a salary of Rs 80 a month.

Monida used to joke how they exploited me because of my innocent looks and sobuj dari (greenhorn). For, I used to be their courier during the year-and-a-half they were in hiding. Most of them had shoot-at-sight orders against them. One of their dens was near Panchanantala, Behala, where they would come to collect food that our families took turns to prepare. Around 150 rotis and a tiffin carrier full of daal. The only way to reach the meeting place, a three bigha vacant plot, was through a very narrow passage, wide enough for only a lean fellow like me to pass through. There was no way any cop from Punjab or Gwalior would find the place. But I used to ferry food for them every day. It seems Monida was right about my 'innocent' looks. I never got caught.

How did music happen?

That was the other bond we shared. Both our mothers were singers. And we shared our love for a wide variety of musical genres. From Bengali music of the late '40s to early '50s (*Chhilo Chaand Meghero Parey* by Suprabha Sarkar) to S.D. Burman and O.P. Nayyar, we used to listen to them all. I remember, we bought a record of songs from the film, *Jewel Thief*, since we loved Dev Anand. Yet, we did not want to be seen listening to Hindi film songs. So, we locked ourselves up in a room to hear the record. Just as we would admire Naina Devi's thumris, we would also appreciate Ali Akbar Khan's sarod or Nikhil Banerjee's sitar or Jimi Hendrix's guitar or Bob Marley's reggae. We would also read a lot, both Bengali and English.

How did the song *Kotha Diya* come about?

Monida wrote this song when he was in Alipore central jail from end-'71 to early 1972. He was assigned cell 52. In cell 51, there was 'Haath kata' Babu of Behala Parnasree. In cell 53, there was Buddhuda, a class 7 dropout. Three of us, a friend Rodney Edgar, his mother and myself used to visit him in jail. Monida would always want lots of bidis and/or cigarettes to distribute among inmates. During his incarceration, and especially when all the inmates would be let out of their cells for roll call or for meals, the others would get on his case. They would taunt him about his long hair, his Presidency College background, his fluency in English and his love for ingraji gaan (English songs), citing these as signs of a privileged upbringing. Someone as 'sophisticated' as him could never be a real Naxal. This went on for long and it became a sort of torture for him. Later, we realised this was one of the many methods used by the Deep State and police to sow seeds of distrust among comrades.

During this time, Monida requested permission for a guitar. The jailer, one Mr Ghosh, allowed it, after which the taunts began to increase. And at one of our visits to see him, he told me about this song. He played it for me and said he would work out the arrangements once he returned home.

Kotha diya bondhu phire na aila, e kemon kotha. Aa ki dosha.

The song is not about romance or some long-lost love, as it is widely perceived to be. It is a lament. It is about the disappointments that 'revolution' spurred, the uprising that did not fulfil its promise. During performances, I always make it a point to reveal its real context.

You all rarely sang about love and romance?

Yes, we always steered clear of that kind of stuff. It was a conscious decision not to use the kind of language that was being used in mainstream songs and poetry, ie, to extol the virtues of spring or neel akaash (blue sky) and express love for one's beloved. We could never ignore social realities and it was this consciousness that was reflected in our music.

What is *Hay Bhalobasha* about?

That one was my second song. I wrote it when I was nineteen years old. One time, during the early '70s, Monida had fled to Goshaba in the Sunderbans. I was there with him for two days. There, we used to survive on flour soaked in water. And because we were 'VIP visitors', we were given a chilli to go with

BAND OF BROTHERS: With MONIDA (right)

it. I remember it as a luxury. But soon, Monida contracted very high fever. After all, he may have devoured Karl Marx and treatises on Maoism, but the harsh realities of a forest were too much for him to bear. Don't forget, he was this middle-class Calcutta boy of Presidency College. So, we had to leave the place. I remember returning on this very small boat that was supposed to drop us off at Diamond Harbour. The boatman had wrapped up a shivering Monida with whatever pieces of cloth, even if battered and torn, he had. The song came to me then. It was the stark realities of life we learnt about. On the one hand we had these typically middle-class loves of writing poetry and listening to music. Yet, there were those for whom a piece of chilli was a luxury to be accorded only to visitors of so-called eminence. We went on to encounter such inequalities on several occasions. But that would be the first and last time I would write about it.

Jokhon dekhi ora kaaj kore grame bondore
Sudhui foshol folaay gham jhoraay mathe prantore
Tokhon bhalo lage na lage na kono kichhui
Sudin kachhe esho bhalobashi eksathe shob kichhui

That song spoke to many of us when we were in college in the mid-'80s, and still does.

Even now, there isn't a single show we do where *Bhalobashi* isn't performed. These days, I am invited as a judge at various music competitions where bands are usually asked to perform one original and one cover. At least three or four songs of Mohiner Ghoraguli are always performed.

Not surprising since your songs are so relevant today.

That's because not much has changed… ISRO and NASA have changed and one can now think of a honeymoon on Mars, I am told. The world is in our fist, thanks to the cellphone. But nothing seems to have improved on the ground. We were in Chhattisgarh recently and found that for poor tribals there, even a meal of kaon seeds (Foxtail millet) and tamarind juice was a luxury at 48 degree Celsius.

During the time Mohiner Ghoraguli was performing original songs, Dilip Balakrishnan and High were playing too. Did you all interact with each other?

Oh, we used to look up to them in awe, Nondon Bagchi and the others. They used to have better equipment than ours. They even had Fender plectrums, while we used to improvise by cutting out small pieces of plastic.

During its time and after, Mohiner Ghoraguli benchmarked Bangla contemporary music like no other. The original line-up performed regularly from 1976 to 1981, a time when the band held several memorable concerts at venues as diverse as Jogesh Mime Academy, Star Theatre, Rabindra Sadan, St Paul's Cathedral, Calcutta International Jazz Festival and Calcutta School of Music. In its second edition, the band came out with an album titled, aptly, *Abar Bochhor Kuri Porey* (Twenty Years On, Once Again). It had many of the classics of the '70s as well as new songs like *Prithibi*, *Telephone*, *Bangalee Korechho*, that saw Mohiner Ghoraguli generate a kind of public following that it had never had. Their songs began getting covered by more and more bands, and today, Bangla bands in Bengal and Bangladesh perform their songs regularly.

Bapida's assessment of the day is that there is more meaningful music coming from the fringes and smaller towns than Calcutta. 'There are many good Bangla bands in Asansol, Burdwan and Jalpaiguri. Chandannagore has eighty-two,' he says without hiding his disdain for most of those playing in the city for their misplaced priorities. For one, English names—'Road Roller', 'Blood'—for a Bangla band gets his goat. He doesn't approve of their singing about wet kisses (*Bheja Chumu*) when the rest of the world is burning.

'People who weren't even born in the '60s and '70s are gathering in huge numbers in Bangladesh, Egypt and Syria to protest against the injustice of totalitarian regimes. Protests against immigrants are suddenly rising in parts of Germany. At home, people are being lynched over lies. How can we ignore such realities and sing about, say, *Amakey amar moto thakte dao* (Let me be as I am, a reference to a popular song of these days), or a roadside Romeo who has to pleasure himself at night, soiling his jeans in the process, for not being able to start his day with a glimpse of this girl. God help us with such ideas of modernity.'

Years ago, Bapida fell awkwardly at home one day and sustained serious injuries. The surgeries did not go well, and for a while he suffered a lot, one time even insisting that he be taken to the studio in an ambulance so that he could record a few songs. For that session, a bed was made for him on the floor and he played and sang reclining himself on a pile of pillows, his wife Sutapa tells us. But he is better now. Although the strums on the guitar aren't that free flowing, his singing is as sharp.

Monida's passing changed everything for them. Bishu is in San Fransisco. Bula is in Calcutta. So is Abraham, running a successful music school.

Bapida doesn't perform as Mohiner Ghoraguli. He doesn't think it's ethical. Instead, he calls his troupe, comprising youngsters half his age, Mohin Ekhon, O Bondhura (Mohin Now, and Friends). They have had CDs out in 2011, 2015 and 2018. He is happy that he has been able to instil a sense of commitment among his bandmates. 'All of them are aware. They realise that an artiste has a commitment to his craft and to himself/herself. It is easy to break this inner covenant citing the demands of the market place. But for those who don't, it may so happen that your home has walls that only have a coat of plaster of Paris and no paint. That's the price. For me, that's hardly a price to pay for not selling out.'

No matter. The walls of his home look nice enough with friends and fans having worked their magic with graffiti. I ask him what song they would sing if Monida were to be here today. Bapida quotes poet Jibanananda Das and says something about how it would take hundreds of years for another Mahatma Gandhi or Charu Majumdar to set foot in this country. 'What happened to journalist Gauri Lankesh? See what Pune police did the other day,' he says, referring to the raids and subsequent house arrest of activists deemed to be 'urban Maoists'.

Before we leave, Bapida is generous enough to play for us a recording of one of their latest songs. Titled *Bhanga Aina* (Broken Mirror), the song is about the culture of projecting oneself on Facebook, he says, akin to staring at a distorted reflection of the self in a broken mirror. I note the crossover to a full-blown electric sound in the composition that is set to a propulsive beat. I would go on to experience that electric sound live exactly a year later when Mohin Ekhon, O Bondhura were performing at what looked like a makeshift hall with a tin shed for roof at Lake Town on the northern fringes of Calcutta. It was to celebrate the band's eighth and the current line-up's third anniversary. A host of young musicians, all well-known names, had gathered there to celebrate Mohiner Ghodaguli and their music. The finale was *Hay Bhalobashi*. Everyone in the audience joined in for what has now come to be regarded as the 'national anthem' for Bangla bands. Mobile phone flashlights were turned on, the crowd swaying to the opening riffs of the song that has been front-loaded with a sharp guitar lick. Bapida was seated, joining in at chorus, while Suman 'Mickey' Chatterjee sang lead vocals, ably accompanied by Prosenjit 'P.P.' Pal on synthesiser, Tannoy 'Bittu' Chatterjee on bass, and Neel Roy Choudhury on drums. Sudip Nag's guitar dutifully receded to the background on cue. And we all sang along.

Bhalobashi Piccaso Bunoyel Daante
Beatles Dylan ar Beethoven sunte
Rabishankar ar Ali Akbar sune
Bhalo lage bhore kuashay ghore phirte

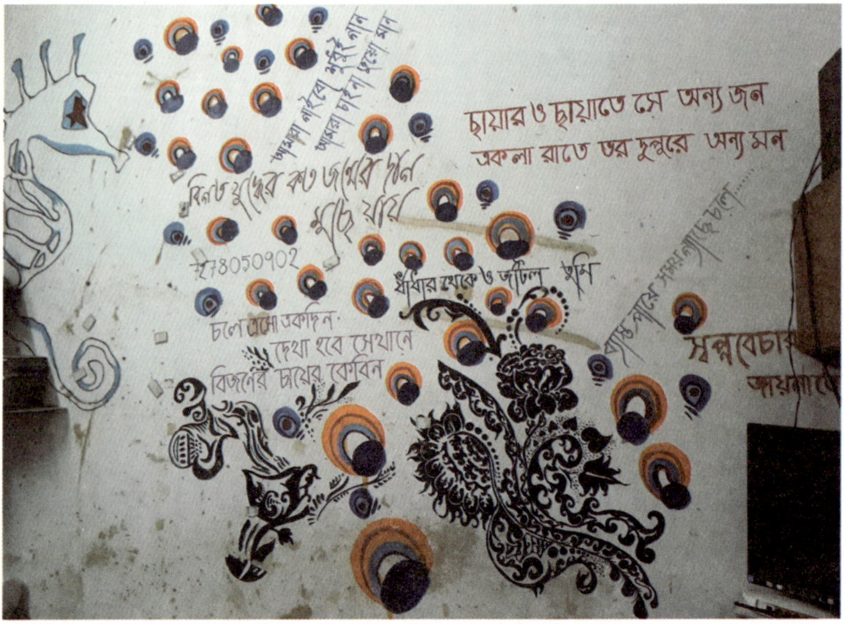

LYRIC & SONG: Bapida's room

The full-throated rendition left behind the melancholy of Mohin's original. Bapida had answered his calling, singing with a bunch of youngsters who weren't even born when he wrote that song. A bridge had been built. They were singing about the same joys and yearnings, but with a renewed sense of confidence, with a bit of head-banging no less. Could they be singing about hope? How could they even dare? After all it was 2019, the year of NRC (National Register of Citizens) and CAA (Citizenship Amendment Act) that seek to determine how Indian we are. Yet if anyone could, it had to be them.

Since then, whenever I hear their songs, I think about that 'friend' who did not keep his word. About those flying horsemen who showed the way, about the rainbow of emotions that binds us to the music of the Beatles, Dylan and Ravi Shankar. This country of ours must find a way to make it worthwhile for our nineteen-year-olds. A Bapi who could pen a song like *Hay Bhalobashi* must be loved, nurtured and respected so that he and others like him who follow can continue doing what they do best. That song yearns for good days. *'Sudin kachhe esho bhalobashi eksathe shob kichhui,'* it says, calling out to a future when we can all go back to liking, loving and respecting everyone and everything together.

21

Restless Native

A day before Mahalaya in September 1996, he found himself walking from Gol Park towards Gariahat, navigating a pre-Puja evening crowd of frenzied shoppers. The flyover that leaps across the South Calcutta landmark wasn't there. So, there was another row of shops on a boulevard running through the middle of the road, selling varied items of clothing, inner wear, bling and what not. Of these, at least five or seven were dalas or small shops selling music cassettes. During that half-hour crawl amid the giggle-gaggle of a mass of people dressed in Puja finery, he could hear music. What did he hear? It sounded familiar, one tune jump-cutting into another as he made his way up the crowd passing by each dala. Whatever it was that was playing, it made him feel good. Why?

More than two decades later, Srikanta is about to tell me. We are at his three-storeyed red coloured house in Calcutta's deep south. I have just been welcomed by a giant framed poster of *Pather Panchali* on the ground floor and, as I climb up the steps, I see one of Ritwik Ghatak. I am led into his Music Room where a smaller black-and white photograph of Ali Akbar Khan has been given pride of place on one of the walls. Secure in back framing, the Ustad's benign presence seems to be a source of guidance, comfort and assurance for the artiste. On the far corner is an array of more photographs. I spot Lata Mangeshkar, Manna Dey, Salil Chowdhury and Nikhil Bandopadhyay. The other side is an open shelf full of awards. We are seated on comfortable drawing room furniture. On the far side is a seating arrangement on the floor. Books, tablas; his place of riyaz.

Articulate, respectful and self-effacing, Srikanta admits he is still jet-lagged. He is just back from the UK performing three concerts and stealing a visit to the Beatles museum in Liverpool. Over tea, he opens up about his serendipitous beginning, loves and learnings and most of all, Rabindrasangeet, a calling he didn't think he needed to answer as a child, but went on to pursue as an adult. I tell him about a concert in Pune circa 2004-2005, the only time I had heard him live, and he connects instantly. 'I remember that show at Bal Gandharva auditorium as one of my most satisfying. The sound and the ambience were remarkably good. I enjoyed performing there.'

For me, a hop-step-and-jump Calcuttan whose then landing point was Pune, that concert was about *Tumi kon kanoner phool, kon gaganer tara*, a beautiful love song Rabindranath Tagore composed in 1886.[1] The poet may have been celebrating an individual, or who knows, the idea of looking up to someone you love graciously, affectionately and respectfully. For me, the song will always be about a time when our family was together. New arrivals, new city, new job and a new beginning.

For Srikanta, 1996 was the year of his new beginning. On January 3 that year, he quit his job as a salesman in North Bengal, having spent close to six years there, logging travel distances of over 2,000 km a month. One of the first persons he went to after that momentous decision, something he shared with his then expecting wife and only a few others in the family, was Dulalda, or Utpal Chakraborty, the owner of The Melody, the iconic music shop on Rashbehari Avenue, where the likes of S.D. Burman and Hemanta Mukhopadhyay would come for adda.

'I had known Dulalda through a friend, and we would often discuss music. Sometimes, he would talk to me about pursuing it seriously, but I did not think much of it. Yet, when I told him that I had quit my job, he was upset with me for taking such a "stupid" and "irresponsible" decision.'

But Dulalda thought it worth his while to send Srikanta first to HMV and then to a much smaller music company Sagarika, after advising him to record a demo tape of his favourite songs at home. At HMV, Subrata Chowdhury, who was then the boss, met him, primarily because Dulalda was a respected name in the music business, and record companies, the few that were around in Calcutta at the time, always paid attention to what he had to say.

Mr Chowdhury told Srikanta he liked his songs but couldn't do anything about them as HMV's plans for the coming Pujas had already been chalked out. 'I was more relieved than disappointed. For I never had any expectations and had, in fact, gone there with great reluctance knowing fully well that a minnow like me had no place in the giant canvas of HMV. Nevertheless, Dulalda seemed a bit surprised that I had been turned down and sent me to meet Anupam Gan, the proprietor of Sagarika.'

Srikanta recalls that Mr Gan called him back within three days of him submitting his demo tape, and started to ask him all sorts of personal questions about his life, family, reasons behind his current state of unemployment, etc. 'Just when I was beginning to lose patience with the grilling, convinced that he was

TORCHBEARER: SRIKANTA ACHARYA

merely playing me when all he needed to say was "no", which I was quite prepared to hear, Mr Gan surprised me. "We are signing you on for five years. You will be our exclusive artiste, which means you cannot sing for any other company."'

The result was that two albums, one of Rabindrasangeet and the other of old Bengali songs, were ready by August-September, and started getting airplay on FM. The first week of *Moner Janala*'s release saw it slip into the last spot of 'Bangla Gaaner Doser Desh', a countdown show aired every Sunday on Times FM. The next week it moved up to Number Three. By the third week, the title track became Number One.

There was media hype too. *Anandabazar Patrika*, the leading Bengali daily of all time, published an article about Srikanta and another singer, who was at the time ruling the market with his covers of old Bengali songs, pitting two music companies, that incidentally had their offices opposite each other on Moti Sil Street, against each other. Sagarika vs Atlantis. Srikanta Acharya and Indranil Sen.

It was all too intimidating. 'I was so unsure of myself. I had not told anyone, but for my wife, that I had two albums out. I was convinced it wouldn't work and did not even tell my closest friends. When Anupamda told me that *Moner Janala* had become a super-duper hit, and that they had already sold over 10,000 copies within seven days and had ordered a fresh lot, I was dumbfounded.'

Dramatic as it was, it was a dream debut.

Tell me about your early years.

For me, learning music wasn't an elaborate affair. As a young boy I learnt Rabindrasangeet. My mother got me admitted to Dakshini (a very well-known music school at Deshapriya Park in South Calcutta), where my sister used to go too. I was there for ten years. Apart from this, I have had no other training in music. My family had nothing to do with music. My uncles were

IIT toppers, who went on to hold high-profile jobs. My father's priorities centred around studies. All he insisted on were studies, studies and studies. It was my mother who thought it fit that we go to a music school. So, whatever I learnt was because of my mother. And after graduating from Dakshini, I did not pursue music seriously at all. That's because I knew music wasn't for me, and that music would get me nowhere. The way we were brought up, there was no way music could occupy a large chunk of our mind space.

Yet I seem to have been drawn to music instinctively. I remember taking part in several college festivals, NRS, Presidency, CNMC, and our very own Xavotsav, and returning with some prize or the other. We were quite the stars in our days at St Xavier's College. But it all ended after college. I got myself a job and forgot about music. I had moved myself far away from it. The detachment was so pronounced that I even gave away my harmonium.

Then occasionally, I would hear people talking about my music. 'Oh, you have given up singing, is it? What a pity, maybe you should have continued.' I kept hearing such comments, and that got me thinking. Has music really left me for good? Shouldn't I give it a shot?

By 1994-95, I realised that no serious pursuit of music could happen with the kind of job I was doing. And by mid-1995, I decided to leave my job. That year after the Pujas, I handed over my resignation, to be relieved after three months in the January of 1996. I stopped work on January 3. On May 10, my daughter was born. But me, I was blissfully unemployed.

By the Pujas that year, you were quite well known. As we now know, your first album was an instant hit.

Yes. To be honest, I did not have to struggle to become known. It happened suddenly and most unexpectedly.

What does Rabindrasangeet mean to you?

It's not that I like all of Tagore's songs. I learnt Rabindrasangeet when I was a child and have been listening to it ever since. But now that I am much older I have come to understand that there is a kind of delicacy in Tagore songs, an X-factor; a kind of reticence and restraint. Once you are able to grasp that, then it becomes very difficult to let go of it. You have to appreciate and admire this restraint to do justice to Tagore while performing his songs. If I am able to sing a Tagore song properly, it offers me a sense of peace and satisfaction. It's as though I want to explore this satisfaction a bit more.

Sometimes, the structure of a Tagore tune is very predictable as anyone who has been listening to, or singing, his songs regularly will tell you. But at times, that is not the case. There comes a sudden deviation in the tune that defies definition. This could be in the form of a note or a word. He blends various aspects of music, which gets me thinking as to how he even conceived of such ideas. The more I think, I realise that he may not have been all that conscious about it at all, which begs the question that if he wasn't conscious about it, then how did he think about it? You know, one komol rekhab here, a shuddho neekhad there.

Also, when I hear compositions of his contemporaries, and think of Tagore's songs purely as a piece of music, I realise that Tagore was 100 years ahead of them. That's why even if one doesn't get the nuances of his lyrics, there is enough in Tagore's music to keep one mesmerised. Yet, I also know that since this is Rabindranath Tagore we are talking about, we can't afford to overlook his words.

Secondly, Tagore songs are replete with vibrant imagery. For performers, it becomes a rewarding challenge to try and tap into this imagery and make sure he/she is able to convey this to the audience. This challenge is alluring. It is what propels performers like me to continue singing Tagore songs till this day.

Thirdly, I now realise that I was unable to do justice to a number of songs that I had recorded, say fifteen years ago. People may have appreciated their renditions then, but I know now I messed them up royally. Consider the song, *Mone ki dwidha rekhe gele chole*. Two decades ago, I would have sung the song at a particular tempo. But now, I tell myself that I will have to sing this slower. That is the only way I can project the imagery of the song better. Similarly, for some other songs, I now realise I was too loud. These days I sing them with a lot more reticence, and in the process, get a better glimpse of their inner beauty. The next step is to connect the listener to this beauty. My greatest reward, therefore, is when people, who profess not being the greatest of Tagore fans, come to me and say that they have begun to rediscover the joys of Tagore after hearing a few of my renditions.

So, there's a kind of magic associated with a Tagore song?

Absolutely. That is precisely why, contrary to what people think, youngsters are listening to a lot of Tagore these days. Many of them are singing them too. And I am sure decades later, they too will rediscover Tagore and sing his songs differently.

How about an example of an unpredictable bend?

Consider *Ei udashi hawar pothe pothe*, a brilliant song with shades of Shudh Kalyan. At '*bou kotha kau tandrahara, bipholo daak diye hoy shara*', there emerges suddenly a komol rekhab, which conventional music pundits would frown upon. But it is exactly this note that helps transcend the music to a spiritual level by bringing out the deep sadness embedded in the pronouncement of 'bipholo byatha.'

In *Sangeetchinta*, his treatise on the craft of music, Tagore writes that his commitment is in creating music as a whole—where lyrics and tune are both an integral part. This can't be achieved if he has to follow a raga to the T. So, instead, he composes what his musical mind is telling him to. But you have to realise that because of his deep knowledge and grooming in Indian classical music since childhood, his ability to make these 'departures' was also supreme.

Also, *Chokkhe amar trishna...* This song is about summer and there is a slight flavour of Sarang, an afternoon raga, to fit the mood of the song. Yet there is a departure in the form of a brilliant introduction of a shuddh and komal gandhaar in the antara (bridge) and aabhog (finale). But I realise now that the beauty of the song is in the manner in which it flows like a symphonic movement. We see how Tagore absorbed the core nuances of Western classical music, blending its characteristics seamlessly into his own music. Hence, if for instance, the Vienna Philharmonic Orchestra was to play the tune of *Chokkhe amaar trishna*, it would be an amazing piece of music: *Jhor utheche topto hawaay, monke shudur shunye dhawaay...* I can almost hear the run of the strings section.

This mix is all over Tagore's oeuvre isn't it?

Tagore has been able to pull off such seamless amalgamation of various influences into what is essentially Rabindrasangeet with seemingly effortless ease on several occasions. At times, I have hit upon this magic in a particular song very late, say, after having performed it for a decade or so.

I have, therefore, come to realise that to grasp the true essence of Tagore and the nuances of his lyrics one needs an intellectual maturity that comes with age. The same people who would in their younger days deride his songs as an uninspiring dirge (pan paney) would come back decades later to say 'No I was so wrong about Tagore'. We did *Valmiki Pratibha* as a child at Dakshini. It is only now that I realise what a mammoth creation it was in the way it blended Western forms of opera with kirtan. '*Shyama ebar...*' is there just as '*Kali, Kali bolo hari...*' Yet these are unmistakably Bengali songs of Tagore.

The reference to *Chokkhe amaar trishna* takes me back to my childhood. I remember listening to Hemanta Mukhopadhyay, courtesy a blue album with a painting of a woman that would play every night at bedtime on our Garrard changer. My all-time favourite memory is of *Ogo Nodi Apon Bege*, the river song; its single-minded journey across gardens and landscapes, a willing chronicler of life's many journeys to be reminisced by generations.

Ogo nodi apon bege pagol para
Ami sthobdho chanpa toru gandhe bhara
Tondra hawa ogo nodi apon money

Chokkhe amar trishna is in the album too. Composed in 1933, the song is a part of Tagore's one-act play *Chandalika*. A travelling monk finds her, Prakriti, drawing water from a well and asks for some. Prakriti quenches his thirst and in the process is so overwhelmed by the recognition he accords her—a social outcast on account of her being an untouchable—that she ends up falling for his beauty and charm. But such a love is not to be. Who will provide the balm for Prakriti's parched soul?

Chokkhe amar trishna ogo, trishna amar bokkho jure
Ami brishti bihin Baisakhi din, sontape pran jai, jai je pure
Jhor uthechey topto hawa-e, hawa-e monke shudur shunney dhawa-e—
Abogunthan jai je ure
Je phool kanon korto alo
Kalo hoe she shukalo
Jhornare ke dilo badha—nishthoor pashaney bandha
Dukkher shikhorchure

(Thirsty my eyes, and thirst in my heart
I am a rainless summer day, the heat burns my soul
A storm in the fiery wind sends my heart far away
The veil flies off
The flower that lit up the garden
Is now dry and blackened
Who damned the waterfall—Trapped by the blazing heat
At suffering's peak?)[2]

Hemanta's version has a gentle lilt to it. But Srikanta seems to have tapped into Hemanta's pathos and built his own rendition of the song around it. The master of yesteryear opening up possibilities. The student of today taking the plunge, daring to rediscover Tagore in his own way.

As I grew older, I would also listen to a lot to *Shokoli phuralo, shokoli pran*, a song of profound grief that was a favourite of my mother. It is about loss and its brutal finality that seemed to have been heightened by the devotional sincerity of the singer, Kanika Bandopadhay. It was an EP that also had *Phule phule*, a romantic song that subsequently found a place in many a Bengali and Hindi film. The recording on the EP was distinctly better than the earlier LPs we had heard. Srikanta recalls hearing that album being played regularly on the radio. 'The piano was played by the legendary V. Balsara. And yes, stereo recording had just about started then which definitely added a dimension to later recordings of Tagore songs.'

By the time I was in senior school, Satyajit Ray and Ritwik Ghatak happened. At a late night public screening of *Komal Gandhaar*, held at a small garden within our housing complex in Salt Lake, I heard *Aaj jyotsna ratey shobai gechhey bone*, a song about staying back when everyone else has left.

Srikanta's album, *Apon Gaan*, has the story behind that composition and several other Tagore songs. Narrated by Ray's favourite hero, Soumitra Chatterjee, the album is a collection of songs with their back stories documented in memoirs of Tagore's many contemporaries. *Aaj jyotsna...* was created one moonlit night when writer-professor Charuchandra Bandopadhyaya was at Bolpur. The others had all gone to Parul Danga for the staging of a play, possibly *Raja*. But he stayed back, unwilling to put in an all-nighter. Yet, that night at Shantiniketan, he woke up twice. First, when he found Tagore in his room covering him with his own shawl, realising he was shivering in the cold. Then later, waking up to the strains of a tune that had come wafting through the breeze. It was a moonlit night. The tune was being hummed by Tagore himself as he paced about in the garden downstairs. Barefeet, Charuchandra tip-toed down and followed Tagore. But the poet did not notice him. He was humming a line repeatedly. '*Aaj jyotnsa raatey shobai gechhey bone... aaj jyotsna raatey shobai gechhey bone*'.

One of the songs I grew up not to be so fond of is *Shedin dujoney dulechhinu bone*, reading it, at best, as a hopelessly mushy love song about lovebirds on a swing in the forest. Srikanta of course has another take on it even though he too, like me, initially thought otherwise.

'Now that you mention it, I must admit I too did not think much of the opening line, "*Shedin dujoney dulechhinu bone*". Then one day, suddenly, one word stood out. "*Jete jete pothey purnima raatey chand uthechhilo gaganey, dekha hoechhilo tomatey amatey ki jaani ki mahalaganey.*" The utterance of the word, mahalaganey (quintessential moment), is the transcending point of the song. From what at first seems like a personal love story between two individuals, that single utterance lifts the song into something universal. "Mahalaganey" transcends the story of these two lovers in our backyard and makes it worthy of every other couple who have been in love anytime, anywhere.'

Is that then the essence of Tagore, the closest to the last word in music, lyric and art, I think to myself. Are we even allowed to ask?

Yet Ritwik Ghatak seems to agree. 'I cannot speak without Tagore... he has understood what I am and he has put in all the words. I read him and I find that all has been said and I have nothing new to say... It just cannot be helped. You can be angry with him, you can criticise him... but in the final analysis, you will find that he has the last word,' the filmmaker told an interviewer shortly before his death in 1976.[3]

Instrumentation and musical arrangements for Tagore songs have undergone a sea change. Earlier, it was a harmonium or esraj. Now, we have a full-fledged band or orchestras backing singers like you.

Instrumentation in Rabindrasangeet has always been a point of contention. It was in the late '50s that Rabindrasangeet began to get popular. It started getting airplay and soon there was a set of artistes who did that exclusively, which means they did not sing anything else. Among those who played a stellar role in popularising Rabindrasangeet were Pankaj Kumar Mullick, who went on to conduct a programme on the craft of singing Rabindrasangeet on AIR, Debabrata Biswas, Hemanta Mukhopadhyay, Kanika Bandopadhyay and Suchitra Mitra.

At the time, the instruments that were used were ones that were available to the artists, and that became popular. However, when Tagore was composing and singing, he mentions having an organ, piano as well as esraj as accompaniment. This trend was not followed later in AIR recordings or even in live singing (one of the reasons could be that the instruments were not amenable to being carried around). As a result, a soundscape for singing Tagore songs evolved. And given the popularity of the songs, that came to be accepted as 'the only' soundscape. This was further institutionalised with the strictures of Visva Bharati Music Board, which became very rigid about the use of music in Tagore songs (while creative use of other kinds of instrumentation in films using Tagore songs actually made the songs more popular).

In the post-copyright era, these restrictions naturally melted away. When we entered the studio, we had instruments that could emulate sounds of the piano, organ, strings and so on. We took advantage of that and our soundscape changed. It's as simple as that.

How did more instruments come into play?

As for orchestration and instrumentation of Rabindrasangeet, I believe, things were made unnecessarily complicated early on. Visva Bharati Music Board had laid down strict diktats on what instruments could be used as accompaniment to Rabindrasangeet like, say, esraj, flute, harmonium and so on. Now, an esraj does not work with all his songs. Also, Tagore is known to have said that he has left little or no 'gaps' in his songs, a statement that has been misconstrued to bolster arguments in favour of limited instrumentation with Tagore songs. It is my belief, based on the little that I have come to understand about Tagore's music, that if Rabindranath were to be alive today, he would have wholeheartedly embraced the idea of orchestration as accompaniment to his songs. It is difficult to believe that Tagore, who was always so open to new ideas, would not have experimented with modern instruments.

Another important factor we tend to ignore is that we have never sought the views of instrumentalists of repute. Shouldn't we have taken their opinion too? I do not believe in the notion that only those who sing Rabindrasangeet know everything that is there to know about Tagore's compositions. Why weren't instrumentalists of repute given a place in the Visva Bharati Music Board? The Board doesn't exist now, but back then, this exclusion was, I believe, a mistake.

What about the various styles of singing Tagore?

The truth is that Rabindrasangeet was at a low point during Tagore's twilight years. The tunes were being distorted to such an extent that Tagore himself is known to have told those close to him that they needed to somehow ensure his songs remained recognisable as his. It was then that a concerted effort was made to create authentic documents spelling out notations (shorolipi) of each song so that there was little scope of deviation.

A gayaki of Tagore songs took on a definitive form after Tagore's demise. A number of gharanas emerged which came to be represented by the likes of Mohordi (Kanika Bandopadhyay), Suchitra Mitra, Shantideb Ghosh, Pankaj Mullick, Debabrata Biswas and Hemanta Mukhopadhyay. They all sang Tagore songs in their own inimitable styles, yet the listener has no difficulty in recognising their renditions as Tagore songs. The reason was that all of them stayed close to the shorolipi of each song. There could have been marginal deviations, but the core tune remained faithful to the notes. This helped preserve the authenticity of Tagore songs.

In fact, such is not the case with Nazrulgeeti (songs of Kazi Nazrul Islam). The same song is sung differently in Calcutta and Dhaka, spurring intense debate over which version is authentic. In the case of Rabindrasangeet, there is one set of notations (pointing to a shelf where all his books of notations have been neatly arranged) which are universally accepted. Hence, there is no scope of dispute over tunes. This is a welcome development. It makes it incumbent on all serious practitioners of Rabindrasangeet to respect the notations and not mess with the tune in the name of improvisation.

Kishore Kumar's *Ami chini go chini tomare* in Ray's *Charulata* comes to mind.

Yes. In that rendition, there is a piano and flute playing. The scene is about Charu, her gradual realisation that she has indeed fallen in love with Amal. She is excited and embarrassed. She is looking at Amal through her fingers after having covered her face with her hands. Then the camera, from the perspective of Amal, moves towards her. We see her. At that very moment Ray uses a violin trill to indicate Charu's state of mind. This is an example of how an instrument can heighten the dramatic intensity of a scene with a song. The same can be said about the considered use of instruments to lift a song.

I can imagine, say, the Vienna Philharmonic Orchestra playing a collection of Tagore songs.

Yes, can there be anything better?

I believe there is a need for orchestration and instrumentation in Tagore songs. More so today when we can listen to music from the world in the comfort of our homes. The soundscape of one nation is flowing into another easily, naturally. My daughter and son listen to music from the world over and not just Rabindrasangeet. If we are to present Tagore's songs to future generations within the sphere of contemporariness, if we are to establish Rabindrasangeet on the world stage as contemporary music, it's time we pay attention to orchestration.

I think the likes of Kishore Kumar and Salil Chowdhury understood that even though they are not the names that come to mind when one talks of Rabindrasangeet.

Among my eternal regrets is that Salil Chowdhury, himself an ardent admirer of Tagore songs, and Ravi Shankar never worked their magic on Tagore songs via orchestration. Both had an extremely keen understanding of instrumentation. Had they considered working on some Tagore tunes, we would have today been left with several classical masterpieces.

Manna Dey loved Rabindrasangeet too. We would have had some great music if Mannada sang more Rabindrasangeet. For instance, in the film *Megh O Roudro*, he sings *Na chahile jare pawa jaay*. Now, that is a masterpiece. Similarly, he has a few EPs like *Oi ashan tale matir pore* or *Ogo swapna swarupini* or *Srabanero gaganero gaye*—absolute gems!

Even though the world speaks of Tagore in superlatives, his music is essentially confined to the Bengal. His ideas are universal, yet his music hasn't really crossed boundaries in the way we think it should have. Why?

Since we are discussing Rabindranath, the lyrics become that much more important. Yet, it was Tagore who said that a song should not be bound by words. He said a song should begin where words end—this from someone who has written over 2,200 songs. But we cannot ignore Tagore's words. The ratio of words to music in his songs, the reticence of his thoughts can be appreciated only if you are equipped to grasp the nuances of the language. One might take to a song because of its tune, but for most of his songs, the poetry elevates them to a higher plane.

Consider *Ami chanchol o hey.*

Ami chonchol o hey,
Ami shudurer piyashi
Din chole jai, ami anmone tari asha cheye thaki bataione—
Ogo, praney mone ami je tahar porosh pabar proyashi
Ogo shudur, bipul shudur, tumi je bajao baykul bashori—
Mor dana nai achi ek thai she kotha je jai pashori

Ami chonchol o hey[4] was first published as a poem in 1902. Tagore put the first two stanzas to tune, composed on piano, fourteen years later for the staging of *Dak Ghar*, an extract of which (*Amol o doi ala*) probably every young Bengali has learnt and enacted at school or at a para function. Just as an ailing Amal, confined to his room, yearns for the outdoors, the song talks of our eternal quest for the unknown; our restless self, harbouring this unquenched thirst to connect with nature's beauty and beyond. Yet we know we can't. For, we are bound within the confines of our own mindspace.

This is among the many songs that I have found myself coming back to for refuge in times of failure, tragedy, grief and contemplation. It has helped me reconcile myself with my limitations, accept, submit and then move on.

Bengalis by nature tend to be too possessive about Tagore. There used to be this statement we would often hear as a child: *Chesta korle* Shakespeare *howa jai, kinto cheshta korley* Rabindranath *howa jai na* (Try hard enough one can be a Shakespeare, but one can never be a Tagore).

There are people who, in order to prove their undying devotion to Rabindrasangeet, decry other forms of music. I do not appreciate that view. I sincerely believe that if one can grasp the true essence of Tagore, one would be just the contrary—not dogmatic and restricted, but rather open and accepting of innovations.

As an aside, I must admit that I harbour a far more immediate concern, and that is whether Bengalis as a race will be able to understand and appreciate Tagore in the years to come. That to me is a far serious worry now, given the way the Bengali language is fast losing its currency in our day-to-day lives.

Tell me about the stalwarts whose rendition of Rabindrasangeet defines our appreciation of Tagore, starting with Santideb Ghosh

I have to admit that I started appreciating Santideb Ghosh's magic much later in life. He had come for the convocation of Dakshini once and I remember feeling that he was extremely protective about Tagore and anything to do with him. Yet, there was a certain openness about him. A few years ago, I managed to see a DD interview of him where he was asked what he felt about Bombay artistes singing Rabindrasangeet, the interviewer half convinced that the master would speak disparagingly about the trend. But no, Santideb babu said he quite liked it!

I think that's because he himself would sing freely, with an open voice. And he liked the way Bombay singers like, say, Asha Bhosle and others, would do the same. Asha Bhosle's Bangla pronunciation and diction may not have been perfect, but there are few who can hold a tune like her. Now, when I hear Santideb Ghosh's songs, I find them truly interesting. There is a lot of drama in his singing.

Suchitra Mitra and Debabrata Biswas?

Suchitradi was a unique mix. Her gayaki was a unique amalgam of Shantiniketan—she imbibed a lot of Santideb Ghosh too—and her days with IPTA (Indian People's Theatre Association). There was flamboyance, reticence and devotion in her renditions. Similarly, Debabrata Biswas was also involved with IPTA. But he was brought up in the ambience of Brahmo Samaj and grew up singing Brahmo Sangeet. This gave a unique dimension to his approach and philosophy of singing Tagore, leaving us with a truly unparalleled set of classics. He was a pioneer, a true radical. When he started using instruments like piano accordion in Tagore songs, there was an outcry. Consider his *Sunilo sagaray*, probably arranged by Dilip Ray. It is beautiful. Those who criticised him did so out of ignorance.

Kanika Bandhopadhyay?

She was this serene, quiet, submissive person who could never see anything wrong with anyone. There were times when I was, say, singing in front of her and she would say, '*besh bhalo hochhchey* (quite good)'. But I knew I was making a hash of it, and would protest telling her, '*Ki bhalo hochchey? Ekabere hochchey na... aapni keno bolchchen bhalo hochchey*' (What, why are you saying good when you know I have messed it up)? Then she would console me and say something like this, '*Aha, ei jaigata ei bhabe ga... baki ta thik achchey*' (Oh ho... sing this part like this. The rest is fine). And this intervention would lift the song to another level. This is where her dynamism lay. It may not have been apparent to many, but it was always there. I say this from personal experience of interacting with her. She wasn't an orthodox person in her approach to music. She was also very open about her own taste in music. She would appreciate all kinds of music. She was a pure soul.

I think we get a sense of that purity when we hear her sing, *Anandadhara Bohiche Bhubane.*

Quite so. You see, these people have grown up with Tagore songs, lived every part of their lives with Tagore. When they sing a Tagore verse, they believe every word of it. Tagore is in their veins. They have nurtured a kind of faith that we as artistes are still aspiring to grasp. That is sadhana. It is this that differentiates them from people like us.

And Rezwana Choudhury Bannya?

Bannyadi is a disciple of Kanika. She was in Visva Bharati on scholarship and learnt Rabindrasangeet by following the same principles as that of Mohordi. She is the torch-bearer. Those who yearn for that Mohordi flavour flock to her concerts. She performs all over the world and is loved by listeners across Bengals (Calcutta and Dhaka). She is very affectionate towards me. We have performed together on occasions.

Shadhu, shadhu.[5]

Like any true-blue music buff, Srikanta has grown up with all kinds of music with an ear out for the instruments; from Pyarelal's violin solo in Mohammad Rafi's *Mein Yeh Sochkar Uske Dar Se* to the piano in *Pyar Diwani Hota Hai* (Sebastian) or Mukesh's *Suhani Chandni Raat* (Louiz Banks). But his devotion to Tagore is total. Feet firmly on the ground, he doesn't take his success for granted even though he admits, somewhat apologetically, it was hardly a struggle. 'But once I got known, an expectation was created. And fulfilling that expectation for the audience became my struggle, something that continues till date.'

So, what was it he had heard that evening, the day before Mahalaya in 1996, while walking through Gol Park? The cassette shops were playing music, remember? 'That evening I heard my songs from *Moner Janala* being played at each one of those shops, one song jump-cutting into another, as I moved

MEMORIES: The Melody at Rashbehari Avenue, Calcutta

ahead navigating the pre-Puja crowd anonymously.' For the first time in months, Srikanta smiled to himself. He had not felt anything like that before. Excited, happy and a bit scared. It was true after all. *Moner Janala*, a collection of his renditions of old Bengali songs, composed by famous people of yesteryear, had indeed become popular.

On Mahalaya, he received a call from a club at Naktala at his then Salt Lake home to negotiate a 'rate' for a possible show on Shashthi a few days later. Piecing together a band courtesy friends within seventy-two hours, Srikanta did not disappoint the club and went on to perform two more concerts at Puja pandals that year. And contrary to his belief, requests for shows kept pouring in through the winter. This singer had found his song.

These days, Srikanta's early rival in the marketplace, Indranil Sen, an accomplished singer with his share of albums and accolades, is a minister in the West Bengal government.

At The Melody on Rashbehari Avenue, I think I managed to snag what was the last copy of *Apon Gaan* Volumes I & II, exactly a week after my conversation with Srikanta. I was the only customer in the shop that afternoon. No one buys CDs these days. They have USB cards, but how long will these sell? Better download all the memories.

22

The Song Remains the Same

A song takes you places. Goopy Gyne Bagha Byne's *Dekho Re* to my younger days at Beltola Road from where I had to walk a mere 300 metres to reach Bijoli cinema in Bhawanipore to catch that evergreen delight about two country bumpkins with hearts of gold who sing their way out of trouble and save a kingdom; *Menoka* and her troubles with her ghomta to Salt Lake where I had heard the doyen of folk Nirmalendu Chowdhury sing that paean to a Shiva-Parvati legend; Hugh Masekela's rare dance track, *Don't Go Lose It Baby*, to Cape Town where I was with former president Abdul Kalam as part of a journalists' delegation; *Sayonee*, the anthemic Sufi rock song by Pakistani band Junoon, to our national capital of Delhi just when India had crossed the rubicon and conducted the Pokhran nuclear tests in 1998; or *Fifteen*, a Daniel Zamir piano-sax duet reminiscent of the foot-tapping immediacy of *Take-Five*, to Tel Aviv, Israel, during a window of relatively less turmoil in West Asia in December 2012.

But what takes you to music? Friends, WhatsApp and YouTube. The link reached me one morning in February 2018. It was from guitarist Amyt Datta. I clicked on it immediately for, it was rare—if ever—for this reticent musician to offer a glimpse of what was on his mind. But since he had, it had to be worth a watch. And Ziba—*Kabir Jam*—eminently was.

The opening notes of the guitar was the hook, instantly transporting me to somewhere in Africa. The beat was unmistakable, the melody skirting the riff that was snaking through the soundscape amid steady but infectious percussive insistence. The bass held it all together, as it is meant to, as Amyt played his solo, a minimalistic exposition of the journey the track was about to let us into. Jazz, philosophy and fun. Amidst this, there's the soaring vocals of a long-haired kaftan-clad dude. His pupils were talking, as if surprised by his own range of vocal histrionics; at times, breaking into a smile, eyes closed in deep appreciation of the canvas held up by his fellow musicians for him to paint on.

Kabir plays on our PC often, allowing thoughts to meander 'like a restless wind inside a letter box'. Our Calcutta is in the throes of yet another journey across the universe of music.

Days later Ziba performed at Phoenix, a cosy little backroom of Astor Hotel on Theatre Road. The sound was good, the crowd young and the beverage in ample supply. Messrs Amyt and Co. were having a blast: Arko Mukherjee, who boasts a husky tenor of incredible range is on vocals, he's the band's world music juke box that is delightfully partial to West African tunes; Aakash Ganguly, who self-taught himself to count Jaco Pastorious, Etienne Mbappe, Richard Bona and Paul McCartney as his influences, is on bass, now playing a top-end Ibanez hybrid (no ridges after the 12th fret); Ritoban 'Ludo' Das is on drums while Deboprotim 'Tukai' Bakshi plays congas and percussion, both students of Monojit 'Kochu' Datta, whose expertise in Latin rhythms led him to form Orient Express.

Kabir Jam, or Sant Kabir's *Ud Jayega*, unveiled an ouvre that was eclectic yet rooted in present times. *Dekho Re* was unrecognisable, the frenetic guitar work not offering so much as a hint that it was indeed the GooGaBaBa track. It did not take me to the dawn break scene from the Satyajit Ray film, of Goopy tentatively trying out the melody with his tanpura and then jumping in joy to find that the boon from the Ghost King (Bhooter Raja) had indeed worked. He could sing. The mellifluous Anup Ghosal was the playback artiste, his renditions of the songs making him an instant hit in Bengal and then a national vocalist of repute for his work on the Dilip Kumar-starrer and Tapan Sinha-directed *Sagina Mahato*.

But the lyrics of *Dekho Re* struck a chord all over again. Arko sang them in a way they stood out, particularly the last line.

Dekho re, jogoter ki bahar,
Jogoter ki bahar, jogoter ki bahar,
Diner alo... diner aloeye kaatey ondhokar

'Oh look at the wonderous universe. See how daylight clears the darkness of night', the words echoing present day sentiment, a silent yet deafening cry from across the world for the light of reason to shine on our dark corners—some of them blacked out by lies, ignorance, intolerance and bigotry. In between, Ziba performed tracks that exemplified their love of places, from Mali to tribal India, the Middle East to Africa, the music coming across as urgent and effervescent, its spontaneity controlled so as not to become an exercise in self-indulgence, something that jam bands often get lost into. Hence, Bob Marley's *I Shot the*

DEKHO RE: ZIBA at DI in January 2019: Aakash (from left), Ritoban, Arko, Deboprotim and Amyt (Picture Rashbehari Das, courtesy *The Telegraph*)

Sheriff takes off from *Manush ekta koler gari*, a Baul song written by Shivananda. A Malian Wassoulou song segues into a Santhali Manbhumi folk tune. They say they're about 'colours, dance and celebration'. They aren't the only ones to tap into these emotions. But they are political, however obliquely. They are among the few that seem to be wanting to speak out. So, their cover of *Roadhouse Blues* has the vocalist dwell on concerns of the city-bred. 'Would you like a cup of tea?' is a question that the lead singer slips in innocuously amid a screaming guitar solo that is matched in pace by the two percussionists. It is asked repetitively. Then, when you least expect it, there comes a statement, as if a news reader on rote. 'Four persons were killed in Bhangor tonight…' referencing the death of two persons in police firing in that hamlet in South 24-Pargana district of Bengal, on the fringes of the city, over the construction of a power grid sub-station.

'So, would you like a cup of tea?' the question is popped again. Welcome to the new normal.

Months later, I heard Ziba again. They were tighter with an eclectic setlist.

- *Ud jayega* (Sant Kabir)
- *I Shot the Sheriff* (Bob Marley) + *Manush ekta koler gaari* (Baul, Shivananda)
- *Diaraby* (Malian traditional, Oumou Sangare) + *Kotodine deen heener bhab* (Baul, Neelkantha, 19th century)
- *Cherie* (Senegalese Fulani, Baba Maal)
- *Mussoulou* (Malian Wassoulou, Oumou Sangare) + *Saltole bela dubilo* (Santhali Manbhumi folk)
- *Couleur Café* (France, Serge Gainsbourg)

- *Namaz Amar* (19th century Fakiri Sufi from Sylhet, Bangladesh, Durbin Shain)
- *Dumbala Dumba* (Romani gypsy, Taraf de Haidouks)
- *Roadhouse Blues* (Doors)
- *Dekho Re* (Satyajit Ray)
- *Allah megh de* (Bengali Bhawaiya folk)

I finally met the band when they were about ten gigs young. No, we did not have tea. Over spirits and brewed indulgences at DI's quaint King's Pub, we talked of new beginnings, songs, politics and what it is like to be in a carnivalesque band.

Ziba is not overtly political. Yet, embedded within songs are several political strains. For instance, the tea question in *Dekho Re*.

Arko: We don't need to be overtly political. It is always the backdrop. The tea question came naturally.

Amyt: We are talking life and beyond. It's a constant search. We are searching for ourselves because you never know yourself. We are looking inwards. We are looking at us.

How did Ziba come about?

Amyt: I wanted to reach out to a more general audience but without losing any of the intellect and integrity of the music I practise. So, I started to think of musicians who could tune in to this idea. Then, very craftily, I handpicked these boys, all of whom I have played with before. I first talked to Ritoban, then Arko; and the percussionist Deboprotim. I always knew that Aakash would be the bass player since he also plays in my quartet.

Deboprotim: Initially, I remember, we were talking about a covers band.

And Arko?

Amyt: I heard him for the first time ten years ago when we were in Darjeeling for the music release of a film. He was singing in the lawn. What was striking was that we could hear him clearly even though it was the hills, a vast expanse of empty space where voices are easily lost. He has this rootsy quality. I liked his diction, Bangla and English. Since then, I have had him in mind. He also has this versatile bag of songs, from shyamasangeet to Bob Marley and Indian classical.

Arko: That was about a decade ago, Amytda (somewhat embarrassed). Basically, I know a bunch of songs. I have travelled and been lucky to have met a lot of musicians who are all very educated and good. Whatever I could gather from them has helped me. I love different sounds. I was, and still am, drawn to West Africa. I also adore pop music.

And the sound of the band?

Amyt: Slowly, I developed an image of this band as an Afro dance band that is very festival oriented. Yet, the music we play is deep. If a listener wants to feel that, then he's got to pay his dues at the altar of music and the painstakingly worked out arrangements.

Ziba marries a song of today with one from the past. How do you decide on them?

Amyt: It's like this. Look at the ceiling with the wood panels (pointing to the rafters of the pub). Tilt your head and focus at a particular angle and you see a man's head and maybe, a peacock's tail. You have to have the eyes to see it.

It's like staring at clouds and discovering a tree and an old man with a flowing beard.

Amyt: Exactly. The musical interactions have to be tastefully executed. Otherwise it becomes a caricature which we do not want.

And the arrangements?

Arko: Luckily, he's (Amyt) the man who is designing the sound. For me, it's easy. I just sing a song to him, one that I know. But then, it could turn complicated and difficult as has happened several times.

Amyt: Yes, re-arranging songs is a big thing for me. I like to take a song and make it my own. There is another layer to the line-up. As you'll realise, I am the only melody instrument. He (Deboprotim) is playing percussion, but he is also like a rhythm back-up. He is like the rhythm guitar player between guitar and Ritoban's drums and Aakash's bass.

All of you play with various people. How is it being in this band?

Arko: Playing with this band is a challenge every day, and it is a good challenge to have. There is no compromise on musicality when it comes to the audience.

Deboprotim: If within the Ziba set-up we were to do, say, a *Mehbooba*, or any other of the many Bollywood hits of yesteryears, we would be touring all over India, and may even the world, by now. But we don't want to do that.

Ritoban: To be honest, for this band, Amytda is the last word. He decides and we try to deliver.

Aakash: For me, this is the kind of music I grew up listening to; like say, Afro-Cuban music. I consider myself privileged to be able to play this music with this band.

Amyt talks of you, Aakash, and Ritoban as these fat pillars that hold the edifice, ensuring that it doesn't crumble.

Aakash: Amytda has this vast knowledge of music. When I am a little lost, he is always there to help with new ideas. But it is very collective, not that individual parts are put together to make up a song.

How is playing with Ziba different from playing with the Amyt Datta quartet?

Aakash: Amytda's music is very new in terms of texture. There's a Mediterranean feel to it. Yet, it is very rootsy. It has the essence of Western and, maybe, even Indian classical music. But none of these is directly implied. It is very original in sound. So, if your ears are big enough to listen to different kinds of music, you will relate to Amytda's music.

Last question to the leader. How is it being in a band of youngsters?

Amyt: A band means harmony as in chords. Two-three notes existing together without fighting, and together we are producing this sound. A band leader is a symbol of leadership. Playing together is conversation, exchanging thoughts. There is a lot to learn in a band. We are five serious men pursuing music as a way of life.

The future's uncertain
And the end is always near.

Let it roll, baby, roll.
Let it roll, baby, roll.
Let it roll, baby, roll.
Let it roll, all night long (Roadhouse Blues, Doors, Jim Morrison)

Ziba went through a transition after the first quarter of 2019. Arko left, somewhat abruptly; but the band was back in business with Malini, a trained classical vocalist, who brought in a different measure of sensitivity to the repertoire. Her rendition of *Couleur Café* at a gig at the Hard Rock Cafe was nuanced. Pretty good, since for those five-odd minutes of celebrating the very French idea of fleeting love Park Street could well have been Rue Montorgeuil, that cobbled street in the centre of Paris humming with bars and restaurants.

AT PRACTICE: AMYT and AAKASH (clockwise from top), DEBOPROTIM, RITOBAN; Ziba's new vocalist MALINI (Pictures Sanjoy Chattopadhyaya, courtesy *The Telegraph*; Prosanto Mohato)

Couleur Café
Que j'aime ta couleur café
(Coffee colour—How I like your coffee colour)

Amid the uncertainty and fuss in India about the presence of a certain Navjyot Singh Sidhu at the swearing-in of newly elected Pakistan Prime Minister Imran Khan in August 2018, there was one name in the proposed guest list that piqued my curiosity. It was of musician Salman Ahmad, the frontman of the Pakistani band Junoon, who had told me of his desire to someday play in Calcutta while they were in New Delhi within days of the Pokhran nuclear tests of May 11 & 13, 1998. Their first cross-border hit, *Sayonee*, went on to capture the imagination of the subcontinent, mirroring a sense of foreboding that had gripped the two nations after Pakistan followed through with nuclear tests of its own—five simultaneous underground N-tests conducted at Ras Koh Hills in the Chagai district of Balochistan province.

Salman's presence at the swearing-in was no surprise. He was always close to Imran Khan, right from the time the Pakistani skipper picked him to join the national side along with such cricketing eminences as Wasim Akram and Rameez Raja for a tour of Bangladesh over three decades ago to the time. Salman campaigned actively for the Pakistan Tehreek-e-Insaaf (PTI) during elections, even performing the party's campaign songs, including the signature, *Naya Pakistan*. But Salman hasn't joined Imran's party, about which he says he has no regrets. 'My music is my politics,' Salman told *The Hindu* in August 2018, in essence emphasising that his song remains the same.[1]

Sayonee
Chain ek pal nahin
Aur koi hal nahin
Sayonee

[Oh (my) love
Can't rest a moment
And there's no solution (in sight)
Oh (my) love]

'Next time we must hold something in Calcutta. Imran Khan told me about how great it was to play there. So, I just want to see the mighty Eden Gardens,' Salman told me in New Delhi in May 1998. With him was bass player Brian O' Connell, in a flowing purple kurta. Both looked rested. I remember feeling disheartened since the prince-of-wails, fluffy-haired lead singer Ali Azmat, wasn't around for the tete-a-tete because of a fever. Ali was familiar to us, the star of the black-and-white video of their song, *Talaash*, that used to be featured regularly on music television for a while. No matter though, his bandmates assured me, 'the life of the party' would be fighting fit by the time they hit the stage.

> 'It's amazing what *Sayonee* has done for us in India,' says Salman even as he puts in a request with the concierge to organise visits to India Gate, Old Delhi, and Taj Mahal—all in one breath.
>
> 'I am told Old Delhi is just like Lahore,' he says, wide-eyed as he holds forth on how 'people-to-people-contact' was the only way to build bridges between our two nations.
>
> 'Daler Mahendi and Pandit Jasraj were in Pakistan recently… and the auditoriums were jampacked,' says the Lahore-born MBBS. What about local protest in Bombay? 'These are little hiccups, look at the big picture and they don't mean a thing.'[2]

Junoon's music has been a modern mix of Sindhi Punjabi folk and qawwali with Sufi lyrics. Their TV-channel busting album of 1997, *Azadi*, which includes *Sayonee*, propelled them into stardom not only in India, but across Southeast Asia. Yet their initial years were bad with Brian and Ali spending months surviving on daal-chawal while Salman's wife Samina toiled to promote the band, printing flyers and organising shows, and at times even physically dragging friends to concerts.

It all paid off in 1996, with Junoon recording their first mega-hit with *Jazba-e-Junoon* (The Spirit of Passion) which went on to become the official song of the Cricket World Cup hosted jointly by Pakistan, Sri Lanka and India. In December, the same year, Junoon had its tryst with the Pakistani government which took serious objection to the video of their Urdu hit *Ehtesaab*. Pegged on growing corruption and the 'need for accountability', the song's video shows children doing menial jobs and fictitious politicians gorging themselves at swanky hotels. Islamabad banned the video but reluctantly allowed the band to play at a free concert in Karachi that was attended by at least 10,000 people.

Their popularity began soaring with the album *Inquilab* (1996), by which time they had decided to let go of the Van Halen–Jimmy Page-isms for distinctly melodious guitar leads, an intricately dominating tabla, a Robert Plant–Nusrat mix of vocals and of course well-structured bass riffs that provided that much-needed framework to facilitate improvisations. Then came *Azadi* (1997) followed by *Parvaaz* (1999) and many more including *Door* (2016).

'We realised MTV and the likes weren't getting us anywhere. We had to focus our music on our people, culture and sensibilities,' Salman had said then, revealing that a longstanding memory of a Led Zeppelin concert at Madison Square Garden while he was a teenager inspired him to take up the instrument. By the time I met them in Delhi in 1998, Junoon had already won over Kanpur and Chandigarh, having performed there as part of a series of concerts billed as The Pepsi Dance Connection. After the next day's gig at Hamsadhwani Theatre, they were to go to Lucknow.

It is 2019, two decades after that New Delhi interaction and Junoon is in the throes of a comeback tour of the US. At home, the sense of foreboding has heightened. The desperate exultations of *Sayonee* still ring true. I often tune in to Salman performing the song on Coke Studio Season 10 (August–September 2017) with Rahat Fateh Ali Khan, son of the legendary Nusrat Fateh Ali, and Ali Noor. It is a full-throated rendition that juxtaposes exemplary musicianship with nuanced vocals, achieving a soul-stirring crescendo that cries out in hope. *Sayonee* tells us not to lose the faith and allow daylight to clear the darkness of night. It is as though, by some sort of divine magic, as only music can create, Goopy, Bagha and Junoon are singing the same song.

Sayonee
Dekho re, sayonee
Jogoter ki bahar
Diner aloeye kaatey ondhokar

Moreover

New Day, Another Song

The last three letters of his name are missing from my autograph. As George Harrison fled the jostling at the Netaji Indoor Stadium cafeteria that evening, the 'i' rolled on and on, the 'son' did not quite make it on paper. A work in progress, I'd like to believe. Quite like the conversations in *Calling Elvis*. How do I even begin to think that we've heard them all? A lost John Coltrane album has been found. At Yale University, they've stumbled upon the complete orchestra parts of Kurt Weill's *Zaubernacht* (Magic Night), his first jab at writing musical theatre when he was only twenty-two. And rivalling the dramatic twists of his Threepenny Opera, the stars are on parade, rocking every step of their way. Big daddies are rocking again. Some like Eric Clapton and the Rolling Stones and U2 didn't quite stop. While others simply joined the bandwagon. It's fifty years of Abbey Road. Jethro Tull is celebrating fifty years too. Jeff Lynne has rediscovered ELO and is playing across the world, Jim Keltner, the drummer who prefers to stay in the wings but has played with them all, is somewhere out there, a storehouse of memories spanning the *Concert for Bangladesh* (1971) to *Concert For George* (2002) and in between, travelling with the Wilburys; Steve Winwood has made appearances at Crossroads; Robert Plant and Jimmy Page sometime team up with former Led Zeppelin bandmate John Bonham's son; Paul Simon and Elton John have wrapped up their final tours, while Peter Frampton is 'coming alive', for one last time, across the US and Europe; Robbie Robertson and Bruce Springsteen are out with biographies; but hey, the effervescent John Mayer has resurrected Dead & Company with Bob Weir and the rest.

I wish I could have met them all.

'It's not a perfect world,' Keith Richards said. We know. John, George and Jim are no more. Chuck Berry, Aretha Franklin, J.J. Cale, Levon Helm, Billy Preston, Leon Russel, Tom Petty, Ray Manzarek are up in the sky. That's some band they're all part of. Me, I am just 'watching the wheels go round and round',[1] á la little Minnie in the film, *Kabuliwala*, dancing to *Kothai amar hariye jaoar nei mana. Mone mone*, willingly losing myself in thought; of a Miles Davis of failing health, affectionately tapping trumpeter Wallace Rooney while playing Gil Evans's arrangements at Montreaux three months before his death in September 1991 and doing what he vowed never to do, ie, look back; Dhani Harrison quietly lauding Eric Clapton as he winds up a searing solo in *While My Guitar Gently Weeps*; and me being surprised by the joy of finding a signed album of Purnadas Baul from my LP collection and going on to discover that the Ebber Hart Webber in the sleeve notes of a CD of Norwegian saxophonist Jan Garbarek I have had with me for years is the Webber who used a violin bow on a self-designed double-bass while playing in Calcutta. It was the same heart-stopping moment of discovery with *Buena Vista Social Club*, Wim Wenders' docu-feature on the Cuban ensemble of yore, tracked down by guitarist Ry Cooder, whose music we heard in college; and later, being similarly gobsmacked after knowing that *Just Dropped In*, the delightfully archaic song that plays during The Dude's dream sequence in Coen Brothers' *The Big Lebowski*, is by Kenny Rogers.

Lovely indulgences, aren't these? So what if the Atticus we look up to is fictional? Let's find inspiration wherever we can and hold on. The spoken word, the written phrase. The poem put to tune, the song sung.

We live in an age of unreason amid unfounded suspicions, hollow proclamations, dictatorial showmanship and crass jingoism. Yet, dispassionately considered, the present terrain isn't exactly unfamiliar. If anything, it is fertile ground for fresh sowing in the hope of a bountiful harvest. Miriam Makeba is remembered in an infectious dance track. Nina Simone is on a jingle on TV, singing about a new day. That's okay. What's important is that the search for songs to fight new battles entrenched in age-old prejudices has well and truly begun. It's time for a new anthem, although there's no knowing how or from where it will come. Could it be that young boy playing the Venezuelan national anthem on his violin alone on a road in Caracas, oblivious to the pelting of stones? Could it be that young Arab with the oud, playing in an acoustic jazz quartet fronted by a Jew from Israel somewhere in Europe? Or would it come from the nameless elderly man gently plucking the strings of his santoor at home in locked-down Srinagar?

Because, let's not forget, this is how it happens. The songs start to ask the questions no one wants to answer. Southern trees bear a strange fruit, Billie Holiday said. How does it feel to be without a home, asked Dylan, who is now resurrecting his mothballed songs of yore at live performances, acknowledging that 'there must be some way out of here' and warning us about 'wildcats growling' and 'wind howling'.

At Delhi's Piano Man Jazz Club, the waiters are taking what is now a customary break while the artiste of the evening plays his tune. It is the one time when patrons are urged to listen. Quietly. Hence, no service. The music is getting its due. In Calcutta, they're getting ready for Dover Lane, the annual festival of Indian classical. Someplace Else and Phoenix, among the active night-out spots for live music in Calcutta, have competition. Skinny Mo's at Manohar Pukur calls itself a Jazz Club. Good for us. A new guitarist is being anointed 'Fender endorsee' every other day and new bands are finding their mojo at the annual Ziro Festival of Music in Arunachal Pradesh. Elsewhere, Amyt Datta is adding a jab of guitar sophistication to Anjan Dutt's life-affirming Bangla story-tunes while Vikramjit 'Tuki' Banerjee's Krosswinds, of Path Gechhe Benke-fame, is conjuring up eclectic setlists for live gigs across the country. Maybe a certain professor of English, Bertie DaSilva, is brooding a possible comeback, but the unstoppable Usha Uthup is working up a *Fever* in her trademark Kanjeevaram sari.

By George, just hit Pause before you Play the next song. And wonder.

Sunset doesn't last all evening
A mind can blow those clouds away
After all this my love is up and must be leaving
But it's not always going to be this way
All things must pass
All things must pass away

Epilogue

The boy on the scooter has got on in years. One Sunday, during one of their usual post-breakfast listening sessions at the Calcutta home, he was playing old favourites for his daughter, around ten at the time, on their old, refurbished Garrard changer, one of the few possessions he and his mother had brought with them from Agartala in 1969 when a family tragedy forced them to move.

Their lives would change forever. Or would they?

Cherry Pink and Apple Blossom was on a 78rpm, the Chipmunks horsing around with *She'll be Coming Round the Mountain* was on a 45 as were Ventures, the Shadows and *Palkir Gaan* (Satyendranath Dutta's poem put to music by Salil Chowdhury, sung by Hemanta Mukhopadhyay). Timir Baran's orchestra was the other regular, his earliest introduction to the sound of the Big Band. Tagore songs followed. And after more of the usuals, the ballad of the river it had to be. As he brought out the record from the familiar blue coloured sleeve depicting a woman near a tree, he recalled his most familiar memory of the song.

'This was the song I would be put to bed to,' he said, hoping the young listener would immediately warm up to the nostalgia.

Ogo nodi apon bege pagol para
Ami sthobdo chapa toru, gondho bhorey...

They heard the song together, she silently while he hummed along. It felt reassuring all over again. Into the second verse and she aired a more immediate concern: 'Relax Papa, don't you fall off to sleep now.'

LOL.

These days, their Sunday morning listening sessions have acquired an extended oeuvre. Classic rock, folk and jazz must vie for playtime with Korean pop!

References

CHAPTER 1

1. A Day in the Life: Excerpted from 'In timeless harmony' by the author, published in *The Telegraph*, April 1991; 'A White Knight's Tale' by the author, published in *The Indian Express*, June 1997; Articles and tributes by Ananda Lal, Nondon Bagchi in brochures and fliers; A Concert for Dilip, Axis, courtesy Lew Hilt and author's personal collection.

CHAPTER 2

1. Minstrels in the gallery: Excerpted from 'We are not for MTV' by the author, published in *The Telegraph*, February 1994.
2. jethrotull.com
3. A night of cobwebby classics: Excerpted from 'Bombay rocks to Jethro Tull tracks' by the author, published in *The Telegraph*, February 1994.

CHAPTER 3

1. Raghupati Raghav on the banjo: An edited version of the author's article first appeared in *The Indian Express*, November 1996.
2. A protest singer, his sports car: Excerpted from the author's interview of Arlo Guthrie, published in *The Indian Express*, April 1998.
3. Guthrie, Arlo. 'Arlo Guthrie/I Can't Help Falling In Love With You'. *YouTube* video, 8:21. June 30, 2008. https://www.youtube.com/sSF89swJ9IU
4. arloguthrie.com

CHAPTER 4

1. Miles meets Marquez: Excerpted from 'A Last Post for the Man with the Horn' by the author, published in *The Telegraph*, October 1991.
2. A love supreme: Excerpted from 'Passion grace and fire', the author's interview of John McLaughlin, published in *The New Indian Express*, February 2003.
3. From an article by the author, published in *The Telegraph t2*, November–December 2015.

CHAPTER 5

1. Drum Machine with Heart: Excerpted from 'The Don Bradman of drums' by the author, published in *The New Indian Express,* March 2003.

CHAPTER 6

1. Palette of possibilities: Excerpted from 'When jazz legends come to town', 'Miles ahead' by the author, published in *The Indian Express,* January 2007.
2. Bob Blumenthal, February 2001, in the sleeve notes of *The Essential Miles Davis,* a two-CD collection brought out by Sony Music Entertainment.
3. Davis, Miles and Troupe, Quincy. *Miles, The Autobiography*. New York: Picador, 1990.
4. *Blue Note Newsletter*: July 25, 2018.

CHAPTER 7

1. Ian Paice's interview to Matt Wardlow of *Classic Rock*, May 1, 2017 in *Keyboard,* November 2013.
2. Skylar Thomas's interview of Don Airey in *Keyboard*, November 2013.

CHAPTER 8

1. Comfortable, not numb: Excerpted from the author's interview of Roger Waters, published in *The New Indian Express,* March 2002.
2. In the flesh: Excerpted from 'Emotionally yours, Floyd' by the author, published in *The New Indian Express,* April 2003.
3. Lyrics by Roger Waters from the album, *Is This The Life We Really Want?*

CHAPTER 9

1. A much shorter version of the interview, 'Bowman's spell, with strings attached', first appeared in *The Telegraph,* February 2018.

CHAPTER 10

1. An abridged version of the interview, 'Cosmic messenger', first appeared in *The New Indian Express,* January 2003.

CHAPTER 11

1. Excerpted from 'Satisfaction is like living a dream', the author's phone-in interview with Keith Richards, published in *The New Indian Express,* April 2003.
2. Rushdie, Salman. *Imaginary Homelands.* London: Granta Books, 1991.

CHAPTER 12

1. An abridged version of the interview was published in *The Indian Express,* February 2005.
2. markknopfler.com

CHAPTER 13

1. A shorter version of the interview first appeared in *The Indian Express,* February 2005.

CHAPTER 14

1. Excerpted from 'I am not singing, my guitar is' and 'A night of love supreme' by the author, published in *The Telegraph,* October–November 2012.

CHAPTER 15

1. Dream beats: Excerpted from the author's interview of Sivamani, published in *The Indian Express* sometime in 1996–97.

CHAPTER 16

1. An abridged version of the interview, 'Ambiance de Amyt', first appeared in *The Telegraph t2,* May 2017.

CHAPTER 17

1. An abridged version of the interview was first published in *The Telegraph,* June 2018.
2. JazzStandards.com
3. Carr, Ian. *Miles David: The Definitive Biography.* New York: Da Capo Press, 1991.

CHAPTER 18

1. An abridged version of the interview was first published in *The Telegraph,* September 2018.
2. 'Jazz: Where it came from, where it's at', by John S. Wilson in an essay originally published in 1975 by USIS, The American Centre, New Delhi.
3. 'What's Behind the New Jazz Resurgence?' by Evan Haga in *Rolling Stone*, July 31, 2018.

CHAPTER 21

1. Geetabaitan.com
2. Tagore, Rabindranath. *Rabindranath Tagore for the 21st Century Reader.* Translated by Arunava Sinha. New Delhi: Aleph Book Company, 2014.
3. Robinson, Andrew. *Satyajit Ray: The Inner Eye.* New Delhi: Oxford University Press, 2004.
4. Sengupta, Samir. *Gaaner Pechoney Rabindranath.* Calcutta: Papyrus, 2017.
5. At Shantiniketan, the tradition is to express appreciation by chanting 'shadhu, shadhu', meaning excellent.
6. Additional reading: Som, Reba. *Rabindranath Tagore: The Singer and His Song.* New Delhi: Penguin, 2009.

CHAPTER 22

1. 'How a cricket buddy brought "junoon" to Imran Khan's party', by Suhasini Haider in *The Hindu*, August 2018.
2. Quotes from the author's interview of the band, 'Pak band in town to test its brand of fusion', published in *The Indian Express,* May 1998.

MOREOVER

1. *Watching the Wheels*, lyrics by John Lennon, album *Double Fantasy.*

Acknowledgements

The seeds of this effort, I now realise, were sown way back in 1996 when a nervous journalist from Calcutta stepped into the hallowed precincts of *The Indian Express* on Bahadur Shah Zafar Marg in New Delhi. Editor Shekhar Gupta not only gave me a job, but subsequently, perhaps realising I wasn't that good at anything else, asked me to write a fortnightly column on music. Thank you Shekhar, for *Calling Elvis* would never have morphed into a book had it not been for that opportunity.

I am indebted to…

The MUSICIANS for their time and all the PROMOTERS, especially VENKAT VARDHAN of DNA Networks for organising India concerts with the biggest of them all.

Everyone associated with THE TELEGRAPH where it all began, editor emeritus Aveek Sarkar for widening our horizons and welcoming back this 'prodigal son' twice over, chief editor Arup Sarkar and editor R. Rajagopal for allowing me to pursue this project and for permission to access TT archives so meticulously catalogued by the incomparable Shakti Roy.

MANINI CHATTERJEE for her friendship, advice and the courage of her convictions.

SANKARSHAN THAKUR for his encouragement—you started this journey, remember, at home over spirits, a hearty meal with Alchie and Mark Knopfler for company.

SHEKHAR BHATIA for making a journalist of me, and granting leave to attend a Jethro Tull concert in Bombay; Ashok Kamath for his generosity and help while I was making the transit to New Delhi, Shampa Kamath for the Miles Davis assignment and lots more, Sumir Lal, Deepayan Chatterjee, Vivek Sengupta, Umesh Anand, L.P. Sahi, Anil Grover, Jaideep 'Jojo' Bose, Chidanand Rajghatta, Yubaraj Ghimire, Surit Doss, Abhijit Dasgupta, Kaushik Mitter for being the seniors we looked up to; Manas Bhattacharya for managing the nitty gritty.

TT NEWSROOM COLLEAGUES past and present, especially Madhushree, Moumita, Sulagana, Rajrupa, Saheli, Manasij, Debina, Mukesh, Pinaki, Animesh Bisoee, Gangulida, Antara, Praduman; photographers Prashant, Manob, Bhola for 24x7 Jharkhand vigil; Pheroze, Anita for being our sheet anchors in Delhi; Sudipta 'Senior' for the shared memories, Subhra for Rabindrasangeet, Upala and Team Graphic for taking so much care, Devdan, 'Comrade' Joyjit, Sumit for adda at DI; Sumit Dasgupta for opening up *t2*, Saumitra Dasgupta for his insights, Uddalok, Arindam, Mathuresh, Santanu Mallick for music exchange; photographers Sanjoy and the evergreen Rashu; Kalida, Raki and everyone else at INFOCOM.

TARUN SHAW for getting us books we didn't know we wanted.

THE INDIAN EXPRESS, especially VIVECK GOENKA for his reassuring presence at the Lalbaug office (Mumbai) and a warm send-off.

Former IE colleagues in Delhi, Pune, Mumbai, especially chief editor Raj Kamal Jha for his ideas and that special turn of phrase; executive editor Unni Rajen Shanker for 'akuri on toast' while on the redesign tour, Praveen Jain and Neeraj Priyadarshi for the photographs that gave life to our reports, Coomi Kapoor for a solid piece of advice that helped me stay afloat, E.P. Unny for cartoons that reveal a lot more than the written word, Pamella Philipose for edit page opportunities, Sourish Bhattacharya for making space in the magazine, Kaveri Bamzai for asking me to write on films, Mr Tripathy for allowing me to set foot on sacred news desk territory; Shalini Langer, Dawa Lhamu, Vinita Deshmukh, Amrith Lal, Sunanda Mehta, Anuradha Masceranhas, Satyajit Joshi, Joy Purkayastha, S. Hussain Zaidi, Sandeep Dwivedi and Kavita Iyer for bearing with me.

THE NEW INDIAN EXPRESS, especially MANOJ SONTHALIA for trusting me with the edition.

T.J.S. GEORGE for his counsel, and the reassuring welcome note that found me the moment I landed in Bangalore.

Former NIE colleagues in Bangalore, the dream team of Rajesh Menon, Ajay Shankar, Sheba Thayil, Anupama Bijur, Max Martin, K.R. 'Baloo' Balasubramaniam; Sushila Ravindranath for opening up the pages of The New Sunday Express, Sudhakar Darbe for his illustrations, photographers Keshav Vitla, Bhargavi and S. Eshwar.

PRESIDENCY COLLEGE, CALCUTTA for broadening our horizons, the professors we had and the friends we made; Mita for being there, Tombi for 'auditioning' me for a place in the college band, Ishanti (Buli) for holding the band together with her piano, Shonamoni for his willing participation, Deepesh,

Bush, Kanchan, Charles, Pronob, Giri, and the statistics department gang of Shibuda, Soma, Sophia, Anuradha, Amit, Bani, Parnasree for the good times.

LA MARTINIERE SCHOOLS, CALCUTTA, for nurturing an atmosphere of true openness where hymns at morning assembly faded into Rabindrasangeet at Bengali cultural evening and dance music at the annual Founder's Day social.

Principals MRS LAWRENCE, who admitted me in a day, and Donald Alney; all our teachers, especially Mr & Mrs Suares, Mrs Peterson, Mrs Innis, who told us about Jonathon Livingston Seagull in class I, 'the gull sees the farthest who flies highest'; Mrs Hymes, one of the kindest souls I have known; Mr & Mrs Hennessy, Mr Milford Hennessy, Mr & Mrs Bose, Mr T.W. Phillips, Mr P.K. Bhattacharya, Mr P.R. Sinha, Mr P. Datta, Mr C.N. Banerjee, Mr D.K. Bhattacharya, Mr S. Sarkar, Mr Some, Mr R.N. Mukherjee, Maha Singh and our music teacher Tony Menezes.

FRIENDS I made at school, Rajeev Kelkar—for the music you so willingly gave, Saktirup for showing up like an angel during those difficult months and for the chance glimpse of Uttam Kumar at Woodburn Road during Puja, Tinku Basu for invites to the Ravi Shankar concert, TN, Rono, Jayjeet, Raja, Supratim, Sudipta Basu, DB, Chester, Harsh, Abhik, Suprotik, Sumit Ray, Sujata (Snooky), Seema, Paula & Sujoy, and Bishakha for all those years together.

MRINALINI DASGUPTA, my boromashi, a woman of rare courage and generosity who turned 98, Beltola Road into a refuge of happy memories; mashis Ila and Nila for their love, Shima for the most precious gift I ever had, my school; Mama and Mami for the holidays in Bhopal, Bombay and Agra; Subrata (Bachhu mama) Banerjee and Karuna Banerjee for their kindness, Sumanta (Bula mama) Banerjee, Samik (Chhotka mama) Banerjee for indulging me, Shampa (Runkidi) Srivastava for always staying in touch, Barsha di, Meghla di and Barin da; Chhotuda & Shyamalidi for the love, Betuda for *Feluda* books and more, Kokila boudi for 'Daffodils' and 'The Lady of Shallot', Daluda & Somadi for pastries from Firpos amid September showers and a lot more of which you know, Tutuda, Laltuda, Mithudi for taking me under their wing; Bobbyda for introducing me to the unbridled joys of theatre on the terrace of 6A, Maharaja Nanda Kumar Road, and that life-changing tryst with Guenter Grass; Shreela boudi for '*khao-khao rob*' and more, Ashokda & Annadidi for always being there, Kajol mama for carrying that boy on his shoulders because he was too sleepy to walk to the Taltola bus stand, Bhuntu and Arjab for Miura, Bunoo & Golu for all the fun, will never forgive you though for the Agra rail ticket fiasco; Chiku, Piku, Chumki & their significant others for being there; Shiladi, Shikhadi and Professor for staying in touch.

D.K. SEN and Sulekha Sen for not saying no, Soubir, Polly, Zoya, Robi, Ben, Sashi and Rishi for family vibes; Bhalo Kaku for introducing me to 'Mohiner Ghoda' Bapida, everyone else in the Sen brigade.

ARUN kaku, kakima; Swati & Pinke for Agartala and Shishu Bihar days.

MAYA mashi, Ishanda, Shayan & Ayan for those wonderful evenings at Lansdown Court.

BINA mashi, Babudada & Mona for that Digha holiday, and for introducing me to Srikanta.

RATNAdi for being there.

VIDYASAGAR NIKETAN for the elders who were always supportive, no one ever complained about a boy creating perpetual racket on the drums at every odd hour; Binuda, Sambhuda, Khokonda, Gautamda, Amitda, GD-da, among many others, for organising the Puja musical soirees; Goblada for elocution lessons, Buroda and Subratada for being our football mentors, friends Preetam, Rupak, Bikram, Mukut, Rana, Lalu, Sumit, Munna, Soumya, Bonny, Ranju, Piyali, Tito, Molly and Sanjoy for the fun times, a la *purano shei diner kotha.*

THE KELKARS, Aunty Usha, Uncle Gopi, Aunty Suman for my home away from home at Keyatola Road; Uncle Deepu and Aunty Reethu Sarawgi for gifting us DI and adda at Circus Range, Uncle Vaz, Dinkie & Deepak, and all the others who make up this amazing family that I count on as my own.

ARIJIT & ROXY for Kolkata trysts, harmonica and Hiltuda connect.

SUBHRO & Sarbani for friendship, music and dinners.

GITA & Abhay for standing by us.

ERROL ABRAHAM for Sunday jam sessions.

ANJUM KATYAL, ANANDA LAL for the support; JHARNAdi, PARNA for help with Tagore.

KABITA LINDENMEYER, SUSMIT & KINGSHOOK BISWAS for Himadri.

BITHIKA for keeping things sane at home.

RAVI SINGH and everyone else at Speaking Tiger, especially Yauvanika Chopra, for embracing, and improving on, The Idea.

SUDIPTA, my first reader, for being You.

SHREYA for the light in her eyes.